Gender Inequality:
A Multidimensional Study

Gender Inequality:
A Multidimensional Study

Swapan Kumar Kolay
Sushila D. Mahant

GYAN

Published, 2019

Published by

Gyan Publishing House
5, Ansari Road
Daryaganj, New Delhi-110002
Phone: 011-47034999, 9811692060
www.gyanbooks.com
E-mail: books@gyanbooks.com

Printed at: G. Print Process, Delhi.

Cataloging in Publication Data—DK
Courtesy: D.K. Agencies (P) Ltd. <docinfo@dkagencies.com>

Kolay, Swapan Kumar, 1966- **author.**
Gender inequality : a multidimensional study / Swapan Kumar Kolay, Sushila D. Mahant.
pages cm
Study conducted in Bastar District of Chhattisgarh, India.
Includes bibliographical references.
ISBN 9788121214872

1. Sex discrimination against women—India—Bastar (District)
2. Women—Legal status, laws, etc.—India—Bastar (District)
3. Tribes—India—Bastar (District) I. Mahant, Sushila D., author.
II. Title.

LCC HQ1237.5.I4K65 2018 | DDC 305.420954137 23

This Book is
Affectionately
Dedicated to
Prof. P.K. Bhowmick

Contents

Preface

We proud Indians of 21st century rejoice in celebrations when a boy is born, and if it is a girl, a muted or no celebrations is the norm. Neediness for a male child is so much so that from the times immemorial we are killing our daughters at birth or before birth, and if, fortunately, she is not killed we find various ways to discriminate against her throughout her life. Though our religious beliefs make women a goddess but we fail to recognize her as a human being first; we worship goddesses but we exploit girls. We don't want to poke in any cultural belief but we want to show the inequality between boys and girls through this book. Exploitation is not only occurs in customs while its a part of health, education and economy. With this point of view I chapter, we described gender disparity at a glance which is based on globally, national level and in tribal context with the inclusion of transgender also. In the II chapter all rules and regulation and prohibition of government are included to due respect of gender sensitisation which is helpful for the reader to acquire sufficient amendment and provisional knowledge about laws for women. Worldwide women are mostly discriminated by wealth, education and health. So we tried to elaborate wage and economic discrimination in chapter III, education inequality in chapter IV and Health discrimination in chapter V. This book is partially covering the socio-cultural discrimination in tribal communities towards women, so the useful methods of data collection for research study are comprised in chapter VI. The Socio-demographic study is the requirement of our study that's why the data at various dimensions is elaborated about study area in chapter VII. The interpretation of gathered data and analysis is stated in chapter VIII which helps to understand the position of tribal women in their communities. At the last concluding chapter is recommendation part which is applicable in uplifting of women in all categories, class and communities. The literal meaning of gender is to beget, to generate. In other words it means social and cultural generation. However, with the emergence of women's studies and the rise of feminist writings and research, it includes biological as well as social and cultural meanings. Thus, a woman has a biological distinctiveness and also some social cultural discrimination against men. We are not hesitating to accept that we are a society of people with double standards as far as our attitude towards women is concerned; our thoughts and preaching are different than our actions. By this research book we are tried to understand the phenomenon of gender inequality; actual facts and figures, their prevalent reasons and searched for applicable solutions.

Dr. Swapan Kumar Kolay
Mrs. Sushila D. Mahant

Acknowledgements

Our deepest gratitude to Prof. S.K. Singh, Vice-Chancellor, Bastar University, Jagdalpur for his elderly and positively support.

Hearty thanks to Prof. G. K. Kshatriya, Prof. A. K. Kapoor & Prof. Salil Basu for their hidden cooperation with morality by silent teaching.

Sincere thanks are also due to the villagers and respondents in particular for the help and co-operation, they have extended all throughout our research study. They have spared many hours of their valuable time and generously placed at my disposal their vast stock of information day-to-day experience and ideas without which our work would not have been completed.

Finally special thanks are extended to all the staff of Anthropology and Tribal Studies, Bastar University, Jagdalpur for their help and coperation.

Dr. Swapan Kumar Kolay
Mrs. Sushila D. Mahant

List of Tables

List of Abbreviations

AIDS	: Acquire Immuno Difficiency Syndrom
ANC	: Antinatal Care
BCG	: Bacillus Calemette Guerin
CBOs	: Community Based Organisations
CDC	: Center for Disease Control
CEDAW	: Convention on Elimination of All Forms of Discrimination against Women
CEO	: Chief Executive Officer
CIA	: Central Intelligence Agency
CRC	: Convention on the Rights of the Child
DAC	: Development Assistance Committee
DDR	: Double Data Rate
DIG	: Deputy Inspector General
DLHS	: District Level Health Servey
DMK	: Dravida Munnettra Kazhakam
DOJ	: Departments of Justice
DPT	: Diptheria Pertusis Tetanus
EC	: Executive Committee
EEOC	: Equal Employment Opportunity Commission
EU	: European Union
FAC	: Forest Advisory Committee
FIR	: First Information Report
FLFP	: Federation Libredela Formation Professionnelle
GAR	: Gross Attendance Rate
GBV	: Gender Based Violence
GDI	: Gender Development Indices
GDP	: Gross Domestic Product
GII	: Gender Inequality Index

GOI	: Government of India
HHS	: Health and Human Services
HIV	: Human ImmunodeficiencyVirus
HRLN	: Human Rights Law Network
ICC	: International Criminal Court
ICDS	: Integrated Child Development Services
ICPD	: International Conference on Population and Development
ICRA	: Indian Civil Rights Act
ICRW	: International Center for Research on Women
ICTR	: International Criminal Tribunal for Rwanda
ICTY	: International Criminal Tribunal for the Former Yugoslavia
IFC	: International Finance Corporation
IGP	: Income-Generation Programmes
IIPS	: International Institute for Population Sciences
ILO	: The International Labor Organization
IMF	: International Monetary Fund
IMR	: Infant Mortality Rate
INGOs,	: International Non-governmental Organizations
IPC	: Indian Penal Code
MDG	: Millennium Development Goal
MMR	: Maternal Mortality Rate
MoEF	: Ministry of Environment and Forests
MTPA	: Metric Tonnes Per Annum
NAR	: Net Attendance Rate
NCRB	: National Crime Records Bureau
NCW	: National Commission for Women
NFHS	: National Family Health Survey
NGOs	: Non-Government Organisations
NHRC	: National Human Rights Commission
NLSA	: The National Legal Services Authority
NMDC	: National Mineral Development Corporation
NPO	: Non-profit Organisation
NPP	: National Population Policy
OBC	: Other Backward Class

ODA : Official Development Assistance
OECD : Organization for Economic Cooperation and Development
OHCHR : High Commissioner for Human Rights
PDS : Public Distribution System
PIL : Public Interest Litigation
PNSDT : Pre-Natals Diagnostic Techniques
PRIs : Panchayat Raj Institutions
PWDVA : Protection of Women from Domestic Violence Act
SAARC : South Asian Association for Regional Cooperation
SC : Schedule Caste
SHGs : Self Help Groups
SOOE : The Salvation of Oppressed Eunuchs
SRS : Sex Reassignment Surgery
ST : Schedule Tribe
TJ : Transitional Justice
TLOA : Tribal Law and Order Act
TPDS : Targeted Public Distribution System
UN : United Nation
UNDP's : United Nations Development Programme's
UNGA : United Nations General Assembly
UNICEF : United Nations International Children's Emergency Fund
UNIFEM : United Nations Development Fund for Women
UNMIL : United Nations Mission in Liberia
US : United State
USA : United State of America
VAWA's : Violence Against Women Act's
WHO : World Health Organisation
WJI : Women's Justice Initiative

Chapter - I

Introduction

Gender is a primary marker of social and economic stratification and, as a result, of exclusion. Regardless of one's socioeconomic class, there are systematic gender differences in material well being, although the degree of inequality varies across countries and over time. As a result, gender inequality is a characteristic of most societies, with males on average better positioned in social, economic, and political hierarchies. For more than two decades, the goal of reducing gender inequality has held a prominent place in international organizations and in national strategy statements. Millennium Development Goal 3 (MDG) reflects the global attention to the issue of gender inequality and has been providing the impetus for governments to eliminate gender inequality in primary and secondary education by 2005 and in all levels by 2015.

There is growing recognition that well being is a multi-dimensional concept and, as noted in chapter 2, goes beyond income, educational attainment and health (the material dimensions) to include agency and empowerment as well as subjective well being. That framework is reflected in the following gender analysis that evaluates gender differences in three key domains: *capabilities*, *livelihoods*, and *agency* (Anand, P., Hunter, G., Carter, I., Dowding, K., Guala, F. and Hee van, M., 2010). The first of these categories capabilities is of intrinsic value and it also generates the preconditions for securing one's economic wellbeing via engagement in production and economic decision making. The second domain livelihoods is comprised of conditions that enable individuals to adequately provide for themselves and their families and includes access to work, wages, access to credit and asset ownership (Barro, R. and Lee, J. W., 2010). The third domain agency (or empowerment) can be understood as the ability of individuals and the groups to which they belong to shape their environment. Thus, gender equality in this domain would imply that women are equally *agentic* as men (Besley, T. and Case, A., 2003). Women's share of managerial positions and trade union membership and of leadership positions in cooperatives, businesses and governing bodies are useful indicators in this domain.

1.1 Gender Inequality; a Paradox

In gender inequality, there is not a simple meaning of it. It means some way of isolation, disparity and discrimination for women. Many historians said that history start from the matrilineal dynasty and woman was known as the God's complete creation. It can be not injustice by saying that women are emotionally stronger than men. We can say that she is the symbol of independent and powerful personality with love, caring, gentleness and intensity of both in love, in hate. Undoubtedly women endure much more pain than men do. No man do goes through even half of the pain a woman goes through during labour. Reasonable and honestly speaking, this is true that motherhood is something that God has blessed only females with. However women have not been treated nicely. Most beneficiary part, in fact 99 percent of them are awarded to boys. The common excuse is that girls are made to be housewives and mother. But this doesn't mean that girls should be totally ignorant about the world, current affairs, history and development in modern era. The girls are discriminated in education and equal status beside men but girls who are well educated make better wives and mothers than uneducated women. That way a lot of people would benefit from a girls' education.

However, what does not get assurance is that fact that so many girls in India, Pakistan, Saudi Arabia, Iran, Iraq and many more eastern countries are having to give up their ambitions, simply because their parents feel that girls should be married and mothers by the age of 18. It is not only education where girls are forced to take backseat in the eastern countries, but the inequality spreads to many other things too.

When we observe about the crime against women, more than half of the total rape cases go unreported. This is because the victims do not want to shame their families by publicizing the abuse they have gone through and they do not want to face embarrassing cross questioning in the court. The society makes the victims pay for someone else's mistakes. Unwed mothers are verbally and physically abused in public places.

Dowry is another very common problem, particularly in India. The groom's family demand enormous sums of money and other valuables from demands enormous sums of money and other valuables from the bride's father, to show that the groom is doing them a big favour by agreeing to married their daughter. If the father is unable to pay, the bride is usually married off anyway but then she is mentally and physically tortured and sometime burnt to death.

Female infanticide is another problem. It is not a new problem; it has existed for thousands of years in the East. It is selective murder. As soon as the baby is born, if it is a girl, she is either buried alive or drowned. However, in West countries, things are dramatically different. Women are not treated as atrociously as in the East. Women in the West have the right to education and they have no limit on how far they want to study. Women in the West have high profile careers and command respect and good pay too. But women in the west do have to deal with discrimination. The most common is unequal pay. This is common almost every career; sports, films, multinational companies, school, etc. They also face problems in getting a job position where they are competing with man. The man is always favoured over the woman.

Apart from disparity between man and woman, we cannot forget about discrimination of transgender in society. We can say that the life of transgender is miserable in society. Many illiterate as well as educated people believe that they are curse of the family; they are not able to accept that they are the outcomes of chromosomal disorder, means a Genetical Disorder. Thus there is a lot of differences in the way women and transgender are treated in the world, but they need special attention from the society for development of civilisation. So, the every chapters in this book, are mainly figuring out the position and status of female by different parameters with also the position of transgender.

1.2 Concept of Gender Inequality

To understand the gender inequality, understanding of the definition is must necessary to justify anybodies mindset. People have various perceptions about the sex and gender. Simply the English language distinction between the words sex and gender was first developed in the 1950s and 1960s by British and American psychiatrists and other medical personnel working with intersex and transsexual patients. Since then, the term gender has been increasingly used to distinguish between sex as biological and gender as socially and culturally constructed. Feminists have used this terminology to argue against the 'biology is destiny' line, and gender and development approaches have widely adopted this system of analysis. "Sex marks the distinction between women and men as a result of their biological, physical and genetic differences...Gender roles are set by convention and other social, economic, political and cultural forces" (http://owa.netxtra.net/indepth/project.jsp?project=206).

From this perspective, sex is fixed and based in nature; gender is fluid and based in culture. This distinction constitutes progress compared with 'biology is destiny'. However, it ignores the existence of persons who do not fit neatly into the biological or social categories of women and men, such as intersex, transgender, transsexual people (*hijras*). Furthermore, for many people the sex categories of female and male are neither fixed nor universal, but vary over time and across cultures. Accordingly, sex, like gender, is seen as a social and cultural construct.

1.2.1 Definitions of Gender and Sex

The parameter or range of definitions of gender and sex consequently based on l the diversity of individual and institutional understandings with debated terms.

"Gender refers to the array of socially constructed roles and relationships, personality traits, attitudes, behaviours, values, relative power and influence that society ascribes to the two sexes on a differential basis. Whereas biological sex is determined by genetic and anatomical characteristics, gender is an acquired identity that is learned, changes over time, and varies widely within and across cultures. Gender is relational and refers not simply to women or men but to the relationship between them" (www.un-instraw.org/en/index.php?option=content&task=view&id=37&Itemid=76).

"Gender refers to the economic, social and cultural attributes and opportunities associated with being male or female at a particular point in time" (World Health Organization, 2001).

"Sex refers to the biological characteristics that define humans as female or male. While these sets of biological characteristics are not mutually exclusive, as there are individuals who possess both, they tend to differentiate humans as males and females" (World Health Organization, 2002).

"Sex in human beings is not a purely dichotomous variable. It is not an evenly continuous one either.... a fair number of human beings are markedly intersexual, a number of them to the point where both sorts of external genitalia appear, or where developed breasts occur in an individual with male genitalia, and so on" (Geertz, Clifford, 1983).

"If the immutable character of sex is contested, perhaps this construct called 'sex' is as culturally constructed as gender; indeed, perhaps it was always already gender, with the consequence that the distinction between sex and gender turns out to be no distinction at all" (Butler, Judith, 1990).

"Gender is not what culture created out of my body's sex; rather; sex is what culture makes when it genders my body" (Wilchins, 2006).

"We believe it is indispensable to deconstruct the binary gender system that shapes the Western world so absolutely that in most cases it goes unnoticed. For 'other sexualities to be possible' it is indispensable and urgent that we stop governing ourselves by the absurd notion that only two possible body types exist, male and female, with only two genders inextricably linked to them, man and woman. We make trans and intersex issues our priority because their presence, activism and theoretical contributions show us the path to a new paradigm that will allow as many bodies, sexualities and identities to exist as those living in this world might wish to have, with each one of them respected, desired, celebrated" (IGLHRC, 2005).

With above definition we are able to say that gender' is a socio cultural term referring socially defined roles and behaviors assigned to 'males' and 'females' in a given society; whereas, the term 'sex' is a biological and physiological phenomenon which defines man and woman. In its social, historical and cultural aspects, gender is a function of power relationship between men and women where men are considered superior to women. Therefore, gender may be understood as a man made concept, while 'sex' is natural or biological characteristics of human beings.

Apart from so much different definition about sex and gender, gender inequality may be defined as discrimination against women based on their sex. In not only Indian society but worldwide women are traditionally considered by the society as weaker sex. She has been accorded a subordinate position to men. She is exploited, degraded, violated and discriminated both in our homes and in outside world. This peculiar type of discrimination against women is prevalent everywhere in the world and more so in Indian society.

1.3 Gender Inequality in India

India is known as the shrine place of so many God and Godess. The cultural diversity with sacred tradition is the special identity of India. An Indian person prays Maa Durga as the symbol of power (Shakti) but why there is girl child is aborted from the life, is a big question. To acquire knowledge about pharmacopeia towards girls from normal people, is our prime ambition to study gender inequality in multidimensional. The World Bank estimated that over the last two decades, around 2.5 lakh girls were killed in India each year because of their sex. When infant and child mortality are driven by biology, fewer girls die than boys, but the third National Family Health Survey (NFHS-3) found that the post neonatal mortality rate for Indian girls is 21/1000, compared with 15 for boys. For the age group 1-4 years, "the child mortality rate for girls, at 23/1000, is 61 per cent higher than for boys, at 14." The World Bank report estimated that, as a result, India lost another 2.5 lakh girls in 2008. These figures put us to shame as a society. This systematic massacre could not happen unless society accepted it and governments turned a blind eye to it. Sections 312 to 317 of the Indian Penal Code list the punishments for causing miscarriage, injuring unborn children, preventing a child from being born or causing it to die after birth, and abandoning a child under 12 years. Over the last 20 years, how many prosecutions have there been under these provisions of the law? There should have been 10 million.

The extent of the violence against the girl as foetus and infant shows how deep the bias in India is against women and why women will be secure only if we as a nation introspect and change. Not only is this not happening, but the 2011 census shows that the sex ratio in the age-group 0-6 had fallen in 27 States and Union Territories from 2001. Millions of girls who are allowed to live are fed and educated less than their brothers. The United Nation's Human Development Report 2013 estimates that 42.5 per cent of our children suffer from malnutrition (as against 3.8 per cent in China). There is also great irony in this because NFHS-3 established that when mothers were undernourished, 54 per cent of their children were stunted and 25 per cent wasted. The more educated they were, the lower the chance of their children being either stunted or wasted. By starving millions of girls so that their brothers can eat marginally better, and by taking them out of school, we have condemned each new generation boys and girls to a fresh cycle of malnutrition. The treatment of little girls moulds the psyche of their brothers, who internalise the view that their needs as males have preference over those of their sisters. What we have come to thereby is the socialisation of violence against women. There are no estimates of the extent of physical violence against the girl child but it would be reasonable to assume that it is extensive.

In 2007, the Ministry of Women and Child Development published a "National Study on Child Abuse," which reported that 53 per cent of the children interviewed had suffered one or more forms of sexual abuse. It would be dangerous to extrapolate from this limited study that over half our children suffer sexual abuse, but it is clearly far more widespread than we admit. What should be of the gravest concern was that in most cases the children reported that the attack was by someone they knew, often a close relative. Data from the National Crime Records Bureau (NCRB) confirms that this pattern continues as the girl becomes a woman. Since the NCRB can only collate cases registered, its data represent just the tip of the crime iceberg. But it reports that in 2012 there were 24,923 cases of rape registered. In 98 per cent of the cases, the victims knew the offenders. This is a logical outcome of a nurturing process in which boys grow up believing, from what they see in their families, that women exist only to satisfy the needs of men.

Society still resists change. NFHS-3 found that the median age for marriage for girls is still just over 16, and commented that this "is an indicator of the low status of women. It is related to lower empowerment and increased risk of adverse reproductive and health consequences." There is enough data to show how adverse these are.

Women, particularly poor women, are most insecure in childbirth when they fulfill the role society has set for them. According to the Millennium Development Goals (MDG), maternal mortality in India which was 301 per lakh of live births in 2001 should be down to 75 by 2015. This will not happen because society doesn't want. In every part of the society, in any class, in any community women are neglected from their parents and other family members. At 27 million live births in India each year, at least 54,000 women die in the process. We also perhaps do not realise how other problems have a compounding effect. We are, for instance, the world leaders in open defecation. Open defecation is also an open invitation to rape. Complaints to the NHRC show how many women are abducted or raped when they go out into the fields at night. In many States, teenage village girls either refuse to go to school or are taken out by their parents because the building has no toilet and their right to education suffers. It has been seen that in any term and condition, women and girls are only blamed for any crime against themselves.

It is sad but to be expected that women have also been indoctrinated to believe that their security depends on good behaviour, as mandated by men. NHFS-3 found that 40 per cent of married women have been subjected to spousal violence. But it also found that 54 per cent of the women it surveyed agreed that wife-beating was acceptable if the wife went out without telling her husband, argued with him, refused sex, neglected the children, did not cook properly, was suspected of being unfaithful or showed disrespect toward her in-laws. On this, NFHS-3 said: "Violence is more likely to be justified if the described behaviour violates what is perceived as acceptable behaviour for women in their gendered roles as wives, mothers and daughters-in-law." And then there are the more obvious acts of criminal violence against women. There is the enormous problem of trafficking; the special insecurities of women in conflict zones. Adivasi and *Dalit* women are branded as witches. There are the continuing tragedies of forced marriages, of girls being killed for marrying boys of their choice or for not bringing in enough dowry, the needless hysterectomies under the *Rashtriya Swasth Bima Yojana.*

Within society as between states, security depends on power. The weakest are the most insecure. Women in India are insecure and remain at risk because in this patriarchal society they are children of a lesser god. For women to be secure the country must change there should be more women in Parliament and in positions of political and executive authority. Every election brings with it hope of renewal, but India will not be transformed, it cannot be secure, developed or respected if the democracy in which it takes pride does not bring about urgent and fundamental change in the lives of its women.

1.3.1 Global Indices

Gender Inequality is also reflected in India's poor ranking in various global gender indices. UNDP's Gender Inequality Index (2014) shows that India's ranking is 127 out of 152 countries in the List. This ranking is only above Afghanistan as far as SAARC countries are concerned. World Economic Forum's Global Gender Gap Index (2014) reveals that India's ranks at 114 in the list of 142 countries of the world. This Index examines gender gap in four major areas:

- Economic participation and opportunity.
- Educational achievements.
- Health and life expectancy.
- Political empowerment.

India's position on these indicators was as follows:

- Economic participation and opportunity: 134th
- Educational achievements: 126th
- Health and Life expectancy: 141st
- Political empowerment: 15th

These two important Global Indices show the sorry state of affairs in India as far as gender equality is concerned. Only in case of 'Political Empowerment' India is doing fine which is a welcome sign. But other indices are very poor and a lot need to be done to improve the same.

1.3.2 Gender Inequality Statistics

Gender inequality manifests in varied ways. And as far as India is concerned the major indicators are as follows:

- Female Foeticide
- Female Infanticide
- Child (0 to 6 age group) Sex Ratio: 919
- Sex Ratio: 943
- Female literacy: 46 percent
- Maternal Mortality Rate: 178 deaths per 100000 live births.

These above mentioned indicators are some of the important indices which show the status of women in our country. *Female foeticide and female infanticide* are most inhuman of acts. And it is a shame that in India these practices are prevailing at large scale. The data shows that despite the law in place via *Prenatal Diagnostic Techniques (Regulation and Prevention of Misuse) Act, 1994 sex* selective abortion is still on the rise. More than 100000 illegal abortions are being performed every year in India mainly for the reason that the featus is of girl child (WHO, 2001). Due to this, there is an alarming trend which has come to the notice in 2011 census report; the report shows *Child Sex Ratio* (i.e sex-ratio of children between the age group 0 to 6) at 919 which is 8 points lesser than the 2001 data of 927. The data indicates that sex-selective abortion is increasing in our country. As far as overall *sex ratio* is concerned, it's 943 in 2011 report as compared to 933 of 2001 which is 10 points increase. Though it is a good sign that overall sex ratio is increasing but it's still tilted against females. *Female literacy* is at 65.46 percent in 2011 as against 82.14 percent of male literacy. This gap indicates a wide gender disparity in India that Indians do not give enough importance to the education of girls.

All these indicators points towards the state of affairs in India regarding gender justice and women's human right. Though every year government starts various schemes and programs apart from existing ones for the benefit and empowerment of women but on the ground there are not enough visible changes. The change will appear only when the mind set of Indian society would change; when the society would start treating male and female on equal footing and when a girl would not be considered as a burden. The following table 1.1 compares the population wide data for the two genders on various inequality statistical measures, according to The World Bank's Gender Statistics database for 2012. Data shows that female group of India as well as in World, is a vulnerable group regarding the occurrence of formal financial institution. Economically women are weaker than men in all over the world but in Indian context women do more physical work and we can see that employees in agriculture where women participation is 59.8 percent and men participation is 43 percent. Not only in the field of agriculture, but self employed trend of women in India is 85.5 percent than the men frequency of 80.6 percent which is comparatively greater. Apart from these ratio women are stood behind in education, government job and other section rather than men.

Table 1.1: Gender Statistic Comparison

Gender Statistic Measure	*India*		*World*	
	Female	*Male*	*Female*	*Male*
Account at a formal financial institution (% of each gender, age 15+)	26.5	43.7	46.6	54.5
Deposits in a typical month (% with an account, age 15+)	11.2	13.4	13.0	12.8
Employees in agriculture (% of total labor)	59.8	43	-	-
Employees in industry (% of total labor)	20.7	26	-	-
Expected years of schooling	11.3	11.8	11.7	12.0
Loan from a financial institution in the past year (% age 15+)	6.7	8.6	8.1	10.0
Lower secondary school completion rate (%)	76.0	77.9	70.2	70.5
Outstanding loan from banks for health or emergencies (% age 15+)	12.6	15.7	10.3	11.6
Outstanding loan from banks to purchase a home, (% age 15+)	2.26	2.35	6.6	7.4
Primary school completion rate, (%)	96.6	96.3		
Ratio to male youth unemployment rate (% ages 15–24, ILO method)	1.13	1.0	1.14	1.0
Ratio to males in primary and secondary education (%)	0.98	1.0	0.97	1.0
Secondary school education, gender of teachers (%)	41.1	58.9	51.9	48.1
Secondary school education, pupils (%)	46	54	47.6	52.4
Self-employed, (% employed)	85.5	80.6	-	-
Unemployment, (% of labor force, ILO method)	4	3.1	-	-
Unemployment, youth (% of labor force ages 15–24, ILO method)	10.6	9.4	15.1	13.0
Withdrawals in a typical month, (% with an account, age 15+)	18.6	12.7	15.5	12.8

Source: World Bank's Gender Statistics Database, 2012.

1.3.3 Types of Gender Inequality in India

The root cause of gender inequality in Indian society lies in its patriarchy system. According to the sociologists, patriarchy is "a system of social structure and practices in which men dominate, oppress and exploit women". Women's exploitation is an age old cultural phenomenon of Indian society. The system of patriarchy finds its validity and sanction in our religious beliefs, whether it is Hindu, Muslim or any other religion. For instance, as per ancient Hindu law giver: "Women are supposed to be in the custody of their father when they are children, they must be under the custody of their husband when married and under the custody of her son in old age or as widows. In no circumstances she should be allowed to assert herself independently".

The above described position of women as per Manu is still the case in present modern day social structure. Barring few exceptions here and there, women have no power to take independent decisions either inside their homes or in outside world. In Muslims also the situation is same and there too sanction for discrimination or subordination is provided by religious texts and Islamic traditions. Similarly in other religious beliefs also women are being discriminated against in one way or other. The unfortunate part of gender inequality in our society is that the women too, through, continued socio-cultural conditioning, have accepted their subordinate position to men. And they are also part and parcel of same patriarchal system. Extreme poverty and lack of education are also some of the reasons for women's low status in society. Poverty and lack of education derives countless women to work in low paying domestic service, organized prostitution or as migrant laborers. Women are not only getting unequal pay for equal or more work but also they are being offered only low skill jobs for which lower wages are paid. This has become a major form of inequality on the basis of gender.

Educating girl child is still seen as a bad investment because she is bound to get married and leave her paternal home one day. Thus, without having good education women are found lacking in present day's demanding job skills; whereas, each year's High School and 10+2 standard results show that girls are always doing better than boys. This shows that parents are not spending much after 10+2 standard on girl child and that's why they lack in job market. Not only in education, in case of family food habits, it is the male child who gets all the nutritious and choicest foods while the girl child gets whatever is left behind after the male members have taken their meals or the food which is low in both quality and nutrition. And this becomes a major health issue in her later years. One of the main reasons for the high incidences of difficult births and anemia in women is the poor quality of food which a girl always gets either in her paternal home or in her in-laws as also is the excessive workload that they are made to bear from their early childhood. So the inequality or discrimination against women is at various levels in the society, either in home or outside home.

1.3.4 Reasons of Gender Disparity

Attaining gender justice is not an easy task in India. From time immemorial, a girl child has been considered as an unwanted entity and a burden that the parents would not mind doing away with. Discrimination against women begins even before her birth. The gruesome evils of female feticide and infanticide prove how brutal the world could be to women. Though the Indian constitution provides equal rights and privileges for men and women and makes equal provision to improve the status of women in society, majority of women are still unable to enjoy the rights and opportunities guaranteed to them. Traditional value system, low level of literacy, more house hold responsibilities lack of awareness, non-availability of proper guidance, low mobility, lack of self confidence family discouragement and advanced science and technology are some of the factors responsible to create gender disparity in our society. The most important causes of gender disparity such as poverty, illiteracy, unemployment, social customs, belief and anti-female attitude are discussed here.

1.3.4.1 Poverty

In India of the total 30 per cent people who are below poverty line, 70 percent are women. Women's poverty in India is directly related to the absence of economic opportunities and autonomy, lack of access to economic resources including credit, land ownership and inheritance, lack of access to education and support services and their minimal participation in the decision making process. The situation of women on economic front is no better and men still enjoy a larger share of the cake. Thus poverty stands at the root of

gender discrimination in our patriarchal society and this economic dependence on the male counterpart is itself a cause of gender disparity.

1.3.4.2 Illiteracy

Despite the notable efforts by the countries around the globe that have expanded for the basic education, there are approximately 960 million illiterate adults of whom two thirds are women .Educational backwardness of the girls has been the resultant cause of gender discrimination. The disparities become more visible between male and female literacy rate, during 2001. The literacy rates for males increased from 56 percent in 1981 to nearly 76 percent in 2001. The corresponding change in female literacy rate from 30 to 54 percent. On the whole the decline

on gender gap peaked in 1981 at 26.6 percent and was 21.7 percent in 2001 is less impressive. The interstate variation in literacy rate for males was much lower in comparison to females. At the state level female literacy rate varies from 35 percent in Bihar to 88 percent in Kerala In states like Arunachal Pradesh, Assam, Bihar, Jammu and Kashmir and Rajasthan, the female literacy rate is below 50 percent.

The progress towards education by girls is very slow and gender disparities persist at primary, upper primary and secondary stage of education. Girl's account for only 43.7 percent of enrolment at primary level, 40 .9 percent at upper primary level, 38.6 percent at secondary level and 36.9 percent at degree and above level. More over girl's participation in education is still below 50 percent Gender differences in enrolment are prevalent in all the state at all levels. They are not able to realize full identity and power in all spheres of life only due to illiteracy.

1.3.4.3 Lack of Employment Facilities

Women are not able to resolve the conflict between new economic and old domestic roles. In both rural and urban India, women spend a large proportion of time on unpaid home sustaining work. Women are not able to respond to new opportunities and shift to new occupations because their mobility tends to be low due to intra-house hold allocation of responsibilities. Rights and obligations within a house hold are not distributed evenly. Male ownership of assets and conventional division of labour reduce incentives for women to undertake new activities. In addition child bearing has clear

implications for labour force participation by women. Time spent in bearing and rearing of children often results in de-Skilling, termination of long term labour contacts. Thus women are not being able to be economically self sufficient due to unemployment and their economic dependence on the male counterpart is itself a cause of gender disparity.

1.3.4.4 Social Customs, Beliefs and Practices

Women are not free from social customs, beliefs and practices. The traditional patrilineal joint family system confines women's roles mostly to the domestic sphere, allocating them to a subordinate status, authority and power compared to men. Men are perceived as the major providers and protectors of a family while women are perceived as playing only a supportive role, attending to the hearth. Boys and girls are accordingly drained for different adult roles, status and authority. In Indian culture since very early periods, men have dominated women as a group and their status has been low in the family and society.

The preference for sons and disfavour towards daughter is complex phenomenon that still persists in many places. Sons especially in the business communities are considered to be economic, political and ritual assets where as daughters are considered to be liabilities. Thus anti female social bias is the main cause of gender disparity in our society. The boy receives a ceremonial welcome on his birth where as everyone is sad at the birth of a girl child. The preference for male child is due to lower female labour participation, prevalence of social evils like dowry and many others causes. The typical orthodox mentality is present even in this modern era leading to sex determination tests and abortion in an illegal way. Parents often think that teaching a girl child to manage the kitchen is more important than sending her to school. Many feel that it is an unnecessary financial burden to send a girl child to school as subsequently she will be married off and shifted to some other family. This orthodox belief of parents is responsible for gender disparity.

1.3.4.5 Social Behaviour

Though many social activists and reformers carried their crusade against all social odds to restore honour and dignity to women, attitudinal disparities still hunt our rural masses. Despite pronounced social development and technological advancement, women in our society still continue to be victims of exploitation, superstition, illiteracy and social atrocities. The social stigma that women are housekeepers and should be confined to the four walls of the house is perhaps a viable cause of gender disparity. They should not raise their voice regarding their fortune for the sake of the prestige of the family. In patriarchal society a lot of weightage is given to men. In the health and nutritional field, male members of family are supposed to take fresh and nutritious food in comparison to women because either they are earning members or head of the family or they are supposed to be more important than female members. This type of social attitude is conducive to create the problem of gender discrimination.

1.3.4.6 Lack of Awareness of Women

Most of the women are unaware of their basic rights and capabilities. They even do not have the understanding as to how the socio-economic and political forces affect them. They accept all types of discriminatory practices that persist in our family and society largely due to their ignorance and unawareness. Article 15 of the Indian constitution states, the state shall not discriminate any citizen on the ground of sex only. The irony is that there still is widespread discrimination which is a form of injustice to women. Hence at the onset of the new millennium let this generation be a historic example by putting an end to the gender based discriminations by unfurling the flag of gender justice in all our action and dealings. As Desai has stated, if women get equal opportunities like men, they can work in every field like men. Today if she lags behind a little, it is not her fault but the fault of traditions which have suppressed them for centuries, owing to this, her own thoughts like also hang around only familial life and her nearest environment also does not provide favourable conditions for her devotion in the outside work. In order to change the situation along with economic growth social progress is also greatly required. Hence the need of the hour is to effectively combat gender disparity as to promote gender equality by sufficiently empowering the women.

1.4 Cultural Factors

Women during the early Vedic period enjoyed equal status with men in all aspects of life. Works by ancient Indian grammarians such as Patanjali and Katyayana suggest that women were educated in the early Vedic period. Rigvedic verses suggest that women married at a mature age and were probably free to select their own husbands. Scriptures such as the Rig Veda and Upanishads mention several women sages and seers, notably Gargi and Maitreyi. In approximately 500 B.C., the status of women began to decline. Although, reform movements such as Jainism allowed women to be admitted to religious orders, by and large women in India faced confinement and restrictions. The practice of child marriages is believed to have started around the sixth century. Indian women's position in society further deteriorated during the medieval period, when child marriages and a ban on remarriage by widows became part of social life in some communities in India. The Muslim conquest in the Indian subcontinent brought purdah to Indian society. Among the Rajputs of Rajasthan, the Jauhar was practised. In some parts of India, some of Devadasis were sexually exploited. Polygamy was practised among Hindu Kshatriya rulers for some political reasons. In many Muslim families, women were restricted to Zenana areas of the house. With different aspects and correlation between women and culture, some disparity is originated from following reasones which are mentioned below:

1.4.1 Patrilocality

Many cultures practice patrilocality whereby a married couple lives near or with the husband's parents. When a woman gets married, she essentially ceases to be a member of her birth family and joins her husband's family. Under this system, parents potentially reap more of the returns to investments in a son's health and education because he will remain a part of their family, whereas a daughter will physically and financially leave the household upon marriage. Co-residence of adult sons and elderly parents is much more common in Asia, the Middle East, and North Africa than in Europe, sub Saharan Africa, and the Americas (Ebenstein, 2014).

Within India, the northern region has a much stronger patrilocal (and patrilineal) system than the south, which is one explanation for why gender inequality is more pronounced in the north (Dyson and Moore, 1983). For example, Chakraborty and Kim (2010) examine the 1901 Indian Census and, that the sex ratio was less male skewed in the south, a pattern that continues to hold today. More generally, Ebenstein (2014) shows that the male to female sex ratio is positively correlated with the rate of co-residence between adult sons and their parents both across and within countries.

If parents fully internalized their daughters' returns to nutrition, health care, and schooling, then patrilocality would not necessarily cause gender gaps in these inputs. In practice, though, the longer duration that parents will core side and pool financial resources with their sons seems to cause them to invest disproportionately in sons. For example, parents are more likely to seek medical care for a sick son than sick daughter. In one study, 405 parents in India who had been advised that their child needed surgery to correct a congenital heart condition were followed up one year later; 70 percent of the boys but only 44 percent of the girls had undergone surgery (Ramakrishnan, et al., 2011). The financial mindset about investing in daughters is encapsulated in an often quoted Indian saying that \raising a daughter is like watering your neighbors' garden." This sentiment is echoed in a Chinese proverb that describes raising a daughter as ploughing someone else's field.

Poverty could exacerbate the tendency to invest more in sons than daughters. Suppose the net returns to surgery are positive for both boys and girls but higher for boys. If a family is liquidity-constrained, they might seek medical care only for their son, but with more available resources, they would seek care for both their son and daughter. (The same reasoning could apply if parents invest more in boys because boys have higher labor market returns to health, and not just when the gender gap is due to cultural practices). Consistent with the idea that poverty can widen the gender gap in investment, Rose (1999) found that favorable rainfall in rural India increased girls' survival more than boys'. Theoretically, parents' marginal spending need not always beneath the disadvantaged group however (Kanbur and Haddad, 1994). Oster (2009) reports that better access to health care initially widens the gender gap in vaccinations in India, but further improvements close the gender gap.

1.4.2 Son Preferable Mindset

Closely linked to patrilocality is the fact that sons traditionally provide old-age support for their parents in societies such as China and India. Ebenstein and Leung (2010) investigate this old age support norm as a reason for the desire to have sons in China. When the Chinese government instituted the Rural Old Age Pension Program, parents now had a better substitute for old-age support from sons, and thus their desire to have a son should have abated. The authors show several patterns in the data consistent with this hypothesized effect. Households without sons are more likely to participate in the pension program (and also to have more savings). In addition, having access to the pension program is associated with a less skewed sex ratio. With the rollout of the pension, the cultural norm that sons not daughters support parents did not change, but its implications for the desire to have a son and the skewed sex ratio did change. When a formal institution for retirement savings arose, the informal method of relying on sons became less important, and therefore this force driving son preference became less relevant.

1.4.3 Girls Marriage Problem

Dowry is a payment that a bride's parents make to the couple at the time of marriage. According to Boserup (1970), dowry systems emerged mainly in societies where women played a lesser role in agriculture. Dowry has disappeared in many societies, notably in Europe, but it has persisted in, for example, South Asia. In fact, over the past several decades, the prevalence of dowry has increased in Bangladesh, and the real value of dowry payments has risen considerably in India (Rao, 1993; Anderson, 2007). In addition, the property rights to dowry as practiced today diver from those seen historically in Europe.

In ancient Rome and medieval Western Europe, the bride held the rights to the dowry; it was her pre-mortem inheritance from her parents (Anderson, 2007). In this formulation, the dowry system was intended to improve the financial well being of females. However, in societies where dowry is used today, the groom typically controls the money dowry is the 12 price of a groom. Dowry is thus a financial cost to parents of having daughters.

Evidence on the impacts of the dowry system on women's welfare is mostly anecdotal. This anecdotal evidence points to the dowry system causing pro-male bias. The prospect of paying dowry is often cited as a key factor in parents' desire to have sons rather than daughters in India, for example (Arnold, et al., 1998; Das Gupta, et al., 2003). The financial burden of dowry indeed seems to loom large in prospective parents' minds. Kusum (1993) describes a billboard that was put up when prenatal sex-diagnostic tests were just arriving in India; a new clinic in the city of Amristar urged parents to invest Rs. 500 now, save Rs. 50,000 later." The 500 rupees today was for an ultrasound test, which would tell the parents if their fetus was female; the 50,000 rupees later |which was obvious enough that it did not need to be spelled out on the billboard was the dowry the parents would save if they aborted the female fetus. Having to pay a dowry for a daughter's marriage should decrease the desire to have daughters but should not necessarily reduce investments in daughters. In principle, parents could recoup their investment in their daughter's health and education in the form of lower dowry demands or a higher quality son-in-law. However, this idealized market solution where parents invest in their daughter's human capital and the groom later compensates them for the investment does not seem to work in practice, perhaps because investments are not fully observable by the groom. In addition, parents have reason to care more about the quality of their daughters-in-law than their sons in law because daughters-in-law will live with them under patrilocality and raise their heirs under patrilineality. Besides reducing human capital investments, the dowry system also results in newly married women sometimes being the victim of violence or, worse, dowry deaths" as punishment for the dowry amount being deemed inadequate by the groom (Bloch and Rao, 2002).

1.4.4 Patrilineality

In a patrilineal system, names and property pass to the next generation through male descendants. This system puts sons on a higher footing than daughters, and the specific feature of land inheritance is especially likely to have effects on gender gaps. For example, in India because widows traditionally do not inherit their husbands' ancestral property, they rely on their sons as their conduit for holding onto the family property and maintaining their standard of living in widowhood. Anderson (2003) and Anderson and Bidner (2014) drawn model that aim to explain the divergent trends in Europe and India and the historical transformation of dowry into a groom price. Having sons is often not appreciably different between women and men. Under the Hindu Succession Act of 1956, sons shared the right to inherit ancestral property in India. In the 1980s and 1990s, the law was amended in four states to make daughters' status equal to sons'. The reforms had some bite: In the sample that Deininger, et al. (2013) analyze, 8 percent of daughters whose fathers died before the reforms inherited land; the proportion increased to 16 percent among those whose father died after the reforms. (About 70 percent of fathers owned land; the fraction of sons who inherited land remained steady at 70 percent before and after the reforms.) As a result of the law changes, women's age of marriage rose, consistent with their having more bargaining power within the family and financial independence (Deininger, et al., 2013). The reforms also increased girls' schooling, presumably because their mothers were more empowered in the household or because education and asset ownership are complements (Deininger, et al., 2013; Roy, 2013). However, the legal reforms also seem to have had some negative consequences for women. Anderson and Genicot (2014) and that they led to a rise in suicides, which they conjecture is due to a backlash effect whereby the increase in female bargaining power sparked marital convicts.

1.4.5 Religious Rituals

In certain belief systems, such as Confucianism in China and Hinduism in India, sons play a special role. Confucianism encourages the patrilineal and patrilocal system in place in China, Vietnam, and elsewhere. But another part of the special role of sons is in rituals. Ancestor worship within Confucianism involves rituals where a son plays an essential part. Similarly, son preference is mentioned in the Vedas, the ancient Hindu texts. In addition, in Hindu societies, it is supposed to be a son who lights a deceased person's funeral pyre and brings him or her salvation. Hindu kinship norms are adhered to more strictly among upper castes than lower castes (Mandelbaum, 1970), and Chakraborty and Kim (2010), in their analysis of the 1901 Indian Census, and a more skewed sex ratio for upper castes than lower castes.

The funeral pyre underpinning of son preference specifically generates a strong desire for one son (with further sons perhaps serving as insurance in case the first son predeceases his parents). Other reasons for son preference such as wanting someone to carry on the family name or widows wanting to retain family land also make the first son especially valuable. Consistent with this idea, Jayachandran (2014) finds that parents in India strongly want to have one son and, once they have one son, prefer a balanced gender ratio, more or less.

1.5 Facts and Figures of Gender Inequality by Different Aspects of Discrimination in India

India ranks 132 out of 187 countries on the gender inequality index lower than Pakistan (123) according to the United Nation Development Programs Human development report 2013. The report said all countries in South Asia, with the exception of Afghanistan were a better place for women than India, with Sri Lanka (75) topping them all. Gender based discrimination against female children is pervasive across the world. It is seen in all the strata of society and manifests in various forms. As per the literature, female child has been treated inferior to male child and this is deeply engraved in the mind of the female child. Some argue that due to this inferior treatment the females fail to understand their rights. This is more predominant in India as well as other lesser developed countries. Sex selection before birth and neglect of the female child after birth, in childhood and, during the teenage years has outnumbered males to females in India and also in countries like Pakistan, Bangladesh and South Korea. There are 1029 women per 1000 men in North America and 1076 women per 1000 men in Europe, but there are only 927 women per 1000 men in India. These numbers tell us quite a harsh story about neglect and mistreatment of the female child in India. Women have a biological advantage over men for longevity and survival, yet there are more men than women. The frequency above support that gender discrimination of female child is a basic facility area. Though the demographic characteristics do not show much or in some cases, anti-female bias, there is always a woman who receives a small piece of the pie.

There are two main inequalities as pointed out by Amartya Sen: educational inequality and health inequality. These are the indicators of a woman's status of welfare. In India irrespective of the caste, creed, religion and social status, the overall status of a woman is lower than men and therefore a male child is preferred over a female child. A male child is considered a blessing and his birth is celebrated as opposed to a female child where her birth is not celebrated and is considered more of a burden. Therefore, education and health care of the female child in India is an important social indicator to measure equality between men and women. According to the 2001 Indian census, overall male-female ratio was 927 females per 1000 males. However, the 2011 Indian census shows that there are 914 females per 1000 males. During the last decade the number female children to male children in the youngest age group fell from 945 per 1000 males to 927 per 1000 males.

It is also observed that gender disparity depending on the location, as the Northern states (particularly Punjab, Haryana, and Himachal Pradesh) seem to be more biased then the Southern states. The sharpest decline for the age group of zero to six years is observed in the Northern States particularly in Punjab (793 per 1000 females) and Haryana (820 per 1000 females). (Amartya Sen, 2001). These new figures point out that the use of new technology contributes to the gender composition. Furthermore, the availability of and access to new technologies provides new ways for parent to achieve such goals of sex determination before birth. Due to the widespread use of this technology the Indian Government banned the sex determination before birth. In spite of these bans imposed by the Government, the law is not widely followed.

A social development report presented in 2010 to the World Bank and UNDP, found that the time a female child and a male child spends on various activities is similar, with the exception of domestic work and social/ resting time; a female child spends nearly three forth of an hour more on domestic work than a male child and therefore lesser hours of social activity/resting than boys. Despite progress in advancing gender equity from a legal standpoint, in practice many women and female children still lack opportunities, and support for the socio-economic advancement (http://www.cdc.gov/healthyyouth/physicalactivity/facts.htm). Historically, the inclusion of young girls and women in education has helped challenge gender stereotypes and discrimination. This suggests that providing space for young girls to develop leadership skills, through education and healthy living is important. This can shape attitudes towards women's capabilities as leaders and decision makers especially in conventionally male domains and male dominated cultures. Because of the sex preference of male children in India, female children are deemed of resources in the areas of health and education.

Though the government in India has launched schemes with great fanfare, the most powerful officials in the country continue to treat educated women as second class citizens who do not even have the right to their hard earned money. In Western nations women typically live about six years longer than men, but this is not true in India. Evidence shows that girls are given less food and health care than boys, especially in Northern India. Girls are breastfed for shorter periods, given less medical attention, fewer consultations and visits to the doctor, and are often taken very late to the hospital in an emergency. Because of some culturally assigned duties, many girls miss out on the chance to improve their overall health. Miller calls this as an extended infanticide, since life sustaining necessities like food, nutrition and health care are denied to the female child. Female children are given less food, both in quality and quantity, and therefore are undernourished compared to male children. This in turn leads to health issues like anemia and intrauterine growth restriction during pregnancy. If a woman gives birth to a female child while malnourished, then the child's survival issues and salon nutritional issues increase. However, the female child's status is the product of general societal attitude towards women at large in India. Girls in India face higher risks of malnutrition, disease, disability, and retardation of growth and development. They have no access to or control over the resources because their work toward raising a family and in the household chores is undervalued. A popular Telugu saying from

Andhra Pradesh says, "*Bringing up a daughter is like watering a plant in another's courtyard*". Due to this understanding, girl is considered a liability and outside commodity and is deprived of good food and nutrition. According to a global study, India is the fourth most dangerous country for a female child in the world.

Experts often argue that women's education is the key to reducing discrimination against girls. However, female literacy rate has risen from 15 to 54 percent, even as the juvenile sex ratio has fallen. Some studies have shown that educated mothers are far more "efficient" in discriminating against their daughters than uneducated mothers. Other studies have shown that though higher levels of maternal education decreases infant mortality for both boys and girls, the effect is larger for girls. Thus, higher levels of maternal education decrease gender differentials in child mortality. On the other hand, there is also evidence that maternal education at the district and household levels is weakly associated with increases in female survival (Rosenzweig and Shultz, 1982). At a macro level, regions with high female literacy states Kerala, Andhra Pradesh, Tamilnadu, Karnataka and Goa, have shown less discrimination towards girls. However, in the past 20 years, high female literacy has not stopped Delhi, Gujarat, and Rajasthan from showing increased discrimination against girls.

The female child in India is often deprived from her right of an education. The number of girls dropping out of school far exceeds the boys because girls are expected to help at home, either with household work like washing and cooking or with taking care of younger siblings. Since girls spend more time performing domestic duties and this increases the gap between female and male equality in rural parts of India, it perpetuates the myth that education is of no help to the girl and her primary job will be to look after the household work, get married early, have children and then raise them. If this is the job she has to do, then education is of no importance to her and it is not imparted. Also, even with education and financial independence, women might not get the same rights and liberties which a man may have. It is through education in the early days of a child that we can bring about behavior changes and open doors to opportunities that will enhance their confidence, personality, and career. Often in these communities, women, in particular, are considered an inferior sex and are raised to accept this belief. Nearly 80 percent of the girls drop out from standards I to V. Out of the 100 girls that enroll in the first year of school, only 42 reach class V. Among Scheduled Castes and Scheduled Tribes, many of those who live below poverty line, only 19 of the 100 girls reach class V. With above background some fundamental indicators are depicted below.

1.5.1 Fundamental Indicator of Gender Inequality

The sex ratio at birth is defined as the number of live female births per 1,000 live male births. A fall in this ratio implies that the number of females born alive is declining relative to the number of males born alive. In evaluating sex ratios in terms of relative female or male deficits at birth, the relevant comparator is not equality in the number of females and males (i.e., a sex ratio of 1,000), however. This is because in most populations more males than females are born (Waldron, 1983; 1998). The sex ratio at birth recorded across most developing countries has been found to vary in a narrow range from 943 to 971 (United Nations Development Programme, 1998). A fundamental indicator of gender inequality in India, and arguably, one of the powerful, is a preference for sons so strong that it is manifested as limiting the birth and survival of girls. The 2001 census data for India revealed a sharp decline in the sex ratio for the population age 0-6, from 945 females in 1991 to 927 females per 1,000 males. The trend in the sex ratio of the under-seven population based on National Family Health Survey data for the period 1992-93 to 2005-06 also provides evidence of continued decline and shows that in 2005-06 the under-seven sex ratio had fallen further to 918 females per 1,000 males (table 1.2).

Table 1.2: Levels and trends of the Sex Ratio in India

Status	*NFHS-1*	*NFHS-2*	*NFHS-3*
	1992-9	*1998-99*	*2005-06*
Trends in the sex ratio (females per 1,000 males) of the population, age 0-6 Years	934	926	918
Trends in the sex ratios at birth for all children born in the five complete calendar years	941	938	919

Note: Females per 1,000 males.
Source: NFHS-1, 2 and 3.

The decline over time in the under seven sex ratio can have one or more of mainly three possible causes: a decrease in the sex ratio at birth through the use of technologies that enable sex selection; an increase in the mortality of girl children compared with the mortality of boy children, suggesting intensification of the already documented discrimination against the girl child (Miller, 1981; Das Gupta, 1987; Kishor, 1993); or a systematic undercount of female children, compared with male children under the age of seven. Even as the role, if any, of the last of these possible causes is debated, it is commonly accepted that the other two causes, fueled by strong son preference and the low status of women in many regions of India, play a substantial role in reducing the under seven sex ratio. Indeed, discrimination against the female child was recognized not just by social scientists but also by policy makers long before the release of the 2001 Census. This is evident in various policy initiatives undertaken earlier. For example, the Pre-Natal Diagnostic Techniques (Regulation and Prevention of Misuse) Act prohibiting the use of prenatal diagnostic techniques for the purpose of prenatal sex determination was passed as early as 1994 in recognition of the widespread use of ultrasound and related technologies to eliminate unwanted female foetuses. Further, the National Population Policy of 2000 explicitly recognized the problem and suggested policy initiatives directed toward ending discriminatory practices that adversely affect the health of the girl child (Ministry of Health and Family Welfare, 2000). Since the pathways to a lower sex ratio of the population age 0-6 mainly involve a low sex ratio at birth and/or excess female mortality after birth, this chapter examines the levels of these and related indicators, including the sex ratio of live births by whether the mother had an ultrasound test during pregnancy. Overall sex ratio at birth can be directly affected by the use of modern technologies that allow couples to have only children of a desired sex. In addition, where strong couple level gender preferences exist, couples are more likely to stop having children only when their desired sex combination of children has been achieved. This stopping behaviour will not affect the overall sex ratio at birth, but will affect the sex ratios at birth of last births. For example, in societies with strong son preference, last births are more likely to be male, and females are more likely to grow up in large families. Thus, an examination of sex ratios of last births provides insight into the pervasiveness of son preference.

1.5.2 Status in the Sex Ratio at Birth

The sex ratio of births that died in each of the five calendar-year periods increased from 991 females per 1,000 males in the period 1987-91 to 1,045 females in the period 2000-04. In the same time period, the sex ratio of surviving births declined from 936 to 910. (Notably, the sex ratio at birth of surviving births closely mirrors the sex ratio at birth for all births, since births that survive constitute a large majority of all births). These data suggest that not only are fewer than expected females being born, but females are increasingly over represented in births that die.

Table 1.3: Trends in the Sex Ratios at Birth of Live Births and Births that have Died in the Five complete calendar years, in India

Status	*NFHS-1*	*NFHS-2*	*NFHS-3*
1992-93	1998-99	2005-06	
Live	936	931	910
Dead	991	1011	1045

Note: Females per 1,000 males.

Source: NFHS-1, 2 and 3.

In India, the sex ratio at birth calculated for all births in the five complete calendar year periods before each of the three National Family Health Surveys not only shows a downward trend in the sex ratio at birth in the five years between 1992-93 and 1998-99, but also shows an acceleration in the decline in the sex ratio between 1993-97 and 2000-04 (table 1.3). In the late 1980s and early 1990s, the sex ratios at birth at 941 and 938 respectively, did not deviate too far from 943, which is the lowest sex ratio at birth within the normal range. However, by the early 2000s the sex ratio at birth in India had fallen well below the normal range to 919. After birth, genetic vulnerabilities result in higher male than female mortality during early childhood in most populations, especially at the neonatal stage. An examination of the trends in the sex ratios at birth by the survival status of the child in the five complete calendar-year periods before each of the three NFHS surveys, however, reveals a strong female disadvantage in survival (table 1.4).

Table 1.4: Trends in the Sex Ratios at Birth for all Children Born in the Five complete Calendar Years in India

Status	*NFHS-1*	*NFHS-2*	*NFHS-3*
1992-93	1998-99	2005-06	
Female	941	938	919

Note: Females per 1,000 males.

Source: NFHS-1, 2 and 3.

1.5.3 Relation between Sex Ratios and Wealth Status

In India the sex ratio at birth, as well as the sex ratio of the population age 0-6 years, varies greatly by household wealth status. In fact, the sex ratio at birth in the five years preceding NFHS-3 is highest, at 954 females per 1,000 males, in the lowest wealth quintile (table 1.5). The sex ratio at birth for births to women in the second wealth quintile, though slightly lower, is also within the normal range for sex ratios at birth (943-971).

Beyond the second wealth quintile, however, the sex ratio at birth falls dramatically by wealth to a low of 854 for births to women in the highest quintile. As expected, the sex ratio of the population age 0-6, which captures the sex ratio of surviving births, also follows a similar pattern.

Table 1.5: Sex Ratio of Population Age 0-6 years and Sex Ratio at Birth for all Births to Women Age 15-49 in the Five Years by Wwealth Quintile in India

Sex Ratio	*Lowest*	*Second*	*Middle*	*Fourth*	*Highest*
Sex ratio of population age 0-6 years	942	947	927	892	856
Sex ratio at birth for births in the past 5 years	954	945	920	889	854

Note: Females per 1,000 males.

Source: NFHS-3.

1.6 Leading Factors of Gender Disparity

We know a lot about gender inequality and its history which tells that how people experience it in their lives, the ways it varies in intensity and form across time and place, the beliefs that make it seem natural, and much more. The outpouring of research and commentary on gender inequality over the past half century has been extraordinary. Unfortunately, despite all this, our understanding of what causes gender inequality remains troubled. Both ordinary people and experts commonly fluctuate between simplistic explanations that founder under close scrutiny and throwing up their hands in frustration over what can seem an enigma beyond human comprehension. Here we will seek to surmount this dilemma. We will explore diverse facets of gender inequality and varied ideas about what causes might be decisive. We will also look carefully at the ways we can identify and verify the causes of social phenomena. Through these efforts we will aim both to enhance our understanding of what produces gender inequality and to improve our general ability to do causal social analyses effectively.

1.6.1 Role of Modern Technology

Sex ratios at birth can diverge greatly from the normal range only with the use of technologies that can help choose or determine the sex of the foetus, such as ultrasound diagnostic testing during pregnancy. In India, 24 percent of all pregnancies in the five years preceding NFHS-3 received an ultrasound test (IIPS and Macro International, 2007). NFHS-3 shows that it is pregnancies to women in the highest wealth quintile that are most likely to receive an ultrasound test: the proportion of pregnancies receiving an ultrasound test increases from only 4 percent and 10 percent for pregnancies to women in the lowest and the second wealth quintile to

21 percent and 38 percent for pregnancies in the next two quintiles, and finally to a high of 62 percent in the highest wealth quintile. While a substantial proportion of ultrasound tests are done for diagnostic purposes, an examination of sex ratios at birth can reveal the extent to which ultrasound testing is being used for sex selection. In India, sex ratios at birth estimated separately for pregnancies with and without ultrasound testing provides clear evidence that many women are using ultrasound tests for sex selection.

Table 1.6: Trends in Sex Ratios at Birth (females per 1,000 males) of Last Births, all other Births and all Births in India

Sex ratios at birth	*Sex ratio at birth*		
	NFHS-1	*NFHS-2*	*NFHS-3*
Last births only	837	791	756
All births except last births	976	981	1,016
All births	935	920	926

Source: NFHS-1, 2 and 3.

The much lower sex ratios at birth at each level of wealth for completed pregnancies that had an ultrasound test, compared with those that did not, provide evidence that ultrasound tests are often being used for the purpose of sex selection at all levels of wealth. Table 1.7 also shows that the sex ratio of completed pregnancies with an ultrasound test to women in the highest wealth quintile (818) is much lower than for pregnancies with an ultrasound to women in any other wealth quintile (854 - 905). This suggests that women in the highest wealth quintile are more likely than women in the lower wealth quintiles to be using ultrasound tests for sex selection. It could be argued that while wealth may only help to increase access to sex selection technology, education has the additional potential to inform and empower women in ways that can reduce son preference. NFHS-3 shows that use of ultrasound tests increases with women's education: For pregnancies in the five years prior to NFHS-3, 9 percent had an ultrasound test if the mother had no education, compared with 58 percent if the mother had 10 or more years of education. In addition, pregnancies without an ultrasound test to women with no education or less than 10 complete years of education result in normal sex ratios at birth, but pregnancies without an ultrasound test to women with 10 or more years of education have an abnormally low sex ratio at birth. This suggests that some educated women may be using sex selection methods that are not being reported. Thus the data shows that more educated women are having disproportionately more sons than daughters, both in absolute terms and compared with women in other educational groups.

Table 1.7: Sex Ratio of Completed Pregnancies with an Ultrasound Test by Quintiles

Ultrasound Test	*Lowest*	*Second*	*Middle*	*Fourth*	*Highest*
No ultrasound test during pregnancy	955	954	923	911	935
Ultrasound test during pregnancy	859	881	905	854	818

Source: NFHS 3.

1.6.2 Sex Ratios at Birth by Birth Order

The sex ratio at birth for a population is a single number, an average for all births in a given time period. This ratio does not differentiate between sex ratios at birth for births with different characteristics or for births to couples with different fertility related desires. This section explores how sex ratios at birth vary by birth order. If son preference exists in a society, evidence of it will typically be found in lower sex ratios at lower birth orders relative to those at higher birth orders and for last births compared with all other births. A caveat regarding a potential source of error is necessary here since this analysis is based on all children ever born (i.e., all births in the survey and not just recent births) to women in the age range of 15-49. Recall error tends to increase the further back in time one goes. The sex ratio at birth will be affected if there is any tendency to recall births of one sex more than births of another sex.

It is expected that sex ratios at birth for first births are less likely than sex ratios of births at higher orders to be affected by factors such as stopping rules' that make it more likely that a couple will stop having children after the birth of a child of the desired sex. The total fertility rate in India of 2.7 children per woman suggests that most women do not stop having children after only one child. Further, since first births are often perceived to be risky, it is also expected that ultrasound and other diagnostic tests would be less likely to be performed primarily for sex selection for first births. Additionally, 7 out of 10 or more currently married women and men in India want at least one daughter. Together these factors suggest that the sex of the first child is less likely to be controlled.

Despite expectations to the contrary, table 1.8 shows that the sex ratio at birth for first-born children has been below normal in all three NFHS surveys and has been declining steadily since NFHS-1. This is also true for births at birth order two. However, in all three surveys, the sex ratio at birth for births at order two is substantially lower than at order one and at any other birth order. The sex ratio at birth for births at order three is also lower than the sex ratio at birth for all births except births at order two. This suggests that substantial proportions of couples with two or three children stop having more children if their last birth is a boy and this has been happening since the early 1990s at the time of NFHS-1. Stopping after two or three children is in keeping with the mean ideal family size of currently married women in India which has been between 2 and 3 children in all three surveys.

Table 1.8: Trends in Sex Ratios at Birth (females per 1,000 males) by Birth order of all Births to Women Age 15-49 in India

Birth Order	*NFHS-1*	*NFHS-2*	*NFHS-3*
1	901	873	843
2	819	765	762
3	832	819	837
4	921	919	961
5	986	1,019	1,026
6	1,002	1,052	1,054
7+	1,039	1,034	1.094
Average	935	920	926

Source: NFHS-1, 2 and 3.

1.6.2.1 Sex Ratios at Birth by Rtate

The sex ratio at birth by state ranges from a low of 728 in Punjab and 756 in Haryana to a high of 1,102 in Jharkhand (table 1.9). There are only five states; Chhattisgarh, Madhya Pradesh, Uttar Pradesh, West Bengal, and Nagaland where the sex ratio at birth lies in the normal range (943-971) and six states where it lies above the normal range. Of the six states with higher than normal sex ratios at birth, all except Jharkhand are in the northeast of the country. Thus, in 18 of the 29 states in India the sex ratio at birth is below normal. Notably, all four of the southern states, including Kerala, have lower than normal sex ratios at birth.

Table 1.9: Sex Ratio at Birth (female per 1,000 males) for all Births in the Five Years preceding the Survey and Sex Ratio at Birth for all Last Births, by State in India

Region/State	*Sex ratio at birth for births in past five years**	*Sex ratio at birth for all last births to women age 15-49*
North		
Delhi	848	681
Haryana	756	540
Himachal Pradesh	901	572
Jammu & Kashmir	912	770
Punjab	728	504
Rajasthan	894	717
Uttarakhand	892	633
Central		
Chhattisgarh	948	807
Madhya Pradesh	968	741
Uttar Pradesh	949	790
East		
Bihar	902	784
Jharkhand	1,102	891
Orissa	932	723
West Bengal	963	819
Northeast		
Arunachal Pradesh	1,009	809
Assam	985	830
Manipur	1,001	834

Source: NFHS-3.

1.6.3 Sex Differentials and Mortality

Sex ratios at birth measure gender inequality in terms of the extent to which the number of female births relative to male births deviates from biological expectations and focus attention on whether girls are being discriminated against regarding their right to birth. However, what about the girls that are born? Does son preference differentially affect girls'survival by subjecting them to gender-based discrimination in access to life sustaining resources, including food and medical care? If such discrimination is common, it will manifest in differential rates of mortality by sex at early ages.

On biological grounds, mortality in infancy should be higher for male infants than female infants particularly in the first month of life. In accordance with this expectation, NFHS-3 shows that the neonatal mortality rate (the number of deaths to children age less than one month per 1,000 live births) in India was 41 for males, compared with 37 for females per 1,000 births in the five years preceding the survey. Further, as table 1.10 shows, male neonatal mortality is higher than female neonatal mortality for births in all wealth quintiles. Excess female mortality becomes evident in India in the period beyond one month of life. In most countries where infant and child mortality is driven by biology alone, female mortality in the first year of life beyond the first month continues to be lower than male mortality. In India, however, the post-neonatal mortality rate (the number of deaths to children age 1–11 months per 1,000 live births) for females is 21, compared with only 15 for boys. Although the female-male differential in post-neonatal mortality is lowest for children born to mothers in the highest wealth quintile, the female disadvantage is, nonetheless, evident in all wealth quintiles.

Table 1.10: Neonatal Mortality in the Five Years preceding by Sex, according to Wealth Quintile

Sex	*Lowest*	*Second*	*Middle*	*Fourth*	*Highest*
Male	50	47	41	36	24
Female	47	42	38	28	20

Source: NFHS-3.

A similar pattern in gender differentials is also observed in the child mortality rate (the number of deaths to children age 1–4 years per 1,000 children reaching age 1 year). In India as a whole, the child mortality rate for girls, at 23 per 1,000, is 61 percent higher than for boys, at 14 per 1,000. As shown in table 1.11, female child mortality is higher than male child mortality in every wealth quintile. However, female child mortality drops more sharply with wealth than does male child mortality. As a consequence, the gender gap in child mortality is virtually nonexistent in the highest wealth quintile. Thus, although wealthier households have a lower sex ratio at birth than poorer households, the data on mortality yield two conclusions: a) girls born in wealthier households are more likely to survive their early childhood than girls born in poorer households; and b) the gender differential in survival is lower in wealthier households than in poorer households. Thus, girls born in poorer households have a much higher probability of dying than boys in poorer households; by contrast, in the wealthiest households, the probability of dying is fairly similar for both boys and girls.

Table 1.11: Children Mortality in the Five Years preceding by Sex, according to Wealth Quintile

Sex	*Lowest*	*Second*	*Middle*	*Fourth*	*Highest*
Male	24	18	11	6	4
Female	41	28	18	9	5

Source: *NFHS-3.*

1.7 Marriage and Spousal Age Differentials

NFHS-3 shows that the vast majority of Indian women and men age 15-49 are married. Only 20 percent of women and 36 percent of men in this age group have never been married. Further, divorce, separation, and desertion is relatively uncommon in India: in this age group, only 1.5 percent of women and 0.6 percent of men are currently divorced, separated, or deserted. Widowhood is the more common form of marital disruption: 3 percent of women age 15-49 are widows and 1 percent of men in this age group are widowers. Among ever-married women, only 2 percent have had more than one marriage; among ever married men, by contrast, the proportion married more than once is almost three times as high, at 6 percent. Thus, in India, marriage is virtually universal and for most adults, particularly women, marriage takes place only once in their lifetime. Men are less likely to be currently divorced, separated, deserted, or widowed than women. This is in part because even though they marry later than women, men are more likely than women to remarry after marital disruption. Table 1.12 focuses attention on an even younger age group women age 20-24 to examine the trends in the age at marriage over time. NFHS-3 data shows that even in this age group, 18 percent of women are married before age 15 and 47 percent are married before age 18. An early age at marriage of women is an indicator of the low status of women in society; at the individual level too, an early age at marriage for a woman is related to lower empowerment and increased risk of adverse reproductive and other health consequences (Mason, 1986; International Center for Research on Women, 2007). An early age at marriage typically curtails women's access to education and cuts short the time needed to develop and mature unhampered by responsibilities of marriage and children. Young brides also tend to be among the youngest members of their husbands' families and, by virtue of their young age and relationship, are unlikely to be accorded much power or independence. An early age at marriage also has many negative health consequences for women. For one, early ages at marriage typically lead to early childbearing. Having a child when the body is still maturing increases the risk of maternal and child mortality. Further, women married very early are typically sexually immature and inexperienced, but are often married to much older sexually experienced men. This combination of early ages at marriage and large spousal age differences can put women at a higher risk of sexually transmitted infections including HIV (Bruce and Clark, 2004). Specifically, young women married early may be subject to a higher risk of infection because of prior sexual experiences of their older partners

Table 1.12: Percent Distribution of Women and Men Age 15-49 by age at first Marriage, according to Educational Attainment and Wealth Quintile in India

Variables	*Age at first marriage: Women*							*Age at first marriage: Men*						
	<15	*15-17*	*18-20*	*21-24*	*25+*	*Not married*	*Total percent*	*<15*	*15-17*	*18-20*	*21-24*	*25+*	*Not married*	*Total percent*
Education														
None	**41.6**	34.8	14.7	2.6	0.7	5.6	100.0	8.9	16.2	29.3	20.2	10.7	14.7	100.0
0-4 years	**26.8**	35.0	18.0	4.4	1.5	14.3	100.0	5.4	11.5	23.9	24.3	12.9	22.1	100.0
5-9 years	**14.3**	28.3	20.9	7.4	1.8	27.3	100.0	4.7	8.6	16.0	17.7	12.9	40.2	100.0
10-11 years	**4.7**	17.8	23.5	12.4	4.0	**37.7**	100.0	2.5	5.2	9.4	15.3	18.1	49.5	100.0
12+ years	1.6	6.5	19.0	23.5	11.3	38.1	100.0	1.9	4.0	7.6	14.9	28.8	42.9	100.0
Wealth quintile														
Lowest	**38.5**	33.3	12.9	2.1	0.7	12.5	100.0	8.2	15.6	26.1	17.0	8.8	24.4	100.0
Second	**33.8**	32.7	14.2	3.2	0.9	15.3	100.0	7.1	12.2	21.6	18.8	10.2	30.2	100.0
Middle	**26.1**	30.3	17.7	5.0	1.5	19.6	100.0	5.3	9.6	17.9	19.0	12.8	35.5	100.0
Fourth	**17.2**	27.2	21.9	8.4	2.7	22.6	100.0	3.1	6.6	13.6	18.6	17.8	40.2	100.0
Highest	**8.3**	17.7	22.7	17.5	6.9	26.9	100.0	1.1	3.1	7.8	16.3	28.2	43.4	100.0
Total	**23.9**	**27.8**	**18.2**	**7.7**	**2.7**	**19.8**	**100.0**	**4.6**	**8.8**	**16.6**	**17.9**	**16.4**	**35.7**	**100.0**

Source: NFHS-3.

combined with their inability to negotiate safe sex due to their own young age and immaturity and, often, the large spousal age difference.

1.7.1 Inequality in Age at Marriage

The median age at first marriage for women in India has been very slow to increase over time from its low level. For women age 25-49, the median age at marriage was 16.1 in NFHS-1; in NFHS-2 it was 16.4 and in NFHS-3 it is 16.8. Thus, in over a decade, the median age at marriage has risen by less than one year. In NFHS-3, the 35 median age at marriage for men age 25-49 is 22.7 years, almost six years higher than for women. However, the median ages at marriage for women and men and the average age difference mask great variation in the age pattern of marriage for both sexes and the decline in marriage before age 15 continues to be common among women in India: even in the age group 25-29, one in four women were married before age 15. This proportion has declined from its high of 33 percent among women age 40- 49, but still continues to be significant. Men, however, are less likely to be married at young ages. For example, only 13 percent of men age 25-29 are married before they are age 18, compared with more than half of women in the same age group. Further, most women 25 and older at least 9 out of 10 are already married in India by age 25, irrespective of their age cohort. By contrast, only about 6 out of 10 men are married by exact age 25. Further, the proportion of men married by age 25 has declined by 14 percent between the 40-49 and 25-29 age cohorts, whereas, the corresponding decline for women is only 3 percent marriage at very early ages. Some of this variation is shown in table 1.13.

Table 1.13: Percentage of Women and Men Age 25-49 first Married by specific exact Ages, according to Current Age in India

Age	*Sex*	*Married by exact age:*			
		15	*18*	*21*	*25*
25-29	Female	25 .4	55 .4	78 .6	91 .3
	Male	4.1	13.4	32.3	58.5
30-39	Female	29.7	62.3	83.1	93.5
	Male	6.2	18.3	39.9	64.9
40-49	Female	32.6	64.4	85.3	94.6
	Male	7.4	19.3	42.5	67.7
Total	**Female**	**29.4**	**61.1**	**82.5**	**93.2**
	Male	**6.1**	**17.4**	**38.9**	**64.3**

Source: NFHS-3.

1.8 Status of Women: Outside the Home

Freedom of movement is severely curtailed for a large proportion of women in India. Only one third of women age 15-49 are allowed to go alone to the market, to the health centre, and outside the community (table 1.14). Freedom to go alone varies most by age and marital status. The young and the never married have the least freedom of movement. Nonetheless, even among women in their 40s only about half are allowed to go alone to all three of these places. Access to spaces outside the home increases with both education and wealth; however, the variation is quite limited. Less than half of women have the freedom to go alone to these places in every education and wealth category.

Table 1.14: Percentage of Women Age 15-49 allowed to go alone to the Market, Health Center and Outside the Community by Background Characteristics in India

Variables	*Women allowed to go alone:*			
	To the market	*To the health center*	*Outside the community*	*To all three places*
Age				
15-19	29.7	23.1	16.8	12.8
20-29	46.2	42.7	32.3	28.0
30-39	62.9	60.3	48.1	43.6
40-49	68.2	65.2	55.6	51.2
Marital status				
Never married	40.7	32.3	25.0	20.3
Currently married	52.8	50.2	39.3	35.0
Divorced/separated/ deserted/widowed	76.1	73.5	68.6	65.6
Education				
None	49.0	45.9	36.3	32.0
0-4 years	47.2	45.9	37.3	32.1
5-9 years	47.1	43.2	33.7	29.5
10-11 years	55.0	49.2	38.5	34.1
12+ years	70.2	64.3	51.9	48.2
Wealth quintile				
Lowest	41.9	39.1	29.8	25.6
Second	42.7	40.5	33.0	27.9
Middle	48.1	44.6	36.2	31.3
Fourth	53.4	49.0	38.9	34.8
Highest	67.6	61.9	48.2	44.8
Total	**51.5**	**47.7**	**37.7**	**33.4**

Source: NFHS-3.

1.9 Women Responses about Money

Less than half, 45 percent, of women age 15-49 have some money of their own that they alone can decide how to use. The proportion having money varies from 39 percent among the never married and 45 percent among the currently married, to 66 percent among the divorced, separated, deserted, or widowed women. Since having money will depend at least in part on the wealth of the household. Table 1.15 shows the percentage of women who have some money they alone control, by wealth quintile. Notably, among all women, the differential by wealth in whether women have some money they control is relatively limited, ranging from 39 percent among women in the lowest wealth quintile to 56 percent in the highest wealth quintile. Thus, having money that women control is not exclusively related to wealth. Variation by wealth quintile in the proportion of women with some money they control is least for women, who are divorced, separated, deserted, or widowed and most for never married women. One possible source of money is, women could have control over its own earnings.

Table 1.15: Percentage of Women Age 15-49 who have access to Money of their own that they can decide how to use by Marital status, according to Wealth Quintile in India

Marital status	***Wealth quintile***					
	Lowest	***Second***	***Middle***	***Fourth***	***Highest***	***Total***
Marital status						
Never married	27.8	31.5	33.5	39.3	49.2	38.6
Currently married	38.9	40.4	41.5	45.7	57.1	44.9
Divorced/separated/ deserted/widowed	63.9	63.4	64.3	65.4	74.6	65.5
Total	**38.9**	**40.2**	**41.0**	**45.1**	**55.5**	**44.6**

Source: NFHS-3.

1.9.1 Access to a Bank or Savings Account that Women Themselves Use

While having a bank or savings account can be thought of as the privilege of wealth, having and using a bank or savings account, irrespective of wealth, is an indicator of women's ability to manage money, as well as interact successfully with modern institutions. Despite India's rapid modernization, few women have a bank or savings account that they themselves use. As table 1.16 shows, only 15 percent of women age 15-49 have a bank or savings account that they use. As expected, this proportion increases sharply with wealth. Nonetheless, even in the highest wealth quintile, only about one in three women have a bank or savings account they themselves use. Whether women have a bank or savings account varies substantially by wealth for women in all age groups, educational categories, and employment statuses being consistently low for women in the lowest wealth quintile and relatively high in the highest wealth quintile.

Nevertheless, even in the highest wealth quintile, less than one in three women have a bank or savings account in all age, education, and employment categories, except for women employed for cash, women with 12 or more years of education, and women who are 30 years or older. Women most likely to have a bank or savings account are the women in the highest wealth quintile who are employed for cash, followed by women with 12 or more years of education. Also notable is that women in the lowest wealth quintile who have 12 or more years of education are more than four times as likely as the average woman in the lowest wealth quintile to have a bank or savings account that she uses.

Table 1.16: Percentage of Women Age 15-49 who have a Bank or Savings Account of their own that they use by Background Characteristics, according to Wealth Quintile in India

Variables	*Wealth quintile*					
	Lowest	*second*	*Middle*	*Fourth*	*Highest*	*All women*
Age						
15-19	2.0	3.4	5.4	9.2	15.8	7.2
20-29	3.4	6.5	9.1	13.6	29.5	13.1
30-39	4.6	9.2	14.4	21.6	43.0	19.4
40-49	5.0	9.4	13.6	21.7	42.4	20.8
Education						
None	3.4	6.6	9.3	13.1	17.3	7.5
0-4 years	4.1	7.0	10.4	17.0	23.9	11.0
5-9 years	4.8	7.0	10.5	14.4	24.0	13.6
10-11 years	8.1	12.0	12.7	18.9	29.5	22.3
12+ years	16.7	18.2	20.7	26.6	47.3	40.9
Employment						
Not employed	3.0	5.3	8.1	12.5	28.1	14.2
Employed for cash	4.7	9.8	15.0	26.8	56.9	19.7
Employed, not for cash	3.3	6.8	9.9	16.7	27.9	9.0
Total	**3.7**	**7.1**	**10.5**	**16.3**	**33.6**	**15.1**

Source: NFHS-3.

1.9.2 Percentage of Women who have a Bank or Savings Account they use by State

The percentage of women who have a bank or savings account in India ranges from 7 percent in Nagaland to 27 percent in Kerala, 30 percent in Delhi, and 42 percent in Goa. With the exception of the latter three states, in no other states do more than one in four women have a bank or savings account that they use. In 14 of the 29 states in India, 15 percent or fewer women have a bank or savings account that they themselves use.

1.10 Gender Relations: Norms and Attitudes

An important element of empowerment is the outright rejection of unequal rights and privileges that derive from and are assigned based solely on a person's sex. Examples of common normatively ascribed rights of husbands include the right to be the key decision maker on major household decisions, the right to control their wives behaviour and bodies, even through violence if necessary; and the right to have sex with their wives when they want. Agreement with these normatively prescribed powers of men over women reflects an acceptance of unequal gender roles, on the one hand, and a lack of awareness about women's entitlement to bodily security and integrity, on the other. Hence, women who perceive as justified the control of husbands *over* their wives can be considered to be less empowered than women who think otherwise (Correa and Petchesky, 1994; Sen and Batliwala, 2000; United Nations, 1995a; 1995b). Although such attitudes do not necessarily imply approval of these rights for men, they do signify passive acceptance of norms that give men these rights. Further, widespread acceptance perpetuates such norms and contributes to the low status of women and the girl child.

1.10.1 Men's Attitudes Regarding Gender Roles in Household Decision making

In NFHS-3, men were asked their opinion about the relative weight that should be given to husbands and wives say in making specific household decisions. Specifically, they were asked whether a wife should have a greater say, an equal say, or a lesser say than the husband when specific decisions are made. For all decisions, most men say that a wife should have at least an equal say. Nonetheless, the share of men who say that women should have a greater say or an equal say differs by decision, as also the proportion who say that a wife should have a lesser say. What is remarkable is that there is virtually no variation in opinions between never married and ever married men. The two decisions in which men are most likely to say that a wife should have a lesser say are decisions regarding making major household purchases and visits to her family or relatives. In the case of these decisions, about one in four of all men say that a wife should have the lesser say. Further, the proportion saying that women should have the greater say is only 5 percent for the decision about major purchases and 12 percent for the decision about visits to her family or relatives.

Men say that women should have the greater say in decisions about purchases for daily needs more often than for any other decision; however, even for this decision, more than one in five say that a wife should have a lesser say. Few men, only 22 percent, agree that a wife should have the greater say in what she does with the money she earns. Most say that a husband and wife should have an equal say, and 14 percent say that the husband should have the greater say. Almost 9 out of 10 men say that wives and husbands should have an equal say in the decision about how many children to have. This proportion is higher than for any other decision. Men's agreement with a wife's equal or greater say in various household decisions varies only somewhat by education. For example, for the two decisions for which most men said that a husband should have the greater say (major household purchases and visits), the proportion who agree that a wife should have at least an equal say varies from 68 percent for men with no education to 82 percent to 83 percent for men with 12 or more years of education. Variation in men's opinions by education is least for decisions about the number of children to have: almost 9 out of 10 men even with no education agree that a wife should have an equal or greater say. Despite relatively high levels of agreement with a wife's equal or greater participation in specific decisions, agreement for all decisions remains relatively low. Half or less than half of currently married men with less than 12 complete years of education and 62 percent of men with 12 or more complete years of education agree that a wife should have at least an equal say in all five decisions. Nonetheless, 95-97 percent of men with little or no education, and 99 percent of men with 12 or more years of education agree that a wife should have an equal or greater say in one or more decisions asked about.

1.10.2 Acceptance of Norms about Men's 'Right' to Beat Their Wives

In order to assess acceptance of norms regarding wife beating, women and men were asked whether a husband is justified in beating his wife for each of the seven reasons, if the wife goes out without telling her husband, if the wife neglects the house or children, if the wife argues with her husband, if the wife refuses to have sex with her husband, if she does not cook food properly, if he suspects her of being unfaithful, and if she shows disrespect for in-laws.

1.10.2.1 Agreement by Reason

By comparing the percentages of women and men who agree with each reason for wife beating, for every reason, women are slightly more likely than men to agree that wife beating is justified. However, the gender differential in agreement for almost all reasons is small, suggesting that the level of socialization regarding this norm is similar for women and men.

Overall, 54 percent of women age 15-49 and 51 percent of men age 15-49 agree with one or more reasons for wife beating. An examination of the level of agreement by reason provides an understanding of what roles are perceived by women and men as key women's roles.

The assumption here is that violence is more likely to be justified if the described behaviour violates what is perceived as acceptable behaviour for women in their gendered roles as wives, mothers, and daughters-in-law. Data from both women and men suggest that being a respectful daughter-in-law and properly looking after the house and children are perhaps essential roles that, when not properly fulfilled, are most deserving of beatings.

1.10.2.2 Agreement by Education

It is expected that women's and men's opinions about gender roles will be strongly affected by their level of education. Indeed, agreement with wife beating falls with education for women and men: almost two thirds of both women and men with no education agree with wife beating, compared with about one third of women and men with 12 or more years of education. Notably, there is very little difference between women's and men's agreement with at least one reason for wife beating at each level of education.

1.11 Gender Differentials in Children's Full Immunization

To be considered as fully immunized, children should have received the following vaccinations before their first birthday: one BCG vaccine, three each of DPT and polio vaccines, and one measles vaccine. In NFHS-3, 42 percent of female children and 45 percent of male children age 12-23 months had received all of these vaccines. Full immunization rates have been rising over time for both boys and girls. However, the increase in full immunization rates between NFHS-1 and NFHS-3 was less for girls, at 7 percentage points, than for boys (9 percentage points). Further, the proportion of male children who are fully immunized in NFHS-3 is 9 percent higher than the corresponding proportion of female children; this differential was 8 percent in NFHS-1 and 6 percent in NFHS-2. This suggests that the gender gap in full immunization not only persists, but may be growing. Some of the key findings in the areas of interest are given in the table. 1.17.

Table 1.17: Prevalent Reasons for Gender Disparity

Son preference	There is strong evidence of continued son preference in India. Girls are under-represented in births and over-represented in child deaths. The sex ratio at birth is much lower in NFHS-3 than it was in NFHS-1. Although, most ultrasound tests are for diagnostic purposes, there is clear evidence that the tests are also being used by women for sex selection of births in all wealth quintiles; nonetheless sex selection of births is more evident among births to women in the highest wealth quintile than among births to women in the other wealth quintiles, particularly the lowest quintile.
Education	There is gender equality in children's school attendance in urban areas; but, in rural areas, the female disadvantage in education is marked and increases with age. School dropout beyond primary school is a major problem, not just for girls, but also for boys. A consequence of high dropout beyond the primary school level is the low educational attainment of adults. Even among the population age 20-29 years, only 27 percent of women and 39 percent of men have 10 or more years of education.
Age at marriage	Age at first marriage continues to be very low in India. The median age at first marriage in NFHS-3 among women age 25-49 is only 16.8 years. In the 13 years since NFHS-1, the median age at first marriage has risen by less than one year. Nonetheless, it is encouraging that in the same time period, there has been a significant decline in the proportions married before age 15 years.
Spousal age difference	Sixteen percent of ever-married women age 15-49 are married to men who are 10 or more years older than them, and for 4 percent the age difference is 15 years or more. Importantly, controlling for education, spousal age difference decreases as age at marriage increases, and this relationship is evident in all three NFHS surveys.
Employment	Only 43 percent of women and 87 percent of men age 15-49 have been employed in the past 12 months. Thus, men are twice as likely as women to be employed. The trend in ever married women's employment shows only a very small per annum increases from 33 percent in NFHS-1 to 44 percent 13 years later in NFHS-3. Most employed women work in agriculture; and only 7 percent are in professional, technical, or managerial occupations. Further, most employed women are working full time and away from home. Almost one in three employed women are not paid in cash for their work. Although the poorest women are most likely to be employed, controlling for wealth, women with high levels of education are more likely to be employed than those with less education. Nonetheless, the relationship of employment and wealth for women suggests that, for many women, employment is largely a result of economic necessity.
Female household headship	Fourteen percent of all households in India are headed by a female, up from 9 percent in NFHS-1, 13 years earlier. Female household heads are less educated and older, on average, than male household

(Contd...)

	heads. Further, households headed by females are over represented in the lowest wealth quintiles and under represented in the highest wealth quintiles. These data suggest that female headed households are more likely to be economically vulnerable than male headed households.
Access to resources	Women's access to resources including media, health care, and money that they control is greatly circumscribed. In addition, only a minority of women are allowed to go alone to various places outside the home. Since women are over-represented in poorer households and under represented in wealthier ones, their per capita resource access is lower than for men. This also means that boys are more likely than girls to be growing up in wealthier households with all the related benefits.
Gender relations	Although a majority of men say that husbands and wives should make decisions jointly, a significant proportion feels that husbands should have the major say in most decisions, particularly in decisions related to large household purchases and visits to the wife's family and relatives. More than half of women and men agree with one or more reasons that justify wife beating. Both are most likely to agree that wife beating is justified if a woman disrespects her in-laws and if she neglects the house or children. Few women and men, however, agree with norms that do not allow women to refuse sex to their husbands.
Decision making	Among women who are employed and have earnings, only one fifth have a major say in how their own earnings are used; and only 7 in 10 have a say in how their husbands' earnings are used. In about one-fifth of couples where both husband and wife have earnings, women earn at least as much as their husbands. However, it is women who earn about the same as their husbands, rather than those who earn less or more, who are more likely to have a major say in the use of their husbands' earnings. Less than two in three currently married women participate, alone or jointly, in decisions about their own health care, large household purchases, purchases for daily needs, and visits to their own family and relatives. Having earnings that women control increases their participation in household decisions. Notably, education is consistently and positively associated with joint decision making and not with decision making alone.
Spousal violence	About two in five currently married women have ever experienced spousal violence in their current marriage, and among them, at least two-thirds experienced violence in the past year. Women who report both physical and sexual violence are more likely to have injuries and be subject to more severe forms of physical violence than women who report experiencing physical but no sexual violence. Joint decision making, rather than decision making alone, is more protective of women with respect to violence. There are few household, couple, or individual characteristics that are consistently related to women's risk of all forms of spousal violence. Despite the large number of potential risk factors examined, only higher education and wealth were

(*Contd...*)

	found to be consistently related to a lower risk of all three forms physical, sexual, and emotional of spousal violence; and husbands' consumption of alcohol and having a mother who was beaten by her spouse were the only ones that were found to consistently and significantly increase the risk of all these forms of violence. Although women who are employed suffer all forms of violence more than women who are not, a large part of this effect is due to the fact that more employed than unemployed women are poor and less educated. Controlling for wealth and education, women's employment is unrelated to physical violence and remains positively associated with spousal emotional violence; notably, however, employment appears to protect women against spousal sexual violence.
Gender and health and nutritional outcomes for children	There is a persistent, if small, gender differential in favour of boys in full immunization coverage. Having a mother who is empowered in terms of having higher education or having a major say alone in the use of her husband's earnings benefits a girl child in terms of her full immunization status more than it benefits a boy child. Thus, these forms of women's empowerment are likely to help reduce the gender differential in full immunization. Gender differentials are not significant in the proportion of children age 0-35 months that were underweight. Notably, controlling for wealth, if a mother experiences spousal physical or sexual violence, the likelihood of a child being underweight is significantly higher for boys but not girls. Thus mothers' experience of violence is likely to increase gender differentials in underweight by increasing the likelihood that boys will be underweight.
Gender and nutritional status of adults	Women are more likely than men, and among couples, wives are more likely than husbands, to be too thin. Risk factors for women being too thin include two of the indicators of women's disempowerment, namely, not having a 129 main say in decisions about large household purchases and experiencing spousal physical or sexual violence. Even controlling for wealth, employed women are more likely than unemployed women to be too thin. However, among employed women, having no earnings or not have a main say over own earnings is associated with an increased likelihood of being too thin.
Gender and current use of modern contraception	Controlling for number of children ever born and other relevant factors, employment, particularly employment for cash, and making decisions mainly alone about large household purchases increase the likelihood that married women are using a modern method of contraception.

1.12 Gender Disparity and Religions

The role of women in Hinduism is often disputed, and positions range from equal status with men to restrictive. Hinduism is based on numerous texts, some of which date back to 2000 BCE or earlier. They are varied in authority, authenticity, content and theme, with the most authoritative being the Vedas. The position of women in Hinduism is widely dependent on the specific text and the context. Positive references are made to the ideal woman in texts such as the Ramayana and the Mahabharata, while some texts such as the Manu Smriti advocate a restriction of women's rights. In modern times the Hindu wife has traditionally been regarded as someone who must at all costs remain chaste or pure. This is in contrast with the very different traditions that have prevailed at earlier times in 'Hindu' kingdoms, which included highly respected professional courtesans (such as Amrapali of Vesali), sacred devadasis, mathematicians and female magicians (the *basavis*, the Tantric *kulikas*). Some European scholars observed in the nineteenth century Hindu women were "naturally chaste" and "more virtuous" than other women, although what exactly they meant by that is open to dispute. In any case, as male foreigners they would have been denied access to the secret and sacred spaces that women often inhabited. Mahabharata and Manusmriti asserts that gods are delighted only when women are worshiped or honoured, otherwise all spiritual actions become futile.

There is a wide variety of viewpoints within the different schools and sects of Hinduism concerning the exact nature and gender (where applicable) of the Supreme person or being; there are even sects that are skeptical about the existence of such a being. Shaktism, for example, focuses worship on the goddess Devi as the supreme embodiment of power, or Shakti (feminine strength; a female form of God). Vaishnavism and Shaivism both worship Lakshmi with Vishnu and Parvati with Shiva respectively as beings on an equal level of magnitude (the male and female aspects of God). In some instances such as with Gaudiya Vaishnavism, specific emphasis is placed on the worship of God's female aspect (Radharani) even above that of her paramour Krishna. Thus it could be said that Hinduism considers God to have both male and female aspects, as the original source of both.

Sex differences in religion can be classified as either "internal" or "external". Internal religious issues are studied from the perspective of a given religion, and might include religious beliefs and practices about the roles and rights of men and women in government, education and worship; beliefs about the sex or gender of deities and religious figures; and beliefs about the origin and meaning of human gender. External religious issues can be broadly defined as an examination of a given religion from an outsider's perspective, including possible clashes between religious leaders and laity; and the influence of, and differences between, religious perspectives on social issues. For example, various religious perspectives have either endorsed or condemned alternative family structures, homosexual relationships, and abortion. External religious issues can also be examined from the "lens of gender" perspective embraced by some in feminism and critical theory and its offshoots.

1.12.1 Gender Inequality in Muslim World: Prevalent Reasons

Throughout recorded history, women have been dehumanized, dispossessed, diminished, degraded, marginalized, disenfranchised, secluded, subjugated, and silenced (Hadhrat Mirza Tahir Ahmad, 1992). In preislamic Arabia, Female infants were buried alive. Female infanticide still occurs in many countries. Under the Pakistani *hudood* ordinances enacted in 1977, a women who bring charges of rape is asked to produce four Muslim male eye witnesses of the incident, and if she fails to produce the witnesses, she is charged and punished for the crime of adultery (John Stuart Mill, 1997). In 2002, the Saudi religious police forced fleeing young girls back into a blazing school building in Mecca, because the girls had not put on their *abayas* (practice). In another part in 2007, the Egyptian government reported that 96 percent of women in that country undergo forced genital mutilation (Asifa Quraishi, 1997). According to a US governmental survey of 2011, over 18 percent of women in the US have been raped at some time in their lives. And recently, we learnt with horror about the Taliban's near-fatal attack on a fifteen year old Pakistani girl for the "crime" of championing the cause of women's education (Black, M.C., et al., 2011). The list of enormities against women is long and excruciating. But their rationalizations are ever worse.

In the Islamic worldview, biological differences between men and women are recognized and the supreme virtue of motherhood is extolled, but for the Quran biology is not destiny. The Holy Quran expresses the moral and spiritual equality of men and women by balancing virtues and rewards for both genders in identical terms.

Surely, men who submit themselves to *God* and women who submit themselves to Him, and believing men and believing women and obedient men obedient women, and truthful women, and men steadfast in their faith and steadfast women, and men who are humble and women who are humble, and men who give alms and women who give alms, and men who fast and women who fast, and men who are chaste and women who are chaste, and men and women who remember Allah much Allah has prepared for all of them forgiveness and a great reward.

The ethical qualities enumerated by the Quran for both men and women also have social and political dimensions with far reaching implications.

It is remarkable that the Quran makes absolutely no statement about the inherent ethical or intellectual superiority of men over women. Nevertheless, the Quran has prescribed different rights and obligation for men and women under some specific conditions. The commandment for the *hijab* is given in two verses (24:31: 33:60) in the Quran; neither explicitly prescribes covering of the face. The Quran commands both men and women to restrain their eyes and guard their chastity, but it requires women to wear a head covering or an outer garment to prevent from being treated as mere sex objects. Further, the specific Quranic command (33:44) for sequestering the wives of the Holy Prophet is not to be applied to all believing women.

The system of the hijab or purdah which comprises a wide spectrum of practices-is seen in the West as emblematic of gender inequality and as a tool for the seclusion and subjugation of women. This perception is often based on the way purdah is practiced in Muslim countries. However, Dannenbaum (Muhammad Zafrulla Khan, 1980) found that some women find the hijab liberating and noted that there is an element of cultural imperialism in the West's criticism of the hijab that does not result in segregation. Many believe that the verse (2:283) relating to witnessing financial transactions imply that two females are equivalent to one male. But according to Hadhrat Khalifatul Masih (Germaine Greer, "*The Female Eunuch*", Farrar, Straus, and Giroux, 2001) and Hadhrat Zafrulla Khan, the provision is concerned only with the preservation of evidence and not with the weight to be attached to the testimony. Nor can this provision be generalized beyond the specified scope of financial transactions.

The Quran (2:229, 4:35) describes respective roles of a married couple and says that husbands and wives have rights in equitable reciprocity, but the husband has a supervisory role in the marriage, since he is responsible for the financial upkeep of the family. However, the supervisory role is limited in legal terms. Furthermore, this relative difference of roles cannot be used to deduce an inferior civil and legal position for women. In the Islamic inheritance laws, the share of a female is half of her male sibling. Clearly, the amounts of inheritance for men and women, in general, are unrelated. The difference in the share is explained by the greater financial responsibility given to men.

Hadhrat Khalifatul Masih II[RA] described the status of women before the advent of Islam; "Before the advent of the Holy Prophet (peace and blessings of Allah be upon him) women in all countries were in the position of slave and chattels, and their slavery could not but have affected adversely even on men" (Hadhrat Mirza Tahir Ahmad, 1992). It is realized that the subjugation of women leads to the suppression of men's minds. Over the centuries, many evils crept back into Muslim societies, as indigenous cultural values, patriarchal traditions, dormant misogyny, and the power dynamics between genders reasserted themselves in the guise of religious orthodoxy.

In order to perpetuate patriarchy the structure of male authority the medieval mindset insists on perceiving women exclusively in relation to their male relatives. In this view, the woman does not have any independent existence or identity – she is almost a possession, often an adversary, invariably an ancillary, always a derived entity. In their relentless pursuit of fundamental gender inequality, the medieval minded clergy inverts the relationship between the Quran and the hadith by using unreliable ahadith to override the Quran.

A hadith from Tirmidhi (Kitab-un-Nikah) is often quoted to support blatant inequality between husbands and wives. This hadith, which was rejected by both Bukhari and Muslim, contradicts the sole Quranic criterion for honor. "It is a fact that there exist a large number of fabricated *ahadith*, which have caused a great deal of disruption in Islam. If there is a hadith which stands in contradiction of what has been stated in the Quran, you should exercise your reasoning to reconcile its interpretation, but where no such reconciliation is possible, the hadith should be rejected and thrown aside, since it cannot be taken to have come from the Holy Prophet (http:/ /www.ghazali.org/ihya/english/index. html).

Hadhrat Khalifatul Masih IV[RA] wrote about the true concept of gender segregation; "Segregation is grossly misunderstood when it is conceived as an imposition or restriction on female members of the Muslim society from fully participating in all spheres of human activities. This is not true" (Germaine Greer, 2001). In other words, *purdah* must not be allowed to create an impediment to women's full participation in all honorable areas of human activities. Moreover, concerning one of the most well known issues, "head scarf", it is not really according to Islam religion since Qur'an itself instruct women to cover their hair, breasts and 'private parts in public and not ask anything more. However, "forcing women to cover their entire bodies as in much of Arabia and Iran - is again cultural rather than Qur'anic, as are many other examples of discrimination against, or maltreatment of, women throughout the Muslim world. These include the practice of removing parts of the female genitals, so-called "female circumcision" or "genital mutilation" which is widespread in Muslim Arabia and Africa. Whilst the Qur'an does place restrictions on Muslim women, it also guarantees them the right to own and inherit property, to participate fully in political affairs and to sue for divorce in short a complete, separate legal identity" (Horrie and Chippindale, 2001). Even though Prophet Mohammed did not discriminate women, after his death, religious scholars, kings and administrators elaborated and exaggerated the idea of men's role as protectors and very much reshaped Qur'anic injunctions in ways that suited them (Halila, 1984).

Hadhrat Khalifatul Masih II[RA] made an observation about the status of women in Islam; "Women, in short, were to have an independent status. All the spiritual rewards were open to her. Even in this life she could take part in the different departments of civil administration. In this regard, she was to have the same consideration paid to her as that accorded to man" (Hadhrat Mirza Tahir Ahmad, 1992).

Hadhrat Khalifatul Masih IV noted the contributions of Islam; "The status of women was raised to such a high standard that they could not be treated as helpless commodities. They were given an equal share in the affairs of life. Whereas previously they were distributed as chattels of inheritance, now they could inherit estates of their fathers. They could also stand up to their husbands and talk back to them. They could reason with them and, of course, had the full right to disagree" (Hadhrat Mirza Tahir Ahmad, 1992).

It is essential to understand that no matter how noble and egalitarian some principles may be the social conditions must be right for those principles to be implemented. For example, the right of a Muslim woman to own and manage her property independently of her husband empowers her by establishing her independent financial and legal position. But if society or the community does not create the conditions for her to acquire and use the skills to manage it, then that God given right is effectively revoked by the society.

1.12.1.1 Historical Factors

Unfortunately, true Islam lasted for only a brief period after its inception. First the Umayyads and then the Abbasids inflicted all kinds of damage on Islam. Later the monarchs ruling Iran continued on the same path; they completely distorted Islam and established something quite different in its place. The process was begun by the Umayyads, who changed the nature of government from divine and spiritual to worldly. Their rule was based on Arabism, the principle of promoting the Arabs over all other peoples, which was an aim fundamentally opposed to Islam and its desire to abolish nationality and united all mankind in a single community, under the aegis of a state indifferent to the matter of race and colour. It was the aim of Umayyads to distort Islam completely by reviving the Arabism of the pre-Islamic age of ignorance, and the same aim is still pursued by the leaders of certain Arab countries, who declare openly their desire to revive the Arabism of the Umayyads, which is nothing but the Arabism of the Fahiliyya (Ahmed, 2002).

1.12.1.2 Colonialism

The impact of colonialism from the last century onwards affected society externally and internally in the most extreme manner. First and foremost, the already existing sexual divisions and roles of labour were further exaggerated. Colonialism imposed foreign values at the same time as it destroyed or eroded native ones. As a result, society collapsed internally, its destiny unsure, its confidence evaporated. Man retreated into the shell of rigid customs and sterile ritual, finding a form of security there. They also forced their women to hide behind burkhsa (shuttlecock veils) and remain invisible in the courtyards of their homes. In India, Mughal princesses were reduced to becoming prostitutes. The stereotype of Oriental females as chattels and playthings was formed. It was a bad time for Islam, a time of retreat. When the European masters began to leave from the middle of the twentieth century Muslim women were to be glimpsed still in various degrees of deprivation and subjugation. They still have to recover. Too much has been damaged. Deprived of economic and hereditary rights, and everywhere behind men in education, women formed into an inferior class. The actual situation of women, their social status and privileges, is usually far removed from the Islamic idea, whether in the tribe, village or the city (Ahmed, 2002). In fact, "the Islamic civilization was virtually wiped out during the era of Colonialism, and thus what is left is a confused jumble of customs, religious ideas, imported governmental structures, political turmoil, and poverty" (Emerick, 2002).

1.12.1.3 Economic Factors

One important point we could miss to take into account is economic impact on gender issues. First, we cannot deny the existence of gender discrimination on labor issue in this world. Before we solve the division of labor and wages problems among men and women, it is very important to introduce women into the labor industry which will keep them out of their confined kitchens where they cannot learn anything and can get no idea to improve their gender role. As long as the women are engaged in Labor force, they can still at least get access to economic opportunities which have lots of impacts on their lives. However, it depends on the type of economy in which the country is introduced for women to get better access to labor markets.

In Middle East oil-rich countries, the economic growth due to oil and mineral extraction is found to be a major cause for underrepresentation of women in the workforce. First of all, oil production did shape the country economy. "When countries discover oil, their new wealth tends to produce an economic condition called the 'Dutch Disease', which is characterized by a rise in the real exchange rate, and a transformation of the economy away from the 'traded sector' (agriculture and manufacturing) towards the "non-traded sector" (construction and services)" (Corden and Neary, 1982). Hence, in oil rich Middle East countries, the traded sector cannot flourish and only non-traded sector becomes dominant. "In many developing countries, women are largely employed in the traded sector, in low-wage jobs in export-oriented factories and agriculture; and they are excluded from many parts of the non-traded sector, such as construction and retail, since these jobs typically entail heavy labor, or contact with men outside the family" (Anker, 1997). Therefore, oil booming resulted in the inability and failure of women to join the nonagricultural labor force in non-traded sector. In fact, the entry of women to the labor force can boost female political influence since women in the workforce get a chance to form and join informal networks by which they can later attain collective action to lobby, influence and change a nation's policy for the betterment of women. In those oil rich Middle East countries, since the women miss chances to join workforce, they are far from acquiring collective bargaining power and they cannot influence in politics and policy making of the country.

Hence, the lack of women's participation in economy has important policy implications. "First, it reduced economic opportunities for women. Second, it reduced their political influence. Third, it may foster Islamic fundamentalism" (Ross, 2008). A recent study of 18 countries found that when Muslim women had fewer economic opportunities, they were more likely to support fundamentalist Islam (Lisa Blaydes and Drew Linzer, 2006). Therefore, here, it is very important to accept and admit historical, colonial and economic causes as the real causes for gender inequalities in Islam.

1.12.2 Feminism and Christianity: Contradiction in Society

Feminism, faith, and religion are all terms that used and misused by members and nonmembers alike, and it is difficult define such complex value systems without oversimplification or misrepresentation. Feminism comes from all angles, as does Christianity, Hinduism, or any other type of religion, value system, or ideology, but like all labels, it is certain that there are those in a group who have opinions that differ from the consensus.

Feminism was originally about political equality at the ballot boxes, but challenges began when it moved, whether consciously or unconsciously, into cultural and religious spheres such as the workplace, home, church and temple. In the beginning, feminism fought for giving women the same political rights that men enjoyed, this was and is a value that everyone, whether a secular feminist, western Christian, or Indian Hindu, would affirm. However, as western feminism evolved and began to incorporate cultural norms such as equality in the workplace and home, the movement began to alienate those of faith.

To the feminist, gender equality means equality in *action* women should be able to do everything men do, and not be treated any differently. Consider feminism's relationship with Christianity, a religion that shares a similar starting point in western culture and allows us to focus in on the disconnect between feminism and faith before its magnification by globalization and manifestations in other cultures. Some feminists say Christianity disrespects women, and some Christians say feminism disrespects religion. In effect, feminism and Christianity are working with two different definitions and expectations of gender equality. These different conceptualizations about what gender is and ought to be create a situation where the two are not on the same page and cannot have a meaningful conversation because they do not even acknowledge what the other is talking about. The Bible, as many Christians interpret it, indicates that God clearly intended man and woman to have different roles. Most mainline traditional Christians will affirm that gender roles are not a social construct and will point to specific passages from the Bible where men and women given different roles by God. However, as God equally values both genders, most Christians do not see this difference in action as a difference in value. Thus, gender roles and gender equality are not mutually exclusive ideas to the Christian, while, to the feminist, gender roles are the very definition of gender inequality. Where feminism sees a problem, Christianity does not see one.

It is true that there is strong disagreement between feminism and Christianity as the two are traditionally and conservatively understood. Feminists may disagree with Christians in their understanding of what gender equality is and ought to be, feminists seem to act in a way that indicates a claim of authority over gender equality and does not leave room for others' values, thinking, and beliefs. Women ought to be as respected and valued as men are on that all are in agreement, but we should agree to disagree on how that is practiced, as long as the basic principle of respect and value is being upheld.

Consider Taylor's theory of cultural modernity, to which our current case of feminism and gender equality is quite similar (Taylor, "Two Theories of Modernity"). As modernity arrives in different cultures, it looks different because the cultures it emerges in come from different starting points. Modernity in Europe does not look the same as modernity in Asia, and to expect the two modernities to look similar is almost laughable. As Taylor writes, "The belief that modernity comes from a single universally applicable operation imposes a falsely uniform pattern on the multiple encounters of non-Western cultures with the exigencies of science, technology, and industrialization" (Taylor, "Two Theories of Modernity"). The same argument can be made of feminism and gender equality. What feminists in the west identify as gender equality will and should produce different results in non-western contexts that reflect the different starting points of cultures. Gender equality *should look* different, and to expect the same kind of feminism in America and in Saudi Arabia is an unrealistic thought at best. Substituting Taylor's modernities with our discussion of gender equality, conclude: "The point of the alternative modernities thesis is that these adaptations don't have to and generally won't be identical across civilizations" (Taylor, "Two Theories of Modernity").

This is the core of the issue feminism faces in today's globalized world. Feminists expect that others will have the same definition and expectation of gender equality, and that gender equality will look similarly across different cultures. Even before globalization made things more pluralistic and complicated, however, feminism never addressed the issue of different understandings of gender equality even with Christianity. Even given shared western culture and societal norms, feminism and Christianity are in unresolved conflict. In a place like India, where religious, cultural, societal norms and values are all different from that of the average western secular feminist, there is even more conflict and it is all the more important to understand what and where the core issue is.

The western secular feminist sees gender equality as sameness in opportunity and action in all spheres, and is advocating for this on the Indian woman's behalf, but has the feminist stopped to consider what the Indian woman deems as gender equality and what she wants for herself. Indeed, "when feminists challenge family structures and work to dismantle them, the women of the temple town see such efforts as directly threatening their sense of identity and personhood. They do not see their conjugal families as oppressive kinship structures but rather as fluid, organic entities that are continually transformed and reconstituted by the essences and qualities of in-marrying women. To a western feminist, gender equality is sameness in the workplace and home, but to an Indian Hindu woman, this is not necessarily the case. The western concept of gender equality is so wedded to the values and beliefs of western culture that Indian female activists now say they do not want gender equality, but female empowerment. From this, it is clear that if feminists cannot agree to disagree with socioculturally similar religions such as Christianity, much less religions such as Hinduism, they will only drive away the very people they want to help.

By first understanding the conflict that exists and recognizing the need for reconsideration and redefinition of what feminism and gender equality mean in the globalized contexts of today's world, we can approach the fundamental object of conflict between feminism and religion from a new perspective. This discussion and clarification of what gender equality means is not merely an issue of semantics but rather, a real, practical step that can be the start to transforming and improving the current conversation, and extend it to the different contexts that globalization presents. Redefining gender equality is not meant to divert attention away from injustice against females, but to do exactly the opposite by redefining the issue, need to re-orienting attention with the true injustices suffered by females around the world. Gender inequality, both in action and in value, is a real issue that we need to understand and address, precisely why a clear and nuanced conversation is needed.

1.13 Transgender: A Socio-cultural Issues in Society

Transgender (***Hijra)*** is a term used in South Asia, particular, in India. In other areas of India, transgender people are also known as *Aravani*, *Aruvani* or *Jagappa* (T*he Global Expat Network India,* 2014). A number of terms across the culturally and linguistically diverse Indian subcontinent represent similar sex or gender categories. While these are rough synonyms, they may be better understood as separate identities due to regional cultural differences. In Odia language a hijra is referred to as *Hinjida*, *Hinjda* or *Napunsaka*, in Telugu, a hijra is referred to as *napunsakudu*, *kojja* or *maada*. In Tamil Nadu the equivalent term is Thiru nangai (mister woman), Ali, aravanni, aravani, or aruvani. In Punjabi, both in Pakistan and India, the term *khusra* is used. Other terms include *jankha*. In Gujarati they are called *pavaiyaa*. In Urdu another common term is *khwaaja sira*.

In Pakistan, the *hijras* identify themselves as either female, male or third gender. The term more commonly advocated by social workers and transgender community members themselves is *khwaaja Sirha* and can identify the individual as a transsexual person, transgender person (khusras), cross dresser (zenanas) or eunuch (narnbans) (Sharma, Preeti (2012a; 2012b). The word "*hijra*" is an Urdu Hindustani word derived from the Semitic Arabic root hjr in its sense of "leaving one's tribe,"(Towle, R. B. and Morgan, L.M., 2006) and has been borrowed into Hindi. The Indian usage has traditionally been translated into English as "eunuch" or "hermaphrodite," where "the irregularity of the male genitalia is central to the definition" (Nanda, S. and Herdt, G., 1996) However, in general hijras are born with typically male physiology, only a few having been born with intersex variations (Lahzar Zanned, 2005). Some Hijras undergo an initiation rite into the hijra community called nirwaan, which refers to the removal of the penis, scrotum and testicles (Cohen, L., 1995).

A common misconception is that a transgender person is therefore gay. However, being transgender involves gender identity and not sexual orientation; a transgender person may be of any sexual orientation. Another important misconception is that one who cross dresses is transgender; however, many cross dressers are comfortable with their assigned sex. Being transgender does not mean having a mental disorder; it is not something that can be cured. In fact, many transgender people experience gender dysphoria, which is a disconnect between one's assigned sex at birth, and with which gender the person identifies.

Transgender people in India face a variety of issues. So far, these communities perceive that they have been excluded from effectively participating in social and cultural life; economy; and politics and decision-making processes. A primary reason (and consequence) of the exclusion is perceived to be the lack of (or ambiguity in) recognition of the gender status of hijras and other transgender people. It is a key barrier that often prevents them in exercising their civil rights in their desired gender. So far, there is no single comprehensive source on the basis of which an evidence-based advocacy action plan can be prepared by transgender activists or possible legal solutions can be arrived at by policymakers. Reports of harassment, violence, denial of services, and unfair treatment against transgender persons in the areas of employment, housing and public accommodation have been discussed in local media, from time to time.

1.13.1 Socio- economic Status of Transgender

Most hijras live at the margins of society with very low status; the very word "hijra" is sometimes used in a derogatory manner. Few employment opportunities are available to hijras. But many get their income from extortion (forced payment by disrupting work/life using demonstrations and interference), performing at ceremonies (toli), begging (dheengna), or sex work ('raarha'), an occupation of eunuchs also recorded in premodern times. Violence against hijras, especially hijra sex workers, is often brutal, and occurs in public spaces, police stations, prisons, and their homes . As with transgender people in most of the world, they face extreme discrimination in health, housing, education, employment, immigration, law, and any bureaucracy that is unable to place them into male or female gender categories. In a study of Bangladeshi hijras, participants reported not being allowed to seek healthcare at the private chambers of doctors, and experiencing abuse if they go to government hospitals. Beginning in 2006, hijras were engaged to accompany Patna city revenue officials to collect unpaid taxes, receiving 4 percent commission (https:/www.ncbi.nlm.nih.gov/pmc/articles/pmc2928103). Since India's Supreme Court re-criminalized homosexuality and bisexuality on 13 December 2013, there has been a sharp increase in the physical, psychological and sexual violence against the transgender community by the Indian Police Service, nor are they investigating even when sexual assault against them is reported (https:/en.wikipedia.org). On 15 April 2014, in National Legal Services Authority v. Union of India, the Supreme Court of India ruled that transgender people should be treated as a third category of gender and as a socially and economically "backward" class entitled to proportional access and representation in education and jobs (news.biharprabha.com).

The governments of both India and Pakistan in 1994 have recognized hijras as a "third sex", thus granting them the basic civil rights of every citizen. In India, hijras now have the option to identify as a eunuch ("E") on passports and on certain government documents (Usmani, Basim, 2009). They are not, however, fully accommodated; in order to vote, for example, citizens must identify as either male or female. There is also further discrimination from the government. In the 2009 general election, India's election committee denied three hijras candidature unless they identified themselves as either male or female.

In April 2014, Justice KS Radhakrishnan declared transgender to be the third gender in Indian law, in a case brought by the National Legal Services Authority (Nalsa) against Union of India and others. The ruling said: (*National Legal Services Authority ... Petitioner Versus Union of India and others. Respondents* (Supreme Court of India 15 April 2014). Seldom, our society realises or cares to realise the trauma, agony and pain which the members of Transgender community neither undergo, nor appreciates the innate feelings of the members of the Transgender community, especially of those whose mind and body disown their biological sex. Our society often ridicules and abuses the Transgender community and in public places like railway stations, bus stands, schools, workplaces, malls, theatres, hospitals, they are sidelined and treated as untouchables, forgetting the fact that the moral failure lies in the society's unwillingness to contain or embrace different gender identities and expressions, a mindset which we have to change.

1.13.2 Rituality and Transgender

Traditional Hindu literary sources do not speak of homosexuality directly, but changes of sex, homoerotic encounters, and intersex or third gender characters are often found both in traditional religious narratives such as the *Vedas*, *Mahabharata*, *Ramayana* and *Puranas* as well as in regional folklore. Hindu mythology has many examples of deities changing gender, manifesting as different genders at different times, or combining to form androgynous or hermaphroditic beings. Gods change sex or manifest as an Avatar of the opposite sex in order to facilitate sexual congress. Non-divine beings also undergo sex changes through the actions of the gods, as the result of curses or blessings, or as the natural outcome of reincarnation. Hindu mythology contains numerous incidents where sexual interactions serve a non-sexual, sacred purpose; in some cases, these are same-sex interactions. Sometimes the gods condemn these interactions but at other times they occur with their blessing. With above background not only in Hindu but in other religions, transgender has special position regarding rituality.

1.13.2.1 Transgender in Hindu

In some versions of the Ramayana, (Bockrath, T., 2003) when Rama leaves Ayodhya for his 14 year exile, a crowd of his subjects follow him into the forest because of their devotion to him. Soon Rama notices this, and gathers them to tell them not to mourn, and that all the "men and women" of his kingdom should return to their places in Ayodhya. Rama then leaves and has adventures for 14 years. When he returns to Ayodhya, he finds that the hijras, being neither men nor women, have not moved from the place where he gave his speech. Impressed with their devotion,

Rama grants hijras the boon to confer blessings on people during auspicious inaugural occasions like childbirth and weddings. This boon is the origin of *badhai* in which hijras sing, dance, and give blessings (Narrain, Siddharth, 2003)

There he assumes an identity of a eunuch-transvestite and performs rituals during weddings and childbirths that are now performed by hijras (Nanda, S., 2003). In the Mahabharata, before the Kurukshetra War, Ahiravan offers his lifeblood to goddess Kali to ensure the victory of the Pandavas, and Kali agrees to grant him power. On the night before the battle, Ahiravan expresses a desire to get married before he dies. No woman was willing to marry a man doomed to die in a few hours, so Arjuna as Brihinala marries him. In South India, hijras claim Ahiravan as their progenitor and call themselves "aravanis" (Narrain, Siddharth, 2003).

Bahuchara Mata is a Hindu goddess with two unrelated stories both associated with transgender behavior. One story is that she appeared in the avatar of a princess who castrated her husband because he would run in the woods and acts like a woman rather than have sex with her. Another story is that a man tried to rape her, so she cursed him with impotence. When the man begged her forgiveness to have the curse removed, she relented only after he agreed to run in the woods and act like a woman. The primary temple to this goddess is located in Gujarat and it is a place of pilgrimage for hijras, who see Bahucahara Mata as a patroness.

One of the forms of Lord Shiva is a merging with Parvati where together they are Ardhanari, a god that is half Shiva and Half Parvati. Ardhanari has special significance as a patron of hijras, who identify with the gender ambiguity (Venkat, Vidya, 2008).

1.13.2.2 Hijras in Islam

There is evidence that Indian hijras identifying as Muslim also incorporate aspects of Hinduism. Still, despite this syncretism, Reddy (2005) notes that a *hijra* does not practice Islam differently from other Muslims and argues that their syncretism does not make them any less Muslim. Reddy (2003) also documents an example of how this syncretism manifests: in Hyderabad, India a group of Muslim converts were circumcised, something seen as the quintessential marker of male Muslim identity.

1.13.3 Transgender Rights

The Tamil Nadu state in India was the first state to introduce a transgender (hijra/ aravani) welfare policy. According to the transgender welfare policy transgender people can access free Sex Reassignment Surgery (SRS) in the Government Hospital; free housing program; various citizenship documents; admission in government colleges with full scholarship for higher studies; alternative sources of livelihood through formation of self-help groups (for savings) and initiating income-generation programmes (IGP). Tamil Nadu was also the first state to form a Transgender Welfare Board with representatives from the transgender community.

In India one group of transgender people are called Hijras. They were legally granted voting rights as a third sex in 1994 (Shackle, Samira. "Politicians of the third gender: the "shemale" candidates of Pakistan". New Statesman. Retrieved 11/05/2013). Due to alleged legal ambiguity of the procedure, Indian transgender individuals do not have access to safe medical facilities for SRS ("On 15 April 2014, Supreme Court of India declared transgender people as a socially and economically backward class entitled to reservations in Education and Job, and also directed union and state governments to frame welfare schemes for them ("Supreme Court's Third Gender Status to Transgenders is a landmark". IANS. news.biharprabha.com. Retrieved 15 April 2014).

On 24 April 2015, the Rajya Sabha passed *The Rights of Transgender Persons Bill, 2014* guaranteeing rights and entitlements, reservations in education and jobs (2 percent reservation in government jobs), legal aid, pensions, unemployment allowances and skill development for transgender people. It also contains provisions to prohibit discrimination in employment, prevent abuse, violence and exploitation of transgender people. The Bill also provides for the establishment of welfare boards at the Centre and State level, and for Transgender Rights Courts. The Bill was introduced by DMK MP Tiruchi Siva, and marked the first time the House had passed a private member's bill in 45 years. The Bill was passed unanimously by the House. However, the Bill contains several anomalies and a lack of clarity on how various ministries will co-ordinate to implement its provisions (http://indianexpress.com/article/india/india-others/rajya-sabha-passes-private-bill-to-protect-the-rights-of-transgenders/99).

Social Justice and Empowerment Minister Thaawar Chand Gehlot stated on 11 June 2015 that the Government would introduce a comprehensive Bill for transgender rights in the Monsoon session of Parliament. The Bill will be based on the study on transgender issues conducted by a committee appointed on 27 January 2014. According to Gehlot, the Government intends to provide transgender people with all rights and entitlements currently enjoyed by Scheduled Castes and Scheduled Tribes (http://www.newkerala.com/news/2015/fullnews-72086.html).

The problems being faced by the Transgender community have also been articulated in a few Public Interest Litigation (PIL) petitions. As per available information, two PIL petitions [WP (C) No. 400 of 2012 & 604 of 2013] have been filed in the Supreme Court of India and one PIL [No. 01 of 2012] in the High Court of Mumbai.

The problems of Transgender community as articulated in the PIL petition WP (C) No. 400 of 2012 filed by the National Legal Services Authority (NLSA) mentioned above, in short, are that Transgender persons are deprived of the fundamental rights available to the other two sexes i.e. male and female, and are not considered as the third sex. They are deprived of many of the rights and privileges which other persons enjoy as citizens of India. The transgender are deprived of social and cultural participation, are shunned by family and society, have only restricted access to education, health services and public spaces, restricted rights available to citizens such as right to marry, right to contest elections, right to vote, employment and livelihood opportunities and various human rights such as voting, obtaining Passport, driving license, ration card, Identity Card etc. The transgender community is treated as a legal non-entity in violation of Article 14, 15, 16 and 21 of the Constitution of India. Other important submissions of NLSA are:

(i) The transgender community, generally known as "Hijras" in this country, are a section of Indian citizens who are treated by Society as unnaturals and generally as objects of ridicule and even fear on account of superstition. All human beings are born free and equal in dignity and ought to be entitled to enjoyment of human rights without discrimination on the basis of sexual orientation or gender identity. Everyone is entitled to equality before the law and equal protection of the law without any such discrimination. Transgenders are also part of society and have equal, rights as are available to other persons. The discrimination based on their class and gender makes the transgender community one of the most disempowered and deprived groups in Indian society.

(ii) In view of the constitutional guarantee, the transgender community is entitled to basic rights i.e. Right to Personal Liberty, dignity, Freedom of expression, Right to Education and Empowerment, Right against violence, Discrimination and exploitation and Right to work. Moreover, every person must have the right to decide his/her gender expression and identity, including transsexuals, transgenders, hijras and should have right to freely express their gender identity and be considered as a third sex.

(iii) The problems, faced by transgenders are discrimination, lack of educational facilities, unemployment, lack of shelter, lack of medical facilities like HIV care and hygiene, depression, hormone pill abuse, tobacco and alcohol abuse and problems relating to marriage, property, electoral rights, adoption. Ministry of Law and Ministry of Social Justice and State Governments need to recognize the deprivation suffered by transgender people and work on much needed reform.

(iv) In 2003, the Hon'ble High Court of Madhya Pradesh upheld the order of an Election Tribunal which nullified the election of a Hijra, Kamala Jaan, to the post of Mayor of Katni, on the ground that it was a seat reserved for women and that Kamla Jaan, being a 'male' was not entitled to contest the seat. It is submitted that all the citizens of India have a right to vote and to contest elections. But in the electoral rolls only two categories of the sex are mentioned male and female. This is unfair to the third sex of India as they are deprived of their statutory right to vote and contest elections.

(v) Transgender, though human beings are not recognized as persons in violation of human rights as they are deprived of their fundamental rights as well as also other civil rights. The lack of recognition isolates transgender, especially eunuchs, in the matter of civil rights. The Constitution of India prohibits discrimination on the basis of sex. Since gender is taken to mean only male and female, the eunuchs and transgender cannot effectively exercise or avail the benefits of constitutional rights and avail of facilities and benefits available to the male and female genders.

(vi) Transgender have very limited employment opportunities. Transgender have no access to bathrooms/toilets and public spaces. The lack of access to bathrooms and public spaces access is illustrative of discrimination faced by transgender in availing each facilities and amenities. They face similar problems in prisons, hospitals and schools.

(vii) So far as criminal liability is concerned, transgender cannot escape punishment when they are accused of committing crimes. The world "person" in the Indian Penal Code and General Clauses Act means all human beings. Persons who can be punished for committing offences include transgender, though they are consciously deprived of their civil rights.

(viii) Transgender have very limited employment opportunities as most jobs are confined to male and female sexes. Transgender, being a third sex, cannot even apply for most of the jobs.

(ix) Transgender persons must be properly documented in census. There is need for statutory reservation in education, elections and employment both in the public and private sectors. They need to be empowered and uplifted by facilities for higher education and vocational training to upgrade their earnings and status in society so as to promote their acceptability in society.

(x) Since transgenders are prone to health risks and setbacks, they need to be provided proper medical facilities, including health insurance and clinics, where free or subsidized treatment should be made available.

(xi) The different manifestations of discrimination and deprivation are a consequence of the practice of recognizing and providing only for the male and/or the female sex. This gets reflected in prescribed forms for applying for various privileges, facilities or amenities, as these do not reflect that a person may belong to a gender, other than male or female."

In the other WP No. 604 of 2013 by Poojya Mata Nasib Kaur ji Women Welfare Society, the petitioner has made similar submissions and referred to transgenders as Kinnars. They have prayed to the Supreme Court to direct the Respondents (Central & State Governments) to inter alia bring a policy for upliftment and for socio-economic development of the Kinnar Communities in India.

The Salvation of Oppressed Eunuchs (SOOE), the petitioner in PIL No. 1 of 2012 in the High Court, Mumbai has brought out some issues, which are different from the above and are as follows:

(i) Eunuchs are forced by their 'gurus' to lead a life of servitude and bonded labourers. A prayer has been made to ensure that the condition of eunuchs living as bonded labour be ended forthwith under the provisions of the Bondel Labour System (Abolition) Act, 1976.

(ii) The word 'rape' in Section 375 of Indian Penal Code (IPC) should include all sexual crimes against women, men, children and transsexuals/eunuchs, as eunuchs are often the targets of some of the worst sex crimes, more so, if they happened to be sex workers. It has, therefore, been prayed to direct appropriate modification/ interpretation of section 375 to include transsexuals and eunuchs in the definition of the term 'rape'.

(iii) There is an order of the Hon'ble High Court, Delhi about Section 377 of IPC, validating rights of the homosexual people and that right has been denied to eunuchs until now, simply because their disability was attempted to be concealed. A prayer has been made in this context for directing appropriate modification/ interpretation of Section 377 of IPC, validating the rights of homosexual people be modified/interpreted to include transsexuals and eunuchs in the definition of the term 'homosexuals'."

In a lecture delivered on Refresher Course for Civil Judges (Junior Division)-I Batch at Tamil Nadu State Judicial Academy on 12.02.2011 "Rights of Transgender People – Sensitising Officers to Provide Access to Justice"1 by Hon'ble Mr. Justice P.Sathasivam, then Judge, Supreme Court of India (presently Chief Justice) had stated thus:

"The Constitution provides for the fundamental right to equality, and tolerates no discrimination on the grounds of sex, caste, creed or religion. The Constitution also guarantees political rights and other benefits to every citizen. But the third community (transgenders) continues to be ostracized. *The Constitution affirms equality in all spheres but the moot question is whether it is being applied* (http://www.hcmadras.tn.nic.in/jacademy/Article/PSJ-CJO-SPEECH-Royappetah.pdf).

The main problems that are being faced by the transgender community are of discrimination, unemployment, lack of educational facilities, homelessness, lack of medical facilities like HIV care and hygiene, depression, hormone pill abuse, tobacco and alcohol abuse, penectomy and problems related to marriage and adoption." The broad remit of the Committee is to suggest appropriate workable solutions to the above problems being faced by the transgender people.

1.13.4 Discrimination of Transgender in Society

Transgender people have been facing inequality and discrimination since before the 1800s. Much inequality has stemmed from the terms used to refer to transgender people. Some Native American tribes had third gender roles including transgender people. When Europeans came over they deemed them "berdaches" which was a derogatory term for a male trying to pass as a women or "passing women" which was a derogatory term for a women who tried to assume a masculine role. The term "transvestite" originated in 1910 from the German sexologist Magnus Hirschfeld. At that time, it was used in a similar fashion to transsexual, a word that not coined until the late 1940s. The term, "transgender", was used in 1971.

The 1950s saw some of the first transgender positive organizations and publications. These helped transgender people deal with the inequality they faced along with day-to-day issues they encountered. The court ruled against allowing a transgender person to change their original sex cited on their birth certificate to match the reassigned gender. It ruled that the only time the sex on a birth certificate could be changed was when there had been an error made when recording it at birth. Over the last decade, more than one person per month has died due to transgender-based hate or prejudice (Transgenderdor.org.).

Transgender people who are going through divorce, inheritance battles or custody disputes are vulnerable to legal challenges. This is because the validity of their marriages is often called into question due to inconsistent laws regulating transgender equality (www.lambdalegal.org.). A tremendous inconsistency in the U.S. is that some states recognize a transgender person's gender transition while other states do not.

Laws vary from state to state concerning the requirements for changing the gender on birth certificates and other identity documents. Laws also vary concerning whether a state will accept such identity documents as conclusive with respect to one's gender identity. In August 2013, Gov. Jerry Brown passed a bill allowing transgender students in California public schools to participate in sex segregated programs and use gender separate facilities, such as restrooms, according to their self-perceived gender (Kamerschen, Caroline, 2013).

1.13.4.1 Avoidance At work

Transgender workers can have a difficult time coping with the traditional workplace due to established gender norms that limit the roles perceived and expected of them. Among fellow employees, there can arise potential teasing and/or discrimination affecting the transgender worker on emotional levels. Employers at times retract job offers and opportunities because of discrimination towards workers of varying gender identities.

In 2012, Mia Macy, former police detective and veteran was denied a ballistics technician position at the federal ATF laboratory because of her transgender identity. After the matter was raised with the U.S. Equal Employment Opportunity Commission, it was decided that transgender people are protected from employee and employer discrimination through the Civil Rights Act. The event left her family house to foreclosure, but she was grateful for the final ruling (Wong, Curtis, 2012).

Furthermore, in law regarding to transgender discrimination in the workplace, the U.S. Senate on November 7, 2013 gave final approval passing legislation actively outlawing private or public sector justification related to promotions, payment and hiring based on sexual orientation or gender identity (Memoli, Michael A., 2013). This is to recognize a more fair field in the workplace noting credibility and achievements without being swayed from factors that not only fail to create direct relations to those aspects, but also ones that are vulnerable to prejudice from employees, employers and associates.

1.13.4.2 Negligence In school and College

Those that identify with transgender at an early age may have troubles when their identity conflicts with the judgment from traditional school protocol whether public or private. Discrimination may come from classmates that tease or physically harm transgender people as a result of transphobia. It's because of incidents such as these that Transgender Day of Remembrance was created to respect and keep in memory gender non-conformists that have been killed through acts of prejudice. It is an annual event held on November 20 that is acknowledged internationally in schools, neighborhoods, churches, etc. Mental and physical strain through varying forms of assault brought upon from peers is an unfortunate possibility to openly transgender students. Even school staffs are included in academia related parties that prefer repressing public displays of transgender action. For example, in November 2013, Jeydon Loredo was temporarily excluded from their La Feria Independent School District yearbook in Texas due to sporting a tuxedo that did not meet "community standards". It was not until Loredo along with his mother took the case to the Human Rights Campaign, a group that stands for the rights of gay, bisexual and transgender citizens, that the school district reversed its decision allowing Loredo to wear his tuxedo for the yearly photograph and have it published into their high school yearbook pictures (Nelsen, Aaron, 2013).

Those who expressed a transgender identity or gender non conformity while in research study reported alarming rates of harassment (78 percent), physical assault (35 percent) and sexual violence (12 percent); harassment was so severe that it led almost one sixth (15 percent) to leave a school and higher education (Transequality.org.)

A lot of the scrutiny and discrimination transgender people face in college can be attributed to transgender people having to choose what category they fall in within the public eye. Some examples of this are choosing what restroom to use. When task groups are sex segregated, having to decide what group to choose. Filling out paper work is also a challenge because even though they feel a certain gender places still may consider them another gender.

Transgender people still face inequality when applying to schools, for example, a transgender person applied to Smith College, was rejected because her home state still identifies her as male. The application fee was returned with a letter stating that "Smith is a women's college and applicants must be female at the time of application" (Garcia, Michelle (2013-03-20). "Women's College Returns Transgender Student's Application". Advocate.com. Retrieved 2013-11-23). Transgender individuals of colour face additional financial, social, and interpersonal challenges as a result of structural racism in comparison to the transgender community as a whole. According to the National Transgender Discrimination Survey, the combination of anti-transgender bias with structural and individual racism means that transgender people of colour experience particularly high levels of discrimination. Specifically, black transgender people reported the highest level of discrimination among all transgender individuals of colour. Studies on the transgender community are extremely rare, and even fewer studies have been conducted on the experiences of transgender individuals of colour. However, some literature has documented the experiences of certain minority groups and the unique challenges they face in everyday life. As members of several intersecting minority groups, transgender people of colour are especially vulnerable to employment discrimination, poor health outcomes, harassment and violence. Consequently, they face even greater obstacles than white transgender individuals and cisgender members of their own race.

1.13.4.3 Inequality in Employment

All transgender people face disadvantages in the workplace, although black transgender people are among the most disadvantaged. 32 percent of black transgender individuals report losing their job due to bias, compared to 26 percent of Latino transgender people, 24 percent of white transgender people and 21 percent of Asian-Pacific American transgender people. In addition, the unemployment rate for transgender individuals of minority races is especially high, with blacks, American Indians, and Latinos experiencing four times higher the unemployment rate of the general population (Grant, Jaime M.; Harrison, Jack; Herman, Jody L.; Keisling, Mara; Mottet, Lisa A.; Tanis, Justin, 2015*)*. Such individuals are also more likely to live in poverty, with 34 percent of blacks and 28 percent of Latinos living on less than $10,000 dollars a year (National Transgender Discrimination Survey, 2015).

1.13.4.4 Inequality in Health

Transgender individuals of color encounter more physical and mental health issues than transgender whites and their heterosexual counterparts. The HIV infection rate for transgender individuals overall is 2.6 percent, two percent over the national average. Within this group, 25 percent of blacks, 11 percent of Latinos and 7 percent of American Indians report being HIV positive (Johnson, Julia R., 2013). Medicaid policies found that exclusions on transition related health expenses, such as hormone therapy and sex change surgeries, have a disproportionately large effect on low income transgender people of colour, leading to increased violence, political disenfranchisement, and poor health outcomes (Arkles, Gabriel; Gehi, Pooja S., 2007).

In addition, due to the rampant institutional and interpersonal discriminatory practices against transgender individuals of color, they often suffer mental health consequences from social and economic inequalities. Because transgender people of colour face double discrimination for their racial and gender identities, they are more likely to be denied jobs and fall into poverty, leaving them to careers of prostitution or other illegal dealings. These structural issues can often lead to increased encounters with the criminal justice system as well as emotional difficulties (Arkles, Gabriel; Gehi, Pooja S., 2007). Suicidal ideation is especially common among transgender people who belong to racial minorities: 49 percent of blacks and 47 percent of Latinos report attempting suicide, compared to 41 percent of transgender individuals of all races.

1.14 Gender Issue amongst Tribals

If the non-tribal society suffers from gender problems, so does the tribal. Generally, the tribals have been studied from the perspective of a few popular problems such as economic backwardness, land alienation, social change, changing stratification and empowerment. During the last five decades, development has also formed a vital part of tribal studies. K.S. Singh very rightly observes in People of India that Indian social anthropology has a rich literature on ethnography and development. This is all commendable. But, the gender issues, as mentioned earlier, throughout the post-independent period, have been neglected. It could also be said that with the acceleration of tribal development, the gender issues have become more severe. Earlier, the tribal society was more or less egalitarian. If there was division of labour in the tribal society as is found in all societies, it was based on age and not sex. A Bhil would voluntarily grind the corn and fetch potable water. The women, on the other hand, kept vigil over the crops. It was an egalitarian society. But, with the increase in tribal development, the division of labour turned to gender bias. The gender problem, therefore, is largely due the new forces of development, social change and modernization. It is urgent for social anthropology to study the gender issues which are manifest in tribal society. In this section, we shell try to throw some light on the tribal problems which results from discrimination of women by men.

1.14.1 Command over Property

Bina Agarwal, a champion of feminist movement, begins her article on gender problems pertaining to right to land with the following question, which is actually the comment made by an informant in the field:

"We want land, all the rest is humbug. Please go and ask the Sarkar (government) why, when it distributes land, we don't get a title. Are we not peasants? If my husband throws me not what is my security"?

The statement made by the landless women in South India raises a basic question: why do tribal women not have right over land? Agarwal has traced the history of the problems arising out of gender relations in matrilineal and bilateral tribal communities. She says that in some of the South Asian communities, such as Garos, Khasis and Lalvngs (in North East India) and Nayars, Tiyyars and Mappilas (in South India), women India enjoy significant rights over land. The land rights that women enjoyed in matrilineal and bilateral communities fell broadly into three categories: First, among Goros, land was a clan's communal property and could not be inherited either by individuals or by joint family units. All clan members resident in the village had rights in this land as individuals, Second, among Khasis, Nayars Tiyyars and Mappilas, land is inherited in the female line, and is held as joint family property and women had no individual rights of alienation. Responsibility for land management was vested principally with older men, usually brothers or maternal uncles. Third, in Sri Lanka, both men and women had individual inheritance rights in land.

If the three categories of land rights enjoyed by the women are analyzed, we observe that "the picture of gender relations among these groups is a mixed one. On the positive side women enjoyed considerable social independence and relative equality in marital relations, indeed, in all the groups, a daughter's right over land and the fact that she either remained in her natal home after marriage or had inviolable rights to return to it if she so chose, provided her with a strong fallback position within marriage. Women could choose their husband and initiate divorce. It could also say that women in these societies had considerable freedom of movement and of public interaction. But, on the negative side, women's property rights in the matrilineal and bilateral communities did not alter the overall gender division of labour: domestic work and child care were still women's responsibilities. The range of sexual mores founds among these communities indicates that rights in land did not guarantee women the some sexual freedom as men. Formal managerial authority over land in a number of matrilineal lay with men. Thus, though rights over land gave certain benefits to women, but their virtual exclusion from property management circumscribed the power they could derive from those rights. The women, therefore, in matrilineal tribes today struggle to get property in land.

In the patrilineal society of tribals women's right in land is altogether denied. The status of tribal women in this regard is on par with that of the caste Hindu women. In North India some movements are reported wherein women demand their right over land. Commenting on the movement in tribal society, Bina Agarwal observes: "*today, for women, to gain effective rights in land will require not only removing existing gender inequalities in the law, but also ensuring that the laws are implemented. It will involve strengthening women's ability to claim and retain their rights in land, as well as their ability to exercise effective control over it*".

However, in a matrilineal society such as that of Khasi, there is no gender discrimination. The law of inheritance is very simple. Ancestral property is passed from the mother to the daughter, specially the youngest one. In this society men have no inheritance right. The Khasi family assigns a central place to women. However, for protection, the mother's brother is considered very important. Despite the dominance of women in Khasi society man is considered to be quite powerful because of his 'physical strength' and the so called 'twelve strength' as the saying goes among Khasis. Man has power and he is taken to be the protector and provider. There is one disability of women which is very striking. Tilput Nongbri, who has written authoritatively on Khasi society, informs us: "although there are no farmal laws which prevent Khasi women from holding public office, they are not allowed to attend traditional village and 'state' *durbars* (customary administrative and judicial councils). A women who dares to voice her opinion on public affairs is regarded as a 'hen that crows' a freak of nature. Men jealously guard their political prerogatives by defining politics as an arena for mature and physically fit persons." Nongbri further informs that the youngest daughter's position in the religious domain is similar to her position in the economic domain. Women are regarded as the trustees of family rights and tradition as well. The Khasis say: "the woman holds the religion. It is women who have to ensure that family rights are organized in their due course. But they have to seek the assistance of their male kin to actually perform the rituals. Priesthood is a male vocation among the Khasis".

In the matrilineal society there is not much gender discrimination. But, in practice, it is the man who most of the things. He is the manager of property. He provides protection. But, there is a fear among the women that with the Khasi conversion to Christianity, the matrilineal system is gradually getting weak. Yet another force which weakens the system is modernization.

1.14.2 Gender Inequality and Stratification

Much work has been done in sociology in the field of social stratification. However, the mainstream stratification studies deal adequately with gender inequality. If we make a thorough analysis of Indian village studies we find that women work very hard both at the domestic level and at the level of agricultural operations. But, unfortunately, the labour of the women is not calculated in terms of wage earnings. Even, in the urban and industrial society, the status of a woman is identified with the status of her husband. This denies equal gender status to both the sexes.

Recently, the 73rd constitutional amendment has empowered women by giving them reserved status in panchayat raj institutions (PRIs). In this new situation, the identity of woman is recognized by her position in panchayat raj. The Scheduled Tribes have taken the benefit of this.

1.14.3 Rape and the Tribal Response: The Case of Literature

The Scheduled Tribe and Scheduled Caste women are often raped by high caste Hindus. This issue has been taken up by Hindi and regional fiction and story writers in their works. It is argued that the tribal feminism has now become very powerful and it has geared itself to respond to incidences of rape.

Derrida, in his concept of deconstruction, has argued that the post-modernists reject and demystify the macro theories. Something of the kind of deconstruction has come about among the Bengali and Hindi writers. It would be interesting to refer to the work of Mahasweta Devi entitled *Dopadi.* This story revoles round a Santhal Naxalite woman who is not prepared to accept the established patriarchal conceptualization of rape. She struggles and shows resistance to the person who raped her. *Dropadi*, the story runs on the lines of Dropadi of Mahabharata but there significant differences .in the story Dropadi is asked by a Sainanayaka in his tent. She stands there with tears in her eyes.

In Mahasweta's story the actions of Dropadi defy the tradition of her namesake Draupadi of the Indian epic Mahabharata. When Draupadi was being stripped in public, Krishna intervenes and converts her sari into unending yards of cloth. Mahasweta has rewritten this episode. Her Dopadi rejects male leadership. She does not want the male to rescue her. Mahasweta's Dopadi dauntlessly asks: you can strip me but how can clothe me again". This response given by the Santhal woman shows that when feminism successfully works among tribals that mark the end of gender discrimination.

1.15 Need of Gender Study

There are a large number of social issues which social anthropology and for that matter social sciences should study. In the history of social sciences it has been unhistorical to study the gender issues. True, sociology and social anthropology have studied the position of women through history. These disciplines paid attention to only half of our general population. But, since the sixties, there has been a flood of studies on gender issues. This has partly been explained by A.R. Desai. He says that in post independent India, the state is obliged constitutionally to transform rural people, Scheduled Castes, Scheduled Tribals and other subaltern groups into more powerful groups. It is a compulsion made by India's Constitution.

Second, It was in the year 1975 that the Declaration of International women's year was announced. The year was extended into a decade and this gave rise to women's studies. Women's centres and researches on various aspects of women's problems have been favourably looked upon, attracting many funding agencies, including state and its various agencies. The Constitution of India seems to be the guiding code for a systematic observation of women's status. It would be worthwhile to find out the origin of gender problem in our Constitution. Interestingly, till as recently as 1981, the index of the Constitution does not contain a category of 'women', to which one may refer for understanding the position of women as provided in the Constitution. In the category 'marriage' there is a passing reference; 'family planning' is indexed along with 'population control', and not with family or women's welfare. The index maker to this government publication does not find 'women', 'marriage' or 'family' worthy of being referred to in the index of the Constitution.

However, it is in Article 15 on fundamental Rights, there is a reference to *women as equal citizen.* It lays down that "the state shall not discriminate against any citizen on grounds only on religion, race, caste, sex, place of birth or any of them". Further, in sub-article (3) of the same Article, it is stated that "nothing in this Article shall prevent the state from making any special provision for women and children".

Thus, the Constitution enjoins equal status to women, as citizens, but also takes into consideration some special disabilities, which the state may endeavour to rectify by affirmative action. Similarly, in Part IV dealing with Directive Principles of State Policy, there are references to the principles to be taken into account wherein concern for women is exhibited. For instance, Articles 39, 42 and 44 refer specifically to certain principles which, though not enforceable in the courts, should provide guidance to the state treating women as equal citizens.

We have discussed some of the indicators of the underlying principles of gender role as perceptible in the Constitution as well as the path of development adopted by the post independent Indian State. A. R. Desai, who has been a staunch Marxist, raises some questions regarding gender issues with reference to the Constitution. These questions need to be quoted:

- Can a state, which proclaims opposition to discrimination based on sex and other elements, permit religious personal laws, which affect the life of women in a basic manner
- On the ground of religion, can diverse practices of discrimination in terms of number, choice of partners, control over body and sexual life, residence, inheritance, succession, property rights, adoption, local and diverse practices discriminatory to women be permitted
- Which of the practices embodied of the personal laws should be called secular and which religious
- Desai has raised some really fundamental problems. Some efforts will have to be made to amend the Constitution for giving a respectable status to women.

Chapter - II

Important Constitutional and Legal Provisions for Gender Sensitisation in India

Gender inequality is not a new phenomenon. It has instead been a ubiquitous characteristic of societies in evidence for millennia, though to varying degrees across countries and over time. Nevertheless, the emergence of a human rights agenda in the mid 20th century and women's movements across the world since the 1960s has contributed to increased global attention to this form of inequality. Here, too, research shows that some forms of gender inequality can slow economic growth and development. In other words, in addition to the negative effects of gender stratification on women's relative capabilities and well being more generally, there are societal costs to continued gender inequality (Seguino, S., 2010).

2.1 An Overview: Constitutional Need for Women

Concern for women's and girls safety and purity" constrains their physical mobility in many developing countries. It is difficult to say how much of the limited mobility is out of genuine concern for women's welfare, aimed at protecting them from harassment and sexual violence, and how much is simply a way to female autonomy. In a cross-country study of mate preferences, men put more weight on their spouse's sexual inexperience at marriage than on physical appearance in India, China, Indonesia, Taiwan, and Iran, while the opposite prioritization was seen in each of the 24 European, North American, South American, and sub-Saharan African countries studied (Buss, 1989). Restrictions on female mobility often seem largely aimed at keeping unmarried women chaste and married women faithful. In any case, they are a proximate cause of reduced female schooling and career opportunities.

One reason parents cite for not educating their daughters is the distance to school. Burde and Linden (2013) evaluate a school building initiative in Afghanistan and that having a school located within one's village itself matters much more for girls' enrollment; a village school essentially closes the otherwise-large gender gap in enrollment. Muralidharan and Prakash (2013) showed that a program that gave girls bicycles to travel to school in India similarly had a sizable impact on girls' school participation. These results suggest that better infrastructure, which comes with economic development, could onset some of the elect that social constraints on girls' mobility have on their education.

Besides distance to school, parents might also want their daughters segregated from male peers or teachers. Kim, et al. (1999) evaluate a program in the Pakistani city of Quetta that subsidized the creation of neighborhood private schools in part to meet parents demand for single-sex schools for their daughters. Similarly, the construction of sex-segregated school latrines boosted adolescent girls' enrollment in India (Adukia, 2014). The construction of "girl friendly schools" and the schools should be equipped with sex segregated latrines, for example, also improved school attendance and academic achievement in rural Burkina Faso (Kazianga, et al., 2013).

In a setting where the genders are socially segregated, the benets of having a same gender teacher might be especially large and same gender effects on test scores for both boys and girls in India (Muralidharan and Sheth, 2013). But girls lose out on the same gender beneath as they progress because there are fewer female teachers at higher grades; one explanation for the female advantage in high school enrollment but disadvantage in college enrollment in the U.S. in the early twentieth century is that college was further from home (Goldin and Katz, 2009). Thus, distance to school mattering more for females is not unique to today's developing countries.

Gender mismatch can explain 10 to 20 percent of the negative trend in girls test scores as they progress to higher grades. Another consideration is that parents feel pressure to marry their daughters early in societies where female chastity is prized by men, which leads to early school dropout. Field and Ambrus (2008) estimate that, in Bangladesh, for every year an adolescent girl's marriage is delayed, she completes an additional 0.22 years of schooling. The risks associated with female mobility both objective risk and socially constructed risk to family honor might also explain the very low FLFP in India. One of the tenets of the Hindu caste system is that women should be protected from pollution", which includes men outside their families. Disallowing women from working outside the home is one way of maintaining their purity (Chen, 1995). Because these restrictions apply more stringently to upper caste women in India, lower caste women often have more professional exibility and autonomy (Field, et al., 2010, 2014; Luke and Munshi, 2011).

Female seclusion (purdah) is also an important tenet of Islam, and Muslim women resemble Hindu women in their low labor force participation and low self reported freedom of choice. A notable contrast is that many of the norms that underlie Hindu parents desire for sons, such as dowry and bequests only to sons, are weaker or non-existent among Muslims. Correspondingly, within India the sex ratio at birth and child survival exhibit less pro-male bias among Muslims than Hindus (Borooah and Iyer, 2005).

2.2 Persistence of Gender Norms when Eeconomic Conditions Change

One type of evidence that gender gaps do not simply react the current economic environment that culture also matters is their persistence even when the economic environment changes. Complementing Alesina, et al. (2013) work on the long-run persistence of gender norms, recent work has shown that gender norms are sticky in the shorter run, e.g., from one generation to the next. Using the U.S. Census for 2000 and U.S. birth records, respectively, Almond and Edlund (2008) and Abrevaya (2009) and evidence of missing girls among U.S. residents of East Asian and South Asian origin. The male-skewed sex ratio is concentrated at higher parity and in cases when all the older siblings are girls, consistent with couples having sex-selective abortions when they are trying to have a son but conceive a daughter. If the preference for sons were driven entirely by the local economic environment, we would not expect it to be manifest among those who have immigrated to a wealthy country. Many of the cultural practices such as dowry and non-employment of women are abandoned upon immigration, so the economic incentives to prefer sons should be less strong for the immigrant communities. Their continued son preference suggests that gender related practices are embodied in preferences or beliefs that might have a long half life.

Fernandez and Fogli (2009) also study immigrants to the U.S. and that a womans fertility is predicted by the average fertility in her country of origin; a similar pattern holds for her labor force participation. Fernandez, et al. (2004) find that if a mother works, her son's wife is more likely to work, further evidence that gender gaps in behavior at least partly react gender norms that are passed along from parents to children. These findings indicate that gender related behaviors depend on cultural background and not just the economic environment one faces.

2.3 Legal and Constitutional Safeguards against Gender Inequality

Indian Constitution provides for positive efforts to eliminate gender inequality; the Preamble to the Constitution talks about goals of achieving social, economic and political justice to everyone and to provide equality of status and of opportunity to all its citizens. Further, women have equal right to vote in our political system. Article 15 of the Constitution provides for prohibition of discrimination on grounds of *sex* also apart from other grounds such as religion, race, caste or place of birth. Article 15(3) authorizes the Sate to make any special provision for women and children. Moreover, the Directive Principles of State Policy also provides various provisions which are for the benefit of women and provides safeguards against discrimination.

Other than these Constitutional safeguards, various protective Legislations have also been passed by the Parliament to eliminate exploitation of women and to give them equal status in society. For instance, the Sati (Prevention) Act, 1987 was enacted to abolish and make punishable the inhuman custom of Sati; the Dowry Prohibition Act, 1961 to eliminate the practice of dowry; the Special Marriage Act, 1954 to give rightful status to married couples who marry inter caste or inter religion; Pre-Natal Diagnostic Techniques (Regulation and Prevention of Misuse) Bill (introduced in Parliament in 1991, passed in 1994 to stop female infanticide and many more such Acts. Furthermore, the Parliament time to time brings out amendments to existing laws in order to give protection to women according to the changing needs of the society, for instance, Section 304 B was added to the Indian Penal Code, 1860 to make dowry death or bride burning a specific offence punishable with maximum punishment of life imprisonment.

So there are varied legislative safeguards and protection mechanisms for women but the ground reality is very different. Despite all these provisions women are still being treated as second rate citizens in our country; men are treating them as an object to fulfill their carnal desires; crimes against women are at alarming stage; the practice of dowry is still widely prevalent; female infanticide is a norm in our homes.

2.4 Preamble

1. "Gender equality, respect for human rights, and environmental sustainability are cornerstones for achieving enduring impacts on the lives and potential of poor women, men, and children. It is vital that all our policies address these issues in a more systematic and coherent way" (Accra Agenda for Action, 2008).
2. Individually and collectively donor agencies and governments have made strong commitments to gender equality and women's empowerment. Donor guidance to operationalised those commitments includes the *DAC Guidelines on Gender Equality and Women's Empowerment in Development Co-operation* (1999), along with the policies and plans developed by individual agencies.
3. In 2007 members of the DAC Network on Gender Equality reviewed the *DAC Guidelines* with the intention of revising them to reflect changed approaches to and practices in development cooperation. It quickly became apparent, however, that the twin track approach of the *Guidelines.*
4. Recent reforms of aid delivery, most notably the Paris Declaration on Aid Effectiveness (2005), have provided new opportunities and mechanisms to translate donor and government commitments into improved practice, results and impacts. The Declaration sets out five principles for reform of aid intended to *"increase the impact of aid... in reducing poverty and inequality, increasing growth, building capacity and accelerating the achievement of the MDGs"*. Achieving these internationally agreed development goals will not be possible without progress on gender equality and women's empowerment. At the same time, implementing the Declaration's overarching partnership commitments is a powerful way of accelerating progress on MDG: gender equality and women's empowerment. Whilst gender inequalities are costly and undermine aid effectiveness and development impacts, gender equality and women's empowerment, on the other hand, are powerful multipliers of development efforts.
5. The Paris Declaration and the Accra Agenda for Action provide the frameworks and good practice principles for fostering gender equality as a priority development issue. Each offers concrete opportunities to ensure that gender equality and women's empowerment initiatives benefit from scaled up Official Development Assistance (ODA). The strengthened partnerships

which are promoted in each will support both the supply side of governance (government policies, strategies and capacities) and the demand side (voice, inclusion and the empowerment of citizens, including women's groups and civil society). The Declaration and the Agenda for Action can be tools to empower women and men and to strengthen the responsiveness of governments to citizens.

6. These *Guiding Principles* focus primarily on the opportunities for using the implementation of the Paris Declaration's principles and commitments to:
   - Harmonise approaches to support for gender equality.
   - Implement concrete actions, focussed on results and impacts.
   - Be responsible and accountable for those actions and for agreed commitments on gender equality and women's empowerment.

The suggested approaches and entry points can be used by policy advisors and programme managers in both donor and partner countries to increase the prospects for achieving results and impacts through work on gender equality and women's empowerment. As well as being development goals in their own right, gender equality and women's empowerment are catalysts for the reduction of poverty and the achievement of all the MDGs.

2.5 National Policy for the Empowerment of Women (2001)

The principle of gender equality is enshrined in the Indian Constitution in its Preamble, Fundamental Rights, Fundamental Duties and Directive Principles. The Constitution not only grants equality to women, but also empowers the State to adopt measures of positive discrimination in favour of women.

Within the framework of a democratic polity, our laws, development policies, Plans and programmes have aimed at women's advancement in different spheres. From the Fifth Five Year Plan (1974-78) onwards has been a marked shift in the approach to women's issues from welfare to development. In recent years, the empowerment of women has been recognized as the central issue in determining the status of women. The National Commission for Women was set up by an Act of Parliament in 1990 to safeguard the rights and legal entitlements of women. The 73rd and 74th Amendments (1993) to the Constitution of India have provided for reservation of seats in the local bodies of Panchayats and Municipalities for women, laying a strong foundation for their participation in decision making at the local levels.

- India has also ratified various international conventions and human rights instruments committing to secure equal rights of women. Key among them is the ratification of the Convention on Elimination of All Forms of Discrimination against Women (CEDAW) in 1993.
- The Mexico Plan of Action (1975), the Nairobi Forward Looking Strategies (1985), the Beijing Declaration as well as the Platform for Action (1995) and the Outcome Document adopted by the UNGA Session on Gender Equality and Development & Peace for the 21st century, titled "Further actions and initiatives to implement the Beijing Declaration and the Platform for Action" have been unreservedly endorsed by India for appropriate follow up.
- The Policy also takes note of the commitments of the Ninth Five Year Plan and the other Sectoral Policies relating to empowerment of Women.
- The women's movement and a wide spread network of non-Government Organisations which have strong grass-roots presence and deep insight into women's concerns have contributed in inspiring initiatives for the empowerment of women.
- However, there still exists a wide gap between the goals enunciated in the Constitution, legislation, policies, plans, programmes, and related mechanisms on the one hand and the situational reality of the status of women in India, on the other. This has been analyzed extensively in the Report of the Committee on the Status of Women in India, "Towards Equality," 1974 and highlighted in the National Perspective Plan for Women, 1988-2000, the Shramshakti Report, 1988 and the Platform for Action, Five Years after- n assessment".
- Gender disparity manifests itself in various forms, the most obvious being the trend of continuously declining female ratio in the population in the last few decades. Social stereotyping and violence at the domestic and societal levels are some of the other manifestations. Discrimination against girl children, adolescent girls and women persists in parts of the country.

- The underlying causes of gender inequality are related to social and economic structure, which is based on informal and formal norms, and practices.
- Consequently, the access of women particularly those belonging to weaker sections including Scheduled Castes/ Scheduled Tribes/ Other backward Classes and minorities, majority of whom are in the rural areas and in the informal, unorganized sector to education, health and productive resources, among others, is inadequate. Therefore, they remain largely marginalized, poor and socially excluded.

2.6 Goal and Objectives

The goal of this Policy is to bring about the advancement, development and empowerment of women. The Policy will be widely disseminated so as to encourage active participation of all stakeholders for achieving its goals. Specifically, the objectives of this Policy include:

- Rating an environment through positive economic and social policies for full development of women to enable them to realize their full potential.
- The *de-jure* and *de-facto* enjoyment of all human rights and fundamental freedom by women on equal basis with men in all spheres – political, economic, social, cultural and civil.
- Equal access to participation and decision making of women in social, political and economic life of the nation.
- Equal access to women to health care, quality education at all levels, career and vocational guidance, employment, equal remuneration, occupational health and safety, social security and public office etc.
- Strengthening legal systems aimed at elimination of all forms of discrimination against women.
- Changing societal attitudes and community practices by active participation and involvement of both men and women.
- Mainstreaming a gender perspective in the development process.
- Elimination of discrimination and all forms of violence against women and the girl child; and
- Building and strengthening partnerships with civil society, particularly women's organizations.

2.7 Policy Prescriptions; Judicial Legal Systems

Legal judicial system will be made more responsive and gender sensitive to women's needs, especially in cases of domestic violence and personal assault. New laws will be enacted and existing laws reviewed to ensure that justice is quick and the punishment meted out to the culprits is commensurate with the severity of the offence.

- At the initiative of and with the full participation of all stakeholders including community and religious leaders, the Policy would aim to encourage changes in personal laws such as those related to marriage, divorce, maintenance and guardianship so as to eliminate discrimination against women.
- The evolution of property rights in a patriarchal system has contributed to the subordinate status of women. The Policy would aim to encourage changes in laws relating to ownership of property and inheritance by evolving consensus in order to make them gender just.

2.8 Decision Making

Women's equality in power sharing and active participation in decision making, including decision making in political process at all levels will be ensured for the achievement of the goals of empowerment. All measures will be taken to guarantee women equal access to and full participation in decision making bodies at every level, including the legislative, executive, judicial, corporate, statutory bodies, as also the advisory Commissions, Committees, Boards and Trusts etc. Affirmative action such as reservations/ quotas, including in higher legislative bodies, will be considered whenever necessary on a time bound basis. Women friendly personnel policies will also be drawn up to encourage women to participate effectively in the developmental process.

2.9 Mainstreaming a Gender Perspective in the Development Process

Policies, programmes and systems will be established to ensure mainstreaming of women's perspectives in all developmental processes, as catalysts, participants and recipients. Wherever there are gaps in policies and programmes, women specific interventions would be undertaken to bridge these. Coordinating and monitoring mechanisms will also be devised to assess from time to time the progress of such mainstreaming mechanisms.

Women's issues and concerns as a result will specially be addressed and reflected in all concerned laws, sectoral policies, plans and programmes of action.

2.10 Economic Empowerment of women; *Poverty Eradication*

- Since women comprise the majority of the population below the poverty line and are very often in situations of extreme poverty, given the harsh realities of intra household and social discrimination, macroeconomic policies and poverty eradication programmes will specifically address the needs and problems of such women. There will be improved implementation of programmes which are already women oriented with special targets for women. Steps will be taken for mobilization of poor women and convergence of services, by offering them a range of economic and social options, along with necessary support measures to enhance their capabilities

2.10.1 Micro Credit

- In order to enhance women's access to credit for consumption and production, the establishment of new and strengthening of existing micro-credit mechanisms and micro finance institution will be undertaken so that the outreach of credit is enhanced. Other supportive measures would be taken to ensure adequate flow of credit through extant financial institutions and banks, so that all women below poverty line have easy access to credit.

2.10.2 Women and Economy

- Women's perspectives will be included in designing and implementing macro-economic and social policies by institutionalizing their participation in such processes. Their contribution to socio-economic development as producers and workers will be recognized in the formal and informal sectors (including home based workers) and appropriate policies relating to employment and to her working conditions will be drawn up. Such measures could include:
- Reinterpretation and redefinition of conventional concepts of work wherever necessary e.g. in the Census records, to reflect women's contribution as producers and workers.
- Preparation of satellite and national accounts.

2.10.3 Globalization

Globalization has presented new challenges for the realization of the goal of women's equality, the gender impact of which has not been systematically evaluated fully. However, from the micro level studies that were commissioned by the Department of Women & Child Development, it is evident that there is a need for reframing policies for access to employment and quality of employment. Benefits of the growing global economy have been unevenly distributed leading to wider economic disparities, the feminization of poverty, increased gender inequality through often deteriorating working conditions and unsafe working environment especially in the informal economy and rural areas. Strategies will be designed to enhance the capacity of women and empower them to meet the negative social and economic impacts, which may flow from the globalization process.

2.10.4 Women and Agriculture

In view of the critical role of women in the agriculture and allied sectors, as producers, concentrated efforts will be made to ensure that benefits of training, extension and various programmes will reach them in proportion to their numbers. The programmes for training women in soil conservation, social forestry, dairy development and other occupations allied to agriculture like horticulture, livestock including small animal husbandry, poultry, fisheries etc. will be expanded to benefit women workers in the agriculture sector.

2.10.5 Women and Industry

The important role played by women in electronics, information technology and food processing and agro industry and textiles has been crucial to the development of these sectors. They would be given comprehensive support in terms of labour legislation, social security and other support services to participate in various industrial sectors. Women at present cannot work in night shift in factories even if they wish to. Suitable measures will be taken to enable women to work on the night shift in factories. This will be accompanied with support services for security, transportation etc.

2.10.6 Support Services

The provision of support services for women, like child care facilities, including crèches at work places and educational institutions, homes for the aged and the disabled will be expanded and improved to create an enabling environment and to ensure their full cooperation in social, political and economic life. Women friendly personnel policies will also be drawn up to encourage women to participate effectively in the developmental process.

2.11 Social Empowerment of Women

Gender empowerment conventionally refers to the empowerment of women, and has become a significant topic of discussion in regards to education development and economics. It can also point to approaches regarding other marginalized genders in a particular political or social context. This approach to empowerment is partly informed by feminism and employed legal empowerment by building on international human rights. Empowerment is one of the main procedural concerns when addressing human rights and development. The Human Development and Capabilities Approach, The Millennium Development Goals, and other credible approaches/goals point to empowerment and participation as a necessary step if a country is to overcome the obstacles associated with marginalised women's poverty and development.

2.11.1 Education

Equal access to education for women and girls will be ensured. Special measures will be taken to eliminate discrimination, universalize education, eradicate illiteracy, create a gender-sensitive educational system, increase enrolment and retention rates of girls and improve the quality of education to facilitate life-long learning as well as development of occupation/vocation/ technical skills by women. Reducing the gender gap in secondary and higher education would be a focus area. Sectoral time targets in existing policies will be achieved, with a special focus on girls and women, particularly those belonging to weaker sections including the Scheduled Castes/ Scheduled Tribes/ Other Backward Classes/ Minorities. Gender sensitive curricula would be developed at all levels of educational system in order to address sex stereotyping as one of the causes of gender discrimination.

2.11.2 Health

A holistic approach to women's health which includes both nutrition and health services will be adopted and special attention will be given to the needs of women and the girl at all stages of the life cycle. The reduction of infant mortality and maternal mortality, which are sensitive indicators of human development, is a priority concern. This policy reiterates the national demographic goals for Infant Mortality Rate (IMR), Maternal

Mortality Rate (MMR) set out in the National Population Policy 2000. Women should have access to comprehensive, affordable and quality health care. Measures will be adopted that take into account the reproductive rights of women to enable them to exercise informed choices, their vulnerability to sexual and health problems together with endemic, infectious and communicable diseases such as malaria, TB, and water borne diseases as well as hypertension and cardio-pulmonary diseases. The social, developmental and health consequences of HIV/AIDS and other sexually transmitted diseases will be tackled from a gender perspective.

To effectively meet problems of infant and maternal mortality, and early marriage the availability of good and accurate data at micro level on deaths, birth and marriages is required. Strict implementation of registration of births and deaths would be ensured and registration of marriages would be made compulsory.

In accordance with the commitment of the National Population Policy (2000) to population stabilization, this Policy recognizes the critical need of men and women to have access to safe, effective and affordable methods of family planning of their choice and the need to suitably address the issues of early marriages and spacing of children. Interventions such as spread of education, compulsory registration of marriage and special programmes like BSY should impact on delaying the age of marriage so that by 2010 child marriages are eliminated. Women's traditional knowledge about health care and nutrition will be recognized through proper documentation and its use will be encouraged. The use of Indian and alternative systems of medicine will be enhanced within the framework of overall health infrastructure available for women.

2.11.3 Nutrition

In view of the high risk of malnutrition and disease that women face at all the three critical stages viz., infancy and childhood, adolescent and reproductive phase, focussed attention would be paid to meeting the nutritional needs of women at all stages of the life cycle. This is also important in view of the critical link between the health of adolescent girls, pregnant and lactating women with the health of infant and young children. Special efforts will be made to tackle the problem of macro and micro nutrient deficiencies especially amongst pregnant and lactating women as it leads to various diseases and disabilities.

Intra-household discrimination in nutritional matters vis-à-vis girls and women will be sought to be ended through appropriate strategies.

Widespread use of nutrition education would be made to address the issues of intra household imbalances in nutrition and the special needs of pregnant and lactating women. Women's participation will also be ensured in the planning, superintendence and delivery of the system.

2.11.4 Drinking Water and Sanitation

Special attention will be given to the needs of women in the provision of safe drinking water, sewage disposal, toilet facilities and sanitation within accessible reach of households, especially in rural areas and urban slums. Women's participation will be ensured in the planning, delivery and maintenance of such services.

2.11.5 Housing and Shelter

Women's perspectives will be included in housing policies, planning of housing colonies and provision of shelter both in rural and urban areas. Special attention will be given for providing adequate and safe housing and accommodation for women including single women, heads of households, working women, students, apprentices and trainees.

2.11.6 Environment

Women will be involved and their perspectives reflected in the policies and programmes for environment, conservation and restoration. Considering the impact of environmental factors on their livelihoods, women's participation will be ensured in the conservation of the environment and control of environmental degradation. The vast majority of rural women still depend on the locally available non-commercial sources of energy such as animal dung, crop waste and fuel wood. In order to ensure the efficient use of these energy resources in an environmental friendly manner, the Policy will aim at promoting the programmes of non-conventional energy resources. Women will be involved in spreading the use of solar energy, biogas, smokeless chulahs and other rural application so as to have a visible impact of these measures in influencing eco system and in changing the life styles of rural women.

2.11.7 Science and Technology

Programmes will be strengthened to bring about a greater involvement of women in science and technology. These will include measures to motivate girls to take up science and technology for higher education and also ensure that development projects with scientific and technical inputs involve women fully. Efforts to develop a scientific temper and awareness will also be stepped up. Special measures would be taken for their training in areas where they have special skills like communication and information technology. Efforts to develop appropriate technologies suited to women's needs as well as to reduce their drudgery will be given a special focus too.

2.11.8 Women in Difficult Circumstances

In recognition of the diversity of women's situations and in acknowledgement of the needs of specially disadvantaged groups, measures and programmes will be undertaken to provide them with special assistance. These groups include women in extreme poverty, destitute women, women in conflict situations, women affected by natural calamities, women in less developed regions, the disabled widows, elderly women, single women in difficult circumstances, women heading households, those displaced from employment, migrants, women who are victims of marital violence, deserted women and prostitutes etc.

2.12 Violence against Women

All forms of violence against women, physical and mental, whether at domestic or societal levels, including those arising from customs, traditions or accepted practices shall be dealt with effectively with a view to eliminate its incidence. Institutions and mechanisms/schemes for assistance will be created and strengthened for prevention of such violence, including sexual harassment at work place and customs like dowry; for the rehabilitation of the victims of violence and for taking effective action against the perpetrators of such violence. A special emphasis will also be laid on programmes and measures to deal with trafficking in women and girls.

2.13 Rights of the Girl Child

All forms of discrimination against the girl child and violation of her rights shall be eliminated by undertaking strong measures both preventive and punitive within and outside the family. These would relate specifically to strict enforcement of laws against prenatal sex selection and the practices of female foeticide, female infanticide, child marriage, child abuse and child prostitution etc. Removal of discrimination in the treatment of the girl child within the family and outside and projection of a positive image of the girl child will be actively fostered. There will be special emphasis on the needs of the girl child and earmarking of substantial investments in the areas relating to food and nutrition, health and education, and in vocational education. In implementing programmes for eliminating child labour, there will be a special focus on girl children.

2.14 Mass Media

Media will be used to portray images consistent with human dignity of girls and women. The Policy will specifically strive to remove demeaning, degrading and negative conventional stereotypical images of women and violence against women. Private sector partners and media networks will be involved at all levels to ensure equal access for women particularly in the area of information and communication technologies. The media would be encouraged to develop codes of conduct, professional guidelines and other self regulatory mechanisms to remove gender stereotypes and promote balanced portrayals of women and men.

2.15 Operational Strategies

First and foremost, gender equality is a matter of human rights. It is also a driver of development progress. Unless women and girls are able to fully realize their rights in all spheres of life, human development will not be advanced. It is well placed to ensure that gender equality and the empowerment of women are integrated into every aspect of its work to support countries to eradicate poverty and reduce inequalities and exclusion with the help of different Action Plans.

2.15.1 Action Plans

All Central and State Ministries will draw up time bound Action Plans for translating the Policy into a set of concrete actions, through a participatory process of consultation with Centre/ State Departments of Women and Child Development and National/ State Commissions for Women. The Plans will specifically including the following:

- Measurable goals to be achieved by 2010.
- Identification and commitment of resources.
- Responsibilities for implementation of action points.
- Structures and mechanisms to ensure efficient monitoring, review and gender impact assessment of action points and policies.
- Introduction of a gender perspective in the budgeting process.
- In order to support better planning and programme formulation and adequate allocation of resources, Gender Development Indices (GDI) will be developed by networking with specialized agencies. These could be analyzed and studied in depth. Gender auditing and development of evaluation mechanisms will also be undertaken along side.

- Collection of gender disaggregated data by all primary data collecting agencies of the Central and State Governments as well as Research and Academic Institutions in the Public and Private Sectors will be undertaken. Data and information gaps in vital areas reflecting the status of women will be sought to be filled in by these immediately. All Ministries/ Corporations/ Banks and financial institutions etc will be advised to collect, collate, disseminate and maintain/publish data related to programmes and benefits on a gender disaggregated basis. This will help in meaningful planning and evaluation of policies.

2.15.2 Institutional Mechanisms

- Institutional mechanisms, to promote the advancement of women, which exist at the Central and State levels, will be strengthened. These will be through interventions as may be appropriate and will relate to, among others, provision of adequate resources, training and advocacy skills to effectively influence macro policies, legislation, programmes etc. to achieve the empowerment of women.
- National and State Councils will be formed to oversee the operationalisation of the Policy on a regular basis. The National Council will be headed by the Prime Minister and the State Councils by the Chief Ministers and be broad in composition having representatives from the concerned Departments/Ministries, National and State Commissions for Women, Social Welfare Boards, representatives of Non-Government Organizations, Women's Organisations, Corporate Sector, Trade Unions, financing institutions, academics, experts and social activists etc. These bodies will review the progress made in implementing the Policy twice a year. The National Development Council will also be informed of the progress of the programme undertaken under the policy from time to time for advice and comments.
- National and State Resource Centres on women will be established with mandates for collection and dissemination of information, undertaking research work, conducting surveys, implementing training and awareness generation programmes, etc. These Centers will link up with Women's Studies Centres and other research and academic institutions through suitable information networking systems.

- While institutions at the district level will be strengthened, at the grass roots, women will be helped by Government through its programmes to organize and strengthen into Self Help Groups (SHGs) at the Anganwadi/ Village/ Town level. The women's groups will be helped to institutionalize themselves into registered societies and to federate at the Panchyat/ Municipal level. These societies will bring about synergistic implementation of all the social and economic development programmes by drawing resources made available through Government and Non-Government channels, including banks and financial institutions and by establishing a close Interface with the Panchayats/ Municipalities.

2.15.3 Resource Management

Availability of adequate financial, human and market resources to implement the Policy will be managed by concerned Departments, financial credit institutions and banks, private sector, civil society and other connected institutions. This process will include:

- Assessment of benefits flowing to women and resource allocation to the programmes relating to them through an exercise of gender budgeting. Appropriate changes in policies will be made to optimize benefits to women under these schemes;
- Adequate resource allocation to develop and promote the policy outlined earlier based on (a) above by concerned Departments.
- Developing synergy between personnel of Health, Rural Development, Education and Women & Child Development Department at field level and other village level functionaries'.
- Meeting credit needs by banks and financial credit institutions through suitable policy initiatives and development of new institutions in coordination with the Department of Women & Child Development.
- The strategy of Women's Component Plan adopted in the Ninth Plan of ensuring that not less than 30 percent of benefits/ funds flow to women from all Ministries and Departments will be implemented effectively so that the needs and interests of women and girls are addressed by all concerned sectors. The Department of Women and Child Development being the nodal Ministry will monitor and review the progress of the implementation of the

Component Plan from time to time, in terms of both quality and quantity in collaboration with the Planning Commission.

- Efforts will be made to channelize private sector investments too, to support programmes and projects for advancement of women.

2.16 Legislation

- The existing legislative structure will be reviewed and additional legislative measures taken by identified departments to implement the Policy. This will also involve a review of all existing laws including personal, customary and tribal laws, subordinate legislation, related rules as well as executive and administrative regulations to eliminate all gender discriminatory references. The process will be planned over a time period 2000-2003. The specific measures required would be evolved through a consultation process involving civil society, National Commission for Women and Department of Women and Child Development. In appropriate cases the consultation process would be widened to include other stakeholders too.
- Effective implementation of legislation would be promoted by involving civil society and community. Appropriate changes in legislation will be undertaken, if necessary.

In addition, following other specific measures will be taken to implement the legislation effectively.

- Strict enforcement of all relevant legal provisions and speedy Redressal of grievances will be ensured, with a special focus on violence and gender related atrocities.
- Measures to prevent and punish sexual harassment at the place of work, protection for women workers in the organized/ unorganized sector and strict enforcement of relevant laws such as Equal Remuneration Act and Minimum Wages Act will be undertaken.
- Crimes against women, their incidence, prevention, investigation, detection and prosecution will be regularly reviewed at all Crime Review fora and Conferences at the Central, State and District levels. Recognised, local, voluntary organizations will be authorized to lodge Complaints and facilitate registration, investigations and legal proceedings related to violence and atrocities against girls and women.
- Women's Cells in Police Stations, Encourage Women Police Stations Family Courts, Mahila Courts, Counselling Centers,

Legal Aid Centers and Nyaya Panchayats will be strengthened and expanded to eliminate violence and atrocities against women.

- Widespread dissemination of information on all aspects of legal rights, human rights and other entitlements of women, through specially designed legal literacy programmes and rights information programmes will be done.

2.17 Gender Sensitization

Training of personnel of executive, legislative and judicial wings of the State, with a special focus on policy and programme framers, implementation and development agencies, law enforcement machinery and the judiciary, as well as non-governmental organizations will be undertaken. Other measures will include:

- Promoting societal awareness to gender issues and women's human rights.
- Review of curriculum and educational materials to include gender education and human rights issues.
- Removal of all references derogatory to the dignity of women from all public documents and legal instruments.
- Use of different forms of mass media to communicate social messages relating to women's equality and empowerment.

2.18 Panchayat Raj Institutions

The 73rd and 74th Amendments (1993) to the Indian Constitution have served as a breakthrough towards ensuring equal access and increased participation in political power structure for women. The PRIs will play a central role in the process of enhancing women's participation in public life. The PRIs and the local self Governments will be actively involved in the implementation and execution of the National Policy for Women at the grassroots level.

2.19 Partnership with the Voluntary Sector Organizations

The involvement of voluntary organizations, associations, federations, trade unions, non-governmental organizations, women's organizations, as well as institutions dealing with education, training and research will be ensured in the formulation, implementation, monitoring and review of all policies and programmes affecting women. Towards this end, they will be provided with appropriate support related to resources and capacity building and facilitated to participate actively in the process of the empowerment of women.

2.20 International Cooperation

The Policy aim at implementation of international obligations/ commitments in all sectors on empowerment of women such as the Convention on All Forms of Discrimination Against Women (CEDAW), Convention on the Rights of the Child (CRC), International Conference on Population and Development (ICPD+5) and other such instruments. International, regional and sub-regional cooperation towards the empowerment of women will continue to be encouraged through sharing of experiences, exchange of ideas and technology, networking with institutions and organizations and through bilateral and multi lateral partnerships.

The principle of gender equality is enshrined in the Indian Constitution in its Preamble, Fundamental Rights, Fundamental Duties and Directive Principles. The Constitution not only grants equality to women, but also empowers the State to adopt measures of positive discrimination in favour of women. Within the framework of a democratic polity, our laws, development policies, Plans and programmes have aimed at women's advancement in different spheres. India has also ratified various international conventions and human rights instruments committing to secure equal rights of women. Key among them is the ratification of the Convention on Elimination of All Forms of Discrimination against Women (CEDAW) in 1993.

2.21 Constitutional Provisions

The Constitution of India not only grants equality to women but also empowers the State to adopt measures of positive discrimination in favour of women for neutralizing the cumulative socio economic, education and political disadvantages faced by them. Fundamental Rights, among others, ensure equality before the law and equal protection of law; prohibits discrimination against any citizen on grounds of religion, race, caste, sex or place of birth, and guarantee equality of opportunity to all citizens in matters relating to employment. Articles 14, 15, 15(3), 16, 39(a), 39(b), 39(c) and 42 of the Constitution are of specific importance in this regard.

2.21.1 Constitutional Privileges

(i) Equality before law for women (Article 14).

(ii) The State not to discriminate against any citizen on grounds only of religion, race, caste, sex, place of birth or any of them (Article 15 (i)).

(iii) The State to make any special provision in favour of women and children (Article 15 (3)).

(iv) Equality of opportunity for all citizens in matters relating to employment or appointment to any office under the State (Article 16).

(v) The State to direct its policy towards securing for men and women equally the right to an adequate means of livelihood (Article 39(a)); and equal pay for equal work for both men and women (Article 39(d)).

(vi) To promote justice, on a basis of equal opportunity and to provide free legal aid by suitable legislation or scheme or in any other way to ensure that opportunities for securing justice are not denied to any citizen by reason of economic or other disabilities (Article 39 A).

(vii) The State to make provision for securing just and humane conditions of work and for maternity relief (Article 42).

(viii) The State to promote with special care the educational and economic interests of the weaker sections of the people and to protect them from social injustice and all forms of exploitation (Article 46).

(ix) The State to raise the level of nutrition and the standard of living of its people (Article 47).

(x) To promote harmony and the spirit of common brotherhood amongst all the people of India and to renounce practices derogatory to the dignity of women (Article 51(A) (e)).

(xi) Not less than one-third (including the number of seats reserved for women belonging to the Scheduled Castes and the Scheduled Tribes) of the total number of seats to be filled by direct election in every Panchayat to be reserved for women and such seats to be allotted by rotation to different constituencies in a Panchayat (Article 243 D(3)).

(xii) Not less than one- third of the total number of offices of Chairpersons in the Panchayats at each level to be reserved for women (Article 243 D (4)).

(xiii) Not less than one third (including the number of seats reserved for women belonging to the Scheduled Castes and the Scheduled Tribes) of the total number of seats to be filled by direct election in every Municipality to be reserved for women and such seats to be allotted by rotation to different constituencies in a Municipality (Article 243 T (3)).

(xiv) Reservation of offices of Chairpersons in Municipalities for the Scheduled Castes, the Scheduled Tribes and women in such manner as the legislature of a State may by law provide (Article 243 T (4)).

2.21.2 Legal Provisions

To uphold the Constitutional mandate, the State has enacted various legislative measures intended to ensure equal rights, to counter social discrimination and various forms of violence and atrocities and to provide support services especially to working women.

Although women may be victims of any of the crimes such as 'Murder', 'Robbery', 'Cheating' etc, the crimes, which are directed specifically against women, are characterized as 'Crime against Women'. These are broadly classified under two categories.

(i) The Crimes Identified Under the Indian Penal Code (IPC).
(ii) Rape (Sec. 376 IPC).
(iii) Kidnapping & Abduction for different purposes (Sec. 363-373).
(iv) Homicide for Dowry, Dowry Deaths or their attempts (Sec. 302/304-B IPC).
(v) Torture, both mental and physical (Sec. 498-A IPC).
(vi) Molestation (Sec. 354 IPC).
(vii) Sexual Harassment (Sec. 509 IPC).
(viii) Importation of girls (up to 21 years of age).

2.21.3 The Crimes identified under the Special Laws (SLL)

Although all laws are not gender specific, the provisions of law affecting women significantly have been reviewed periodically and amendments carried out to keep pace with the emerging requirements. Some acts which have special provisions to safeguard women and their interests are:

(i) The Employees State Insurance Act, 1948.
(ii) The Plantation Labour Act, 1951.

(iii) The Family Courts Act, 1954.
(iv) The Special Marriage Act, 1954.
(v) The Hindu Marriage Act, 1955.
(vi) The Hindu Succession Act, 1956 with amendment in 2005.
(vii) Immoral Traffic (Prevention) Act, 1956.
(viii) The Maternity Benefit Act, 1961 (Amended in 1995).
(ix) Dowry Prohibition Act, 1961.
(x) The Medical Termination of Pregnancy Act, 1971.
(xi) The Contract Labour (Regulation and Abolition) Act, 1976.
(xii) The Equal Remuneration Act, 1976.
(xiii) The Prohibition of Child Marriage Act, 2006.
(xiv) The Criminal Law (Amendment) Act, 1983.
(xv) The Factories (Amendment) Act, 1986.
(xvi) Indecent Representation of Women (Prohibition) Act, 1986.
(xvii) Commission of Sati (Prevention) Act, 1987.
(xviii) The Protection of Women from Domestic Violence Act, 2005.

2.21.4 Special Initiatives for Women

The Women and Child Development Ministry of the Government of India has taken a number of legislative as well as programmatic measures to enhance the safety and development of women in the country.

2.21.4.1 National Commission for Women

In January 1992, the Government set up this statutory body with a specific mandate to study and monitor all matters relating to the constitutional and legal safeguards provided for women, review the existing legislation to suggest amendments wherever necessary, etc.

2.21.4.2 Reservation for Women in Local Self Government

The 73rd Constitutional Amendment Acts passed in 1992 by Parliament ensure one third of the total seats for women in all elected offices in local bodies whether in rural areas or urban areas.

2.21.4.3 The National Plan of Action for the Girl Child (1991-2000)

The plan of Action is to ensure survival, protection and development of the girl child with the ultimate objective of building up a better future for the girl child.

2.21.4.4 National Policy for the Empowerment of Women, 2001

The Department of Women & Child Development in the Ministry of Human Resource Development has prepared a "National Policy for the Empowerment of Women" in the year 2001. The goal of this policy is to bring about the advancement, development and empowerment of women.

2.22 The Violence against Women Act's (VAWA's) Tribal Provisions

In *Oliphant v. Suquamish Indian Tribe*, 435 U.S. 191 (1978), the Supreme Court held that tribes do not have inherent authority to prosecute crimes committed by non-Indians in Indian Country. *Oliphant* is a judge made, non-constitutional law and generally remains the current law. The Violence Against Women Act (VAWA) partially reverses the *Oliphant* rule by recognizing the inherent authority of federally recognized tribes to prosecute non-Indians in tribal court for domestic violence crimes against tribal members or Indians residing in Indian Country.

In VAWA's tribal provisions, Congress requires tribes to have certain processes and protection to qualify for the recognition of jurisdiction. VAWA also provides procedural safeguards to domestic violence criminal defendants that must be observed by implementing tribes. VAWA allows tribes to elect whether to take advantage of these tribal provisions permitting the assertion of tribal jurisdiction over domestic violence crimes committed by non-Indians. Tribes who do not wish to take advantage of VAWA's tribal provisions do not have to implement any changes. Also, regardless of whether a tribe decides to take advantage of VAWA, federal and state authorities, where applicable, can still prosecute the same non-Indian defendant for the same crime.

2.22.1 VAWA's Jurisdiction; Definitions

VAWA is defined the different type of crimes, dependents, victims, procedure and way of violence on women which are given below:

2.22.1.1 Types of Crimes

To satisfy the requirements of VAWA, tribes may have to amend their tribal codes to recognize special domestic violence crimes as different from assault between two strangers. VAWA requires a "dating or domestic relationship" between the perpetrator and victim for VAWA's special criminal jurisdiction provisions to apply.

Tribes that implement VAWA also can prosecute non-Indians in tribal courts for violation of a protective order, but the violation must occur in

Indian Country. Additionally, the protective order on which criminal jurisdiction is based must be issued:

(1) To prevent violent or threatening acts; or
(2) Contact, communication, or physical proximity with or to the victim. Given this definition, VAWA likely does not permit prosecution of a non-Indian spouse for violating a domestic violence protective order outside of the tribe's Indian Country lands. Such crimes remain under the state or county's exclusive criminal jurisdiction.

2.22.1.2 Types of Defendants

A non-Indian can be subject to VAWA's special tribal domestic violence jurisdiction only if he or she:

(1) Resides in Indian Country;
(2) Is employed in Indian Country;
(3) Is the spouse, intimate partner, or dating partner of a tribal member; or
(4) Is the spouse, intimate partner, or dating partner of an Indian living in Indian Country.

In the case of employment within Indian Country, it is an open question whether the employer must be the tribe or can be a company owned by the tribe or a tribal member or even a company owned by a non-Indian.

2.22.1.3 Types of Victims

To take advantage of VAWA's special domestic violence criminal jurisdiction, the victim must be a tribal member or an Indian that resides in the prosecuting tribe's Indian Country. If both the perpetrator and the victim are non-Indians, VAWA does not recognize tribal jurisdiction over the non-Indian perpetrator.

2.22.1.4 Place of Criminal Act that Serves as the Basis for Special Criminal Jurisdiction

The alleged criminal act or violation of the protective order must occur in Indian Country. *See* Pub. L. 113-4, § 904 (c). VAWA's tribal provisions adopt the definition of Indian Country found in the federal criminal code, 18 U.S.C. § 1151, meaning that acts that a non-Indian committed against a tribal member off-reservation cannot provide the basis for a tribal court prosecution under VAWA. Additionally, any attempts to exercise special domestic violence criminal jurisdiction over crimes that occur on non-Indian owned fee land within a reservation may be rejected if challenged.

2.22.2 VAWA's Procedural Requirements

Congress also specified several procedural protections that a tribe must provide non-Indian criminal defendants under VAWA.

2.22.2.1 Right to a Jury Selected from a Fair Cross Section of the Community

A tribe must provide and protect a defendant's right to trial by a jury selected from a fair cross section of the community, including non-Indians. Accordingly, tribes seeking to implement VAWA's tribal jurisdiction provisions will need to ensure that they can summon an adequately representative pool of potential jurors. Non-Indian tribal employees may be considered as part of the community for this purpose.

2.22.2.2 Right to Counsel for Indigent Defendants

A tribe must provide indigent defendants with effective counsel if any term of imprisonment is imposed. This means that if the tribe wants to imprison someone for a domestic violence crime (even for a day) and the person cannot afford an attorney, the tribe must pay for a law-trained attorney.

2.22.2.3 Law Trained Judges

To qualify for this jurisdictional grant, the presiding judge of the criminal proceeding must be: (1) law-trained and (2) a state licensed attorney. While not express, this requirement likely applies to appellate judges reviewing trial court decisions.

2.22.2.4 Inform of Right to File Writ of Habeas Corpus in Federal Court

The tribal court must also inform a detained defendant that he/she has the right to have a federal court review the defendant's case by petitioning for a writ of habeas corpus at any point.

2.22.2.5 Other Provisions of the Indian Civil Rights Act

A tribe also must ensure that it provides all the rights to the defendant required under the Indian Civil Rights Act (ICRA), including equal protection.

2.22.2.6 Catch All Procedural Safeguard Provision

Congress included opaque language that requires tribes to recognize and protect "all other rights whose protection is necessary for Congress to recognize and affirm" the tribes' inherent authority to prosecute non-Indians for crimes of domestic violence against tribal members or Indians residing on-reservation.

It is unclear what these "other rights" are. This lack of clarity likely will provide a source for future federal court challenges to tribal court prosecutions under VAWA. But this catch all, vague phrase will likely prove beneficial, as it may give federal courts the ability to recognize the constitutionality of VAWA as a whole while striking down or overturning particular tribal court prosecutions on a case by case basis.

A cautious approach would be to interpret this provision as requiring tribes to provide the same protections that federal courts require of states. For instance, the Congressional Research Service has indicated that these "other rights" may include the right to indictment by a grand jury a right not included in ICRA (or required of the states). It may also require that tribes make publicly available laws, rules of evidence and procedures. This is not an exhaustive list. Tribes should consult with legal counsel to determine the likely extent of this provision.

2.22.3 Additional Issues

VAWA creates and supports comprehensive, cost effective responses to the pervasive and insidious crimes of domestic violence, sexual assault, dating violence and stalking. Since its enactment in 1994, VAWA programs, administered by the Departments of Justice (DOJ) and Health and Human Services (HHS), have dramatically improved federal, tribal, state, and local responses to these crimes.There is some additional issues are mentioned below as a criteris of the implementation of VAWA.

2.22.3.1 Time Limits

Most tribes will have until 2015 to make any necessary institutional changes to take advantage of VAWA's tribal provisions. And any tribe can petition the Attorney General to exercise VAWA's special domestic violence criminal jurisdiction immediately under a pilot program. Any tribe wishing to participate in the pilot program must show that the tribal system provides adequate procedural safeguards.

2.22.3.2 Geographic Limits

Congress chose not to extend VAWA's special domestic violence criminal jurisdiction to tribes in Alaska, except for the Metlakatla Indian Community.

2.22.3.3 Non-Jurisdictional Provisions in VAWA

VAWA also provides several grants to tribal governments and tribal coalitions to protect victims of domestic violence before criminal prosecutions occur. Unsupported victims, statistically, will not testify in a domestic violence prosecution.

2.22.3.4 Tribes in Public Law 280 States

Tribes can also take advantage of other recent legislation related to criminal jurisdiction in Indian Country. Under Section 221 of the Tribal Law and Order Act (TLOA), Tribes in mandatory Public Law 280 states can request that the United States reassume criminal jurisdiction over that tribes fee or trust land. If the federal government grants the tribes request, the federal government can prosecute cases that fall under the Indian Country General Crimes Act and Major Crimes Act on that reservation. But the reassumption of federal criminal jurisdiction does not alter state or tribal jurisdiction. This means that the state still has the same criminal jurisdiction over Indian Country delegated to it under Public Law 280. Additionally, tribes that have sought and obtained a re-assumption of federal jurisdiction will not benefit from VAWA, such a tribe will still have to implement separate procedures to take advantage of VAWA's tribal provisions.

The federal reassumption would allow federal, state, and tribal prosecutors to prosecute the same criminal defendant for the same act. Coordination among the different law enforcement officers is one of the keys to successfully implementing TLOA's re-assumption provisions.

Having federal prosecutions means longer and more severe sentencing possibilities for crimes when compared to state and tribal penalties. But federal prosecutions represent fewer prosecutions numerically.

If a tribe wants the federal government to reassume jurisdiction, the tribe must send a written request to the U.S. Department of Justice, Office of Tribal Justice. The request must be signed by the tribe's chief executive officer. Tribes, as well as federal, state, and local entities, have a chance to make comments on the request. The Deputy Attorney General makes the decision whether to reassume jurisdiction based on an evaluation of whether re-assumption will make the tribal community safer. The decision takes about five months. If a decision is denied, the tribe can resubmit a request.

For "optional" Public Law 280 states, Section 221 of TLOA is irrelevant because federal and state prosecutors already have concurrent jurisdiction in those states. TLOA also does not change tribal jurisdiction. A tribe could not exercise criminal jurisdiction over a non-Indian for any reason under TLOA. Optional Public Law 280 states that tribes can request retrocession if the tribe does not want the state to exercise criminal jurisdiction in Indian Country, but the state must concur with that request. Retrocession is rarely used today and this option is not available for mandatory Public Law 280 states.

Because constitutional challenges to VAWA's tribal provisions are expected, tribes that implement VAWA need to take great care to carefully observe all its procedural as well as other requirements. Understandably, in the inevitable cases that follow, tribal proponents fear that bad facts may make bad law. So it is incumbent on Indian Country to ensure adherence to the highest standards universally to protect the hard won tribal jurisdiction provisions in VAWA.

2.23 Women's Justice

The violation of women's fundamental rights through physical, mental, emotional, and sexual violence against women has become almost commonplace in the Indian context. Violence against women has taken particularly acute forms in circumstances where populations are already marginalized, such as in areas affected by armed conflict, areas undergoing mass displacement. Women in the Tribal belts and amongst Dalit populations are already vulnerable, and become even more so in areas affected by conflict. There is therefore a pressing need for the judiciary to recognize and address the particular forms of violence levied against women who are 'doubly marginalised' by caste, class, religion, or in situations conflict. Customary routinely laws discriminate against women, both by denying justice to victims of violence and by dispossessing women from their shares in land and property. A number of laws that protect women from discrimination have also either inadequate, or have not been properly implemented. HRLN has been intimately connected with the women's movement for over two decades. The Women's Justice Initiative (WJI) is our national network of lawyers and social activists, using the law to oppose all forms of gender based discrimination and violence against women and to increase women's access to the justice system as a vital means to their empowerment.

The framework of 'women's justice' involves not only the prevention of specific forms of violence and discrimination against women, but also encompasses all other human rights, including the right to food and health; disability, housing labour rights; dalit/ tribal/ adivasi rights; environmental justice; criminal justice, etc. With this holistic vision of equality and gender justice, WJI works directly with poor and marginalized women as well as through legal education, advocacy and policy analysis to continue the struggle for women's rights.

In order to achieve our objectives, the WJI adopts a multi-pronged strategy to deal with the various facets of women's rights violations. The WJI engages in strategic litigation through PILs in the High Courts and the Supreme Court for systematic changes as well as the implementation of policy and women's rights laws. Through legal aid and counselling we provide women with representation women in cases including divorce, domestic violence, matrimonial remedies, guardianship, custody, adoption, property rights, sexual harassment, etc. The WJI is also active in opposing bail of the accused in cases of violence against women, particularly in cases of rape, dowry harassment, domestic violence, and acid-attacks. Lawyers working with the WJI provide legal counselling to women at various women's crime cells, and to women prisoners. We provide legal expertise as member of several committees, including as members of several sexual harassment complaint committees across the country. The WJI also runs a number of help lines throughout the country that provide legal counselling as well as some and psychosocial support to women.

WJI responds to situations of crisis through emergency dispatch of legal teams for support in crisis affected zones, through investigative missions and through legal fact findings, which often become the basis for further litigation to address severe women's rights violations. We also consistently monitor and review the implementation of laws and policies related to women.

Through legal education and training for social activists, mahila panchayats, police personnel, lawyers, law students, paralegals, etc., we work to integrate womens issues into the general discourse on justice and human rights. Judicial colloquia and legal consultations is a crucial aspect of our work, to sensitize judges and strategize the development of women's rights law in India. The WJI also supports campaigns to influence public opinion, policies and legislation in support of a violence free society for women. A core operational element of the WJI is the degree to which the team works in solidarity with other organizations. As such, WJI has nurtured deep partnerships with grassroots women's NGOs, supporting them in the collective struggle to address the public denial of women's rights.

2.23.1 Issues of Concern

(i) Rape and sexual assault
(ii) Domestic violence
(iii) Sexual harassment in the workplace and in educational institutions
(iv) Matrimonial disputes, custody, divorce
(v) Womens property and inheritance rights
(vi) Reproductive and sexual health rights of women/ adolescent girls
(vii) Pre-birth sex selection and elimination of female foetuses
(viii) Trafficking for commercial sexual exploitation, domestic work, marriage, etc.
(ix) Child marriage
(x) Child Sexual Abuse
(xi) Witch hunting
(xii) Acid attacks
(xiii) 'Honour' based crimes against women/ 'honour killings'
(xiv) Equal employment opportunities for women and labour rights.
(xv) Rights of doubly marginalized sections of women like HIV+ women, dalit and tribal women, women prisoners, lesbians, bisexuals, disabled women.
(xvi) Any other gender based discrimination/ exploitation.

2.23.2 Major Impacts

The WJI is combating the various facets of violence against women through the legal system. In a precedent setting verdict on a case of an acid attack, brought by WJI lawyers to the Karnataka High Court, the court created legal history by treating the throwing of acid as an attempt to murder (rather than an attempt to cause grievous injury) and imposed a life sentence on the perpetrator, ensuring that cases of acid-throwing attract stricter punishment, without bail. In a remarkable judgment, Somaru Patel vs. State, for the first time in judicial history, the court awarded a life sentence under Section 6 of the Immoral Traffic (Prevention) Act, 1956 for the forceful detention of women for prostitution. In another historic case filed in the Delhi High Court, Shramjivi Mahila Samittee vs. State and Others, the court directed the petitioner to form guidelines for placement agencies for domestic workers, which were drafted by the WJI and submitted to the court for implementation.

HRLN is at the forefront on litigation on women's issues across the country, playing a pivotal role in implementing the guidelines given by the Supreme Court on sexual harassment. The case of Shivani Thakur vs. State of Punjab, filed by HRLN's unit in Chandigarh, received an order that resulted in the State of Punjab instituting sexual harassment grievance committees in all its departments. HRLN's landmark PIL in the Supreme Court, in the case of Medha Kotwal Lele vs. Union of India received orders mandating only a single enquiry in cases of sexual harassment to curb the victimization of the complainant. The WJI has also made history by bringing reproductive rights into the ambit of legally enforceable rights through a number of landmark cases and PILs. Order of Shanti case can be included.

The WJI is particularly active in circumstances of extreme violation of women and has used the legal system to ensure rights and provide substantive reliefs in such cases. For example, in a writ petition filed in West Bengal against a shelter home where a woman was refused entry due to her HIV positive status, XY Vs Union of India, the court directed the directorate of Social Welfare to clarify what steps have been taken to establish more shelter homes for positive woman (http://www.hrln.org/hrln/womens-justice-.html#ixzz3ia8VHyyu).

2.24 Policy and Performance in Chhattisgarh

The Chhattisgarh Government has a full fledged department of Women and Child Welfare, which is responsible for womens welfare in the state. However, the activity of the several other departments also touches on womens welfare and these must be taken in to account to get a comprehensive picture of womens welfare in the state. The NCW had circulated a questionnaire to all concerned departments to assess the performance of the state in terms of women's well been. The detailed departmental responses to this questionnaire are appended to this study. The Department of Child Welfare is the lead department for Women and Child Welfare. According to the departments administrative report of 2003-2004 the following major schemes are run by the department:

2.24.1 Integrated Child Development Services (ICDS)

Under which 146 blocks of the state are covered, 152 child developments programmes and 20289 Anganbadi centres are run. Up to March 2004 4.89 lakh pregnant and lactating women apart from 22.80 lakh children were the beneficiaries.

2.24.2 Kishori Shakti Yojana

This is for girls aged 11-18. Details are not immediately available.

2.24.3 Swayam Siddha Scheme

This scheme run in 17 block and 100 Womens Self Help Groups are organized in each block. Various training programmes and other activities are organized for the members. At present there are 1708 SHGs linking 21805 women who have a total saving of 49.27 lakh Rupees. 3939 women are stated to have started economic activities on their own.

2.24.4 Mini Mata Poshan Ahar Yojna

This programme is operationalized under the National Nutrition Mission and provides 6 kg. of grain per beneficiary (defined as women below 40 kg. body weight and adolescent girls below 35 kg. body weight). Currently this programme runs only in Surguja District.

2.24.5 Prime Minister Gramodaya Yojna

This provides for 80 gm. of ready to eat food for children between 6month and 3 years. Currently this is operational only in Rajnandgaon and Surguja Districts.

2.24.6 Iron Fortified Salt Supplementation

This is operationalized through146 projects and benefits 15 lakh women.

2.24.7 Ayushmati Scheme

This provides for free medical aid to women living below the poverty line. In 2003-2004, 11445 women were benefited by scheme.

2.24.8 Balika Samridhi Yojna

Under this scheme, for the first two girl children born to families below poverty line, the government deposits Rs. 500/- per child in a joint account scheme. In 2003- 04 the total no. of beneficiaries was 20226 and Rs. 101.09 stood deposited in joint accounts.

2.24.9 Dattak Putri Education Scheme

The scheme links girls children whose families can not afford the cost of their education with supportive families or voluntary organizations to make available to the girls Rs. 300 per year for primary education, and Rs. 400 per year for secondary education, apart from assistance in terms of books and clothes. The number of beneficiaries in 2003-04 was 35654.

2.24.10 Mahila Jagriti Shivir

These are organized at village Janpad and district panchayat level and are intended to inform women about their legal rights and various schemes for their development. In 2003-2004, 1305 such camps were held and 449041 women attended them.

2.24.11 Grants to Voluntary Organizations

Recurring and nonrecurring grants are provided to voluntary organizations for running Balwadis, Libraries and for organizing training in tailoring. At present 64 organisations are recognized by the govt. for this scheme.

The government of Chhattisgarh has constituted a commission for women in the state vide a gazette notification. However, both the first state government as well as the second elected government that assumed power in 2003 have appointed only one chairperson each, and in both cases a full fledged and empowered commission has failed to get off the ground. There is no jail exclusively for women. The four central jail together had 9553 women prisoners. There is only one family court in the state, in Raipur. There are three Mahila Police Stations. A DIG at police headquarter is responsible for monitoring cases against women. The school education department reports that it runs 1517 primary, 81 secondary, and 149 higher secondary schools for girls within a 5 km. distance from the girls .place of residence.. The Tribal Welfare Department runs an additional 26 secondary and 29 higher secondary schools for girls within the same distance range. 26 vocational schools for girls are run by the education departments and 3 by the tribal welfare department.

Chapter - III

Discrimination in Wage and Economic Status of Women

Gender inequality pervades the world. In considering the dimensions of economic gender inequality, women still make less than men in the formal work sector, are more likely to live in poverty, are less likely to participate in the formal work sector, and do a larger share of work in the household sector. The dimensions of political gender inequality include women's lower representation in elected office and lower representation in political and corporate appointments. Social gender inequality has numerous dimensions, some of which are less favorable to men while others are less favorable to women: men are more prone to violence, imprisonment, and disability, while women are more likely to be the victims of domestic violence and sexual assault; in some countries men have lower educational attainment than women, while the pattern is reversed in other countries. Demographic gender inequality includes the fact that men live shorter lives on average than do women (65 years for men, 69 years for women CIA, 2010), but there is also concern that many women are never given the chance to be born, and in the younger generations men now outnumber women, by large numbers in China and India in particular (with gender ratios respectively of 113 men and 117 men per hundred women in the under 15 age range (CIA, 2010).

While many of the costs of gender inequality are ultimately born by particular individuals, they can also be calculated at a society, or even worldwide level. If individuals of different genders are not given equal opportunity to develop their potential, then societies forego the increased level of output and ultimately wellbeing that would derive from their higher productivity. If societies do not invest equally in educating and training men and women, do not give those equal opportunities to engage in more productive forms of work, and do not give them equal opportunities to advance to more productive positions over time, then the societies do not harness the full potential of their members.

According to the Gender Inequality Index (GII), 2010 report, discrimination and underrepresentation of women in health, education, politics, work and other parts of life has repercussions for the development of their capabilities and their freedom of choice. Four of these aspects form the index which puts them in a globally measurable and comparable form: reproductive health is measured by the maternal mortality ratio and adolescent birth rates; female empowerment is measured by proportion of parliamentary seats occupied by females; education is expressed by the proportion of adult females and males aged 25 years and older with at least some secondary education; the economic status is included as labour market participation and measured by labour force participation rate of female and male populations aged 15 years and older. Using these aspects, the index shows human development costs of gender inequality. A higher the GII value relates to more disparities between females and males within a country. While gender inequality remains a problem even in the more equal societies, it is a major barrier to human development in others, with the worst performing in the two highest quintiles of the data (having index values of 0.45 and above) covering a substantial part of the global population, most notably the African continent and the Indian subcontinent. The cartogram shows this in its real human dimensions. The main map is a gridded population cartogram in which every square of land is resized according to the total number of people living in that space. The transformed map therefore shows the gender inequality index on an equal population projection, emphasizing where how many people live in the more equal or unequal societies. This highlights the high need for action combating gender gaps for a large share of the world's population in order to overcome systematic disadvantages of women and create a more equal and sustainable world.

The goal of this chapter is to perform such a calculation, in which the costs to human society of gender inequality, measured as a percent of actual GDP worldwide and for sub regions, are calculated for the years 2011 through 2050.

The nineteenth century saw the rise of the women's suffrage movement across western countries and a general push for equal treatment of women and men under the law. In 1893 New Zealand became the first country to extend the right to vote to women; most countries followed suit in the first part of the twentieth century e.g., Denmark in 1915, the U.S. in 1920, while other countries were much later e.g. Liechtenstein in 1984; Kuwait in 2005.

Many other forms of legal discrimination against women persisted beyond suffrage, however. It was only in1963 that the US passed the Equal Pay Act, making it illegal to pay women and men different wages for equal work; it took a while for other countries to follow suit e.g., Ireland in 1976; Japan in 1987. Not surprisingly, women's participation in paid work was fairly limited before the latter half of the twentieth century. Participation rises steadily throughout, but at an accelerated rate after1940, with a recent downturn in participation since 2000. Women as a percentage of the labor force have leveled out at around 46 percent.

Table 3.1 shows comparable contemporary data for sets of countries sorted by per capita income level. It is notable that there is still a wide range of participation rates found in present day so that countries have not converged on a specific higher level of female participation in paid work. Interestingly, there is a convex shape with regards to women's participation, with lower participation rates for the middle income countries compared to both the low and high income countries. Men's participation shows much less variation across income levels, but drops for higher-income groups.

Table 3.1. Labor Force Participation Rates by Sex and Proportion of Labor Force that is Female, Countries grouped by Income Level

Variables	*Labor force/population*		
	Women	*Men*	*Women/labor force*
Low income	68	85	0.45
Lower middle income	54	84	0.38
Middle income	54	83	0.38
Upper middle income	53	79	0.41
High income	64	80	0.44

Notes: Source is http://genderstats.worldbank.org/; data are from most recent available year, 2007-2008, for persons 16-64.

One possible precondition for higher rates of participation in the labor force, as well as higher female earnings, is higher levels of female education. Table 3.2 shows the US ratios of women to men among high school graduates and among tertiary degree recipients over the period from 1870 to 1950 where they are also increasing, albeit at a low rate, their labor force participation. Interestingly, over this period, women actually predominate over men in the pool of high school graduates, but have lower rates of tertiary degree percipiency and actually lose ground on this measure after WWII.

Table 3.2. US Ratio of Females to Males among High School Graduates and Bachelor and First Professional Degree Recipients

Year	*High School*	*Bachelors and First Professional*
1870	1.28	0.17
1880	1.18	0.24
1890	1.31	0.21
1900	1.5	0.24
1910	1.48	0.29
1920	1.53	0.52
1930	1.22	0.66
1940	1.11	0.7
1950	1.1	0.31

Source: Digest of Education Statistics-1991.

This pattern of relatively high rates for women relative to men of secondary education is still seen today across most countries. Relative rates by gender of tertiary education vary more substantially across countries. All country groups exceed the tertiary ratio seen in the US as of 1950, but have lower secondary ratios than in the US over the period reflected in table 3.2. Thus education alone is clearly not the fundamental precondition for women's participation in the paid labor force, but education enrollment rates do rise with income level for both genders. Table 3.3 indicates secondary and tertiary enrollment rates (more readily available than degree completion rates) forests of countries sorted by per capita income level (as in table 3.1). It has been noted that in any income group education enrollment is lower than male.

Table 3.3. Education Enrollment Rates by Sex and Countries grouped by Income Level

Income	*Secondary*			*Tertiary*		
	Females	*Males*	*Ratio*	*Females*	*Males*	*Ratio*
Low income	34	41	0.83	4	6	0.67
Lower middle income	61	65	0.94	18	19	0.95
Middle income	67	69	0.97	25	24	1.04
Upper middle income	89	86	1.03	47	38	1.24
High income	100	101	0.99	74	60	1.23

Source: *http://genderstats.worldbank.org/; data are from most recent available year, 2006-2008 Finally*

Finally, we can again contrast the growth in relative earnings in the US since the nineteenth century, to comparable contemporary data for a range of countries as shown in table 3.4. Notably, the US path is not a steady upward trend, pointing out that progress is not always linear, or irreversible. In table 3.4, it is clear (as in table 3.1) that the world has not yet converged on a standard gender earnings ratio, with a wide range of outcomes still occurring across different countries. These ratios are higher than the US in many cases, though it is also the case that yearly earnings ratios are lower than these hourly ratios due to working women's lower hours in paid work. The world clearly still does not yield equal outcomes for women and men.

Table 3.4. Nonagricultural Hourly Earnings Ratios, Women to Men, selected Countries

Country	*Women/men*
Sweden	0.89
New Zealand	0.87
Denmark	0.86
Australia	0.86
France	0.83
Bulgaria	0.83
Netherlands	0.81
Finland	0.8
Egypt	0.78
Germany	0.76
Iceland	0.75
Singapore	0.73
Canada	0.72
South Korea	0.64
Japan	0.52

Source: *ILO, http://laborsta.ilo.org; data are from 2000-2008.*

3.1 The Challenge

It is always mind-stretching to construct a reasonable alternative to the current state of the world, let alone consider what a gender neutral world might have looked like 110 years ago, or what it might look like 40 years into the future. This brings up the standard question of whether to focus on gender equality in outcomes or in opportunities. For instance, a world in which economic outcomes were equal would be a world in which women and men participate equally across all sectors of activity, whether paid or unpaid, and make the same rate of pay. However, in a world where opportunities were gender neutral, men and women would receive the same amount of education and training and have the same chances in life for economic, personal and social advancement. But they could make choices that would lead to outcomes being significantly differ on average by gender, such as women choosing to enter certain occupations at higher rates than men (and vice versa), choosing to spend more time in household production rather than in paid work, and thus ending up with different average earnings than men.

It is thus a challenge to interpret the differential economic outcomes by gender that to see in the world, as some component of them can be due to free choice rather than to gender discrimination in access to education in training, to gender discrimination in hiring, or to gender discrimination in pay (by which mean that equally productive women and men are nonetheless paid different wages). In deciding what proportion of observable differences are due to free choice on the part of individuals as opposed to constraints imposed on individuals through the discriminatory actions of others, to rely on the results of some forty years of research by economists and other social scientists that attempts to calculate the proportion of the gender earnings gap that is due to each cause. It is also make assumptions regarding what proportion of women might have worked in the labor force at each point in time. But considering the case of equality of outcomes, in which women would work at the same rate in the formal sector as do men and would be paid the same wage rate as are men. This result gives a potential maximum value for the gains that society could reap through achieving gender equality, not simply neutrality.

Swamy, et al. 2001 find that women are less involved and accepting of bribery, and thus there might be gains from putting them in charge of more governmental bodies and agencies. In addition, if women leaders were less likely to lead their countries to war or other armed conflicts, there might be quite significant efficiency gains related to the lower level of societal violence.

There are also some very difficult questions relating to how the entire path of development might have been altered if gender equality had been already achieved in 1900. For instance, if women had been working more in paid labor in 1900, the world might well have begun demographic transition down to replacement level birthrates much sooner (since we know that higher rates of female labor force participation in the formal sector are strongly related to smaller family sizes). Another factor not dealt with is the phenomenon that as women's participation rise in the work force, men tend to work less, often starting work later in their life span and retiring earlier.

3.2 Gender Inequality in Participation in Paid Work

Worldwide, women participate less in the formal or paid work, sector of the economy than do men. The International Labor Organization (2009) estimates total worldwide female participation in the paid work force at 40 percent, with generally a lower rate in the less developed countries (closer to 35 percent) and a higher rate in the more developed countries (closer to 45 percent in the OECD).

This lower participation of women than men in the formal sector appears in large part due to their having much greater work responsibilities in the informal, or household, sector. Whether these responsibilities are assumed by free choice, by following of social norms, by coercion, or by lack of opportunities in the formal sector (whether due to gender discrimination or general lack of opportunities) can vary by person and by society. For the developed nations, it appears that women now exhibit free choice to participate to a greater degree in the household sector (as compared to men); for less industrialized nations, particularly where women may receive less schooling or training that is useful for paid work, the matter of choice is much less clear. However, studies across a wide variety of societies and times show that when opportunities for women's work expand in the paid sector, with the concomitant rise in women's wages, that women increase their participation in paid work significantly. This is well documented for the rise of manufacturing employment, particularly in textiles, in the U.S. and the U.K. (Goldin, 1990; Simonton, 1998; Costa, 2000). Thus rising wages and rising female participation in the labor force rise hand in hand, implying that there are gains to the society from women's movement into the paid work sector at these times.

It is also the case that at many times there have been formal restrictions against women's full participation in paid employment, including work hours regulations (quite common from the turn of the 20th century up through the 1920s and 1930s), marriage bars (requiring women to resign when they married) and banning of women from certain industries and occupations (often because they were banned from receiving the necessary training, such as bans on women's entering law school). Thus the current level of labor force participation for women represents for the most part a significant increase over the course of the twentieth century, a trend that will be reflected in our calculations below. This increase in participation will be modeled as partly due to decreased restrictions on women's participation i.e., the factors leading to costs and partly due to expanded opportunities for labor force participation, which will be viewed as a neutral force. These restrictions could be formal and society wide, as outlined above, and household or family specific, if an individual woman is restricted by members of her family (husband, parent, brother) from participating in paid work. So both formal and informal restrictions comprise social inequality for women.

3.3 Gender Differences in Wages

There is an enormous literature that documents the existence of and explores the causes of the gender wage gap, mainly for recent years (1970 – 2010), but also for historical periods. The gender wage gap exists at all times and places. In the calculations below first benchmark the current gender pay ratio at 60 percent in developing countries and 75 percent in developed countries (women's to men's earnings) based on my own earlier surveys of gender wage gap studies (Jacobsen, 2007) and rely on calculations from Goldin (1990) and other sources to estimate the pay ratio worldwide Going back to 1900, fewer systematic studies exist of the pay ratio, particularly for countries other than the U.S. and the U.K.

Interestingly, studies for both developed and less developed countries are quite consistent in attributing about forty to fifty percent of the gender wage gap in general to observable differences in characteristics, leaving as much as fifty to sixty percent unexplained and thus potentially attributable to discriminatory factors in the labor market (though of course they could also be due to nondiscriminatory unobserved factors; for one thing women may choose jobs with relatively more desirable characteristics such as lower probabilities of injury, or women may have the same level of formal education but less valued specific training, such as a less mathematical technical college major comparative literature instead of engineering (Jacobsen, 2007). However, even some of the differences in measured characteristics can either be attributable to underinvestment in women, such as lower rates of education and training, including lower levels of on the job training. Also, factors such as whether a person is married or has children often affect earnings, but need not necessarily do so depending on support structures in the household sector, and thus are still potentially endogenous and capable of being reengineered so that women could reach higher earnings levels. For example, if spouses share household work more evenly, or if other family members who are not in the workforce assist with child care and other household chores, these factors need not affect either spouse's earnings. Thus even part of the difference ascribed to measured characteristics could still be considered related to societal factors that increase gender inequality.

3.4 Valuing Household Production

While it has been intimated in the above sections that shifting women increasingly out of the household sector and into the paid work sector leads to efficiency gains, such shifts are not costless as there is a significant opportunity cost in many cases of household work thus not being done. This could include less in-home production of food preparation, child care, and home-based agriculture such as growing kitchen gardens. In developed countries much food preparation and child care has moved to the formal sector and a smaller proportion of people produce a significant share of their own food. Thus the gain in shifting women between sectors needs to be measured net of the loss of household production that is given up in exchange. Some of this may be mitigated as well over time as higher levels of capital in the household sector, such as has happened in countries like the U.S., can increase efficiency in this sector as well, but then that can also reduce the net improvement in shifting women between sectors. Wagman and Folbre (1996) point out for example that the gain in well being in the U.S. over the latter half of the twentieth century may be significantly over estimated if it is measured solely as gain in GDP per capita without any offset for lost household production, given that a large percentage of the gain in this period came precisely from women moving in to the workforce in much higher numbers.

Landefeld, et al. (2009) use an innovative approach of recent time use data combined with a variety of estimates regarding the value of time spent in household production to come up with a range of values for the value of household production as a percent of measured GDP. They come up with a range for 12 to 62 percent of GDP.

A broader view that considers not only household production but unpaid work writ larger would increase these numbers. Richard Anker (1987), in his preface to Goldschmidt Clermont's definitive book on valuation of unpaid work (1987) maintains that national income estimates would be increased by 25 to 50 percent on average if unpaid work were taken into account. Thus it is quite clear that ignoring the shift in resources out of this sector would lead to a significant overestimate of the efficiency gains from employing more women in the formal sector.

These numbers had been taken as a cue to benchmark the opportunity cost of shifting people from the unpaid sector into the paid sector as fifty percent of the additional value of their paid work. As such, it represents not a cost of attaining gender equality, but simply an adjustment so that only net gains from the shift are counted as the benefit from attaining gender equality.

3.4.1 The Costs Calculation of Gender Inequality: 1900 to 2010

The numbers mentioned above that delineate the differences in male and female paid work participation rates, earnings rates, household production, and educational attainment. A couple of additional numbers are necessary in order to finish the calculations necessary to calculate the costs of gender inequality. First, an estimate of how much of gross domestic product and equivalently gross domestic income is attributable to labor rather than capital. Pakko (2004) indicates that labor has accounted for a relatively steady 70 percent share of U.S. national income over the past fifty years where good data are available. Recent data for a set of OECD countries puts labors share in this set at about 65 percent of GDP on average (with the U.S. on the high end at 70 percent) (Azmat, et al, 2007). One might expect labors share to be higher in lower income countries which are characterized by lower capital stocks. However, it may well be lower in some other countries depending on other factors affecting labors share such as regulations on earnings; for instance Cajing. com.cn (2010) argues that labors share in China is less than 56 percent and dropping. At any rate, the percent change in GDP is the percent share of labor income, which taken as 70 percent, times the change in labor income generated by an increase in women's earnings and participation.

Women comprise 15 percent of the labor force in 1900, rising to 25 percent in 1950 and 40 percent in 2010. These numbers are averaged from a somewhat higher rate in the more developed countries and a somewhat lower rate in the less developed countries, with increasing convergence over the period. In 1900 in the U.S., women comprised 18 percent of the labor force, rising to 30 percent by1950 (U.S. Bureau of the Census, 1976, Series D13; Economic Report of the President, 1997, Table B 34). Assuming these numbers mark the high end of the participation range, adjusted accordingly based on level of development over time and country to come up with the worldwide numbers.

For gender earnings ratios, a worldwide gender earnings ratio of 50 in 1900, 45 in 1950 (as wages actually dropped for women relative to men compared to the earlier manufacturing era see Goldin 1990, 60-62), and a rise back up to 60 in 2010. For each woman that enters the market labor force, an offset of 50 percent for reduced non market production, and an offset of 10 percent for additional education and training. As an example of the estimation technique, the calculations for 2010 are:

(1) The assumed proportion of women in the workforce is 40 percent and the counterfactual is that there would be as many women as men in the workforce if it were not for gender inequality. Thus the new labor force can be calculated as an additional 20 women for every hundred people currently in the workforce (of which 40 are women and 60 are men, so an additional 20 women would yield equal numbers of women and men). Thus the workforce would increase by 20 percent.

(2) The assumed gender earnings ratio is 60 percent and the counterfactual is that women would be paid the same as men if it were not for gender inequality. Thus the new wage bill can be calculated as an additional 40 cents for every $1.60 currently paid to workers (of which $.60 is paid to women and$1.00 to men), where the workforce now consists of equal numbers of women and men. Thus the new wage bill is now 25 percent larger.

(3) Thus the total earnings paid to workers would be fifty percent larger (1.20 times 1.25 = 1.50) if it were not for gender inequality.

(4) Assuming that the wage bill is seventy percent of earnings, GDP now increases by 0.7 and 0.5, or 0.35, so is thirty five percent bigger.

(5) Subtracting out half of this change to compensate for foregone household sector production, the net increase in production is 17.5 percent of GDP.

(6) subtracting out ten percent of this change to cover education and training costs for the labor force increase, since the labor force increased by 20 percent, the additional educational and training cost is 1 or 2 percent of GDP, so the net change in total value due to gender inequality is 15.5 percent of GDP.

For 2010 these adjustments yield a net change in total value due to gender inequality of 7 percent of GDP. Similar calculations are performed for the other years from1900 up to 2010. The only which provides a one-shot contemporary estimate of instant adjustment to full equality (Tzannatos, 2010). Using a two sector model of the formal labor market (male occupations and female occupations), Tzannatos calculates a country level average GDP gain of 4 percent, with regional differences ranging from a loss in the Nordic countries of 3 percent of GDP to a gain in High income Asian countries of 6 percent of GDP. In his model, male wages decrease while female wages rise (always by more than the male wage decrease, and up to 32 percent of the labor force has to be reallocated, mostly from female sector into male sector occupations. His estimates, benchmarked to the late 1990s and early 2000s, do not include a reallocation of women out of the informal or unpaid sectors into the formal sector, and thus not surprisingly provide a lower bound to my calculations, which allow for female shifts into formal sector positions as well.

An alternative approach to measuring the effects of gender inequality on economic growth is taken by Klasen and Lamanna (2009), who estimate regressions of country level GDP growth rates in the 1960-2000 period on measures of gender inequality, focusing in particular on education and labor force participation gender gaps. They find that these gaps explain part of the difference in growth rates between countries, and thus reduction of these gaps would lead to higher growth rates. Here there is no offset for reduced household production as women increase their formal labor market participation.

The Klasen and Lamanna regression based approach could also be extended by including other societal gender differences of the types illustrated in the World Economic Forum's series of gender gap reports (cf. Hausmannet, et al., 2010), which includes measures of political participation gaps such as the gender ratio of parliament seats, and life expectancy differences. Thus one could measure the effects of a range of gender differences on GDP growth rates across countries. Again, this approach is somewhat more limited in serving as a basis for extrapolation out of recent experience (as the reports currently incorporate only about five years of data), particularly back to 1900.

3.4.2 The Costs Calculation: 2010 to 2050

Results going forward in time are calculated using the same technique as in the above historical calculations. For women as a percent of the labor force, the estimate of 42 percent in 2030 and 45 percent in 2050. For the gender earnings ratio, the estimate of 65 percent in 2030 and 70 percent in 2050. Results going forward in time are calculated using both the low GDP growth and high GDP growth scenarios and comparing the different paths in terms of relative to 1900 figures.

3.4.3 Costs Calculation of Gender Inequality: 1900 to 2050

The results of my estimations are summarized below in Tables 3.5 and 3.6; give the numbers at the benchmark years for the challenge. Table 3.5 the total/global loss for each year due to gender inequality as a percentage of GDP in the given year. Recall again that there is no "minimum loss" scenario depicted graphically, because the minimum loss would be zero at all points in time. Table 3.6 presents the total/global loss for each year due to gender inequality as a percentage of GDP in 1900 and as a total dollar figure as well. They also show results for both a high GDP growth and a low GDP growth scenario going forward from 2010 to 2050, where the low growth scenario assumes world GDP growth of 2.5 percent per annum over this period, and the high-growth assumes world GDP growth of 3.5 percent per annum.

Table 3.5. Global loss from Gender Inequality as Percent of GDP (in percent) in the given Year

Scenario	***Year***				
	1900	**1950**	**2010**	**2030**	**2050**
Maximum estimate	37	32	16	13	9
Medium estimate	17	15	7	6	4

Table 3.6. Global loss from Gender Inequality as Percentage/ total in Billions of 1900 GDP

Scenario	Year				
	1900	**1950**	**2010**	**2030**	**2050**
Maximum estimate-high growth	37%	88%	429%	695%	1019%
Maximum estimate-low growth	37%	88%	421%	561%	678%
Medium estimate-high growth	17%	39%	202%	331%	493%
Medium estimate-low growth	17%	39%	199%	267%	328%
Maximum estimate-high growth	$736	$1730	$8301	$13,703	$20,093
Maximum estimate-low growth	$736	$1730	$8301	$11,068	$13,365
Medium estimate-high growth	$328	$776	$3916	$6529	$9713
Medium estimate-low growth	$328	$776	$3916	$5273	$6460

***Note:** high growth assumes 3.5percent GDP growth per annum from 2009 to 2050; low growth assumes 2.5% GDP growth per annum from 2009 to 2050.*

As women have been increasing both their labor force participation and their earnings relative to men, the costs of gender inequality as a percent of current GDP have been dropping. However, these costs have been rising as a percent of 1900 GDP because the total amount of world GDP is so much higher now than in 1900. Thus the total dollar value of the loss is quite substantial by 2010, ranging from a low estimate of $5 trillion to a high estimate of over $13 trillion in 1900 dollars.

There are several obvious critiques of this exercise as we move back in time from the better-known present, where labor force participation rates are more similar between men and women. One is whether it is possible that the labor market of 1900 could really have employed this much higher number of women relative to the size of the labor force at that time. Of course in this scenario, it is not necessary to assume that gender equality only suddenly started in 1900. If gender equality had in fact started much earlier than 1900, the labor market would have had more time to adjust to this level of employment. Similarly, while it may be implausible to assume that the capital labor ratio would have stayed the same in 1900 (thus providing the same relative returns to the higher level of labor), again if the formal labor market had had a higher inflow of women earlier than 1900, the capital-labor ratio would have had longer to adjust (i.e., investment in capital for the formal sector might have also been quite different in the 19th century). However, if either of these adjustments had not occurred, the returns to expanding female labor in the early stages of these calculations would have been lower.

Similarly, demographic and educational attainment effects of equality in the beginning of the 20th century could have started much earlier, thereby likely causing an earlier demographic transition to lower fertility rates and changing the productivity of labor in the nonmarket sector as well as potentially changing the overall population growth rate. There could also have been many accompanying demographic changes in such variables as marital rates and age at first marriage, marital dissolution rates, child and adult mortality rates, life expectancies, and household size. Again, such additional effects are out of the scope of the current limited modeling exercise, and arguments could be made in both directions regarding whether incorporation of demographic dynamics would increase or decrease the calculated amounts in this paper. However, to the extent that many of such changes related to a lower fertility rate would have tended to reduce both women's containment to the nonmarket sector and women's productivity in the nonmarket sector (fewer marriages, smaller families) while increasing human productivity in general (with smaller families, higher educational attainment and better health per child), one would tend to think that the results in the paper are a lower bound rather than an overestimate of the gains from earlier gender equality. It is harder to see how these changes would have reduced total output per person.

Fundamentally, an analysis such as the one undertaken in this paper, whether calculated as a partial equilibrium analysis or a general equilibrium analysis, will not satisfy all readers, and readers may well decide that the numbers presented herein are either too low or too high relative to what they believe to be the case, or that the time path is not as they would have construed it. However, it is also the case that this paper attempts to put range values on which other more detailed studies may then compare with in the future. This paper also makes clear that it is unlikely that the costs of gender inequality are zero and also that they are not unlimited in scope and size.

3.5 Women's Work Worldwide Inequality

Women's experience of work and the sources of their livelihoods vary across the world. However, in all countries women face barriers to equal rights both at work and in the home.

1. In the USA in 2009, 89 per cent of the S&P 500 (Standard and Poor's stock market index of the top 500 companies) had at least one woman director on their board, but women comprised on average only 16 per cent of board directors (Spencer, 2009).
2. In Latin America, 50 per cent of women work and 21 per cent increase in ten years, due in part to a leap in exported goods (UN, 2009). In flower and vegetable greenhouses in Ecuador, Guatemala, and Mexico, women are the majority of workers but are often hired repeatedly on short term contracts. In sectors such as fruit production, women are typically brought in for seasonal job (Raworth, 2004).
3. Colombia is the world's second biggest flower exporter, employing 110,000 workers, 65 per cent of them women (Ferm, 2008). During peak times a female worker has to work up to 80 hours a week, earning as little as $1 a day.
4. In Italy, Spain, and Portugal, women spend three to four times the amount of time on domestic work than men (UN, 2009).
5. In Kenya, women own half of all small and medium enterprises, but these experience less growth than male-owned businesses, due to a lack of support and resources (IFC, 2009).

6. In 14 of the countries in the EU group of 27, there is no woman CEO in any of the top 50 publicly quoted companies (Bettio and Verashchagina, 2009). In the EU, the pay gap increases with age, level of educational attainment, and years of service. For example, it exceeds 30 per cent in the 50–59 age group compared with only 7 per cent for those under 30 (EC, 2007).
7. Eastern Europe is the only region where the proportion of women in industry exceeds 20 per cent (UN, 2009).
8. In sub-Saharan Africa nearly 80 per cent of women workers are in vulnerable employment (UN, 2009). In Mali, 67 per cent of women work in agriculture (ILO, 1997). Girls marry young and inherit only one eighth of their husbands' land, which is usually poor in quality (World Bank, 2010).
9. A study in Nagpur, India showed that 62 per cent of women had experienced violence in the past year and that 9 per cent had suffered injuries serious enough to prevent them from working in a job, in the household, or both, for an average of seven days per incident (ICRW, 2000).
10. In Southern Asia, 36 per cent of women participate in the labour market. Less than 50 per cent of these are on a payroll, and are concentrated in informal, subcontracted, and home-working economies (UN, 2009). In Bangladesh, women make up 80–90 per cent of the textiles industry (Action Aid, 2007). Although Bangladesh achieved gender parity in primary level education in 2005, 30 per cent of female factory workers are illiterate (compared with 17 per cent of men) and earn on average 21 per cent less per hour than men (Kapsos, 2009).
11. In Asia, women spend just under 1.45 hours a day preparing meals, while men spend just 15 minutes (UN, 2009).
12. Gender differences in access to land, credit and labour disadvantage women in China where firm managers prefer to sign export contracts with men because women have limited access to productive assets, lack statutory rights over land, and have less authority over family (and therefore over potential farm labour) (World Bank, 2012 p 227).
13. In Asia, the Philippines and Thailand both have comparatively high proportions of women among directors and chief executives, with 48 and 32 per cent respectively; the Republic of Korea has the lowest proportion in the region, with just 3 per cent.

Averaged over all occupations, women in the Republic of Korea earn 68 per cent of what men earn (UN, 2009).

Income is perhaps one of the most basic indicators of gender inequality. Very few countries have achieved parity in employment in contrast to the concentration of most secondary education ratios around 1 (where the global mean in 2010 was 0.976 compared to 0.693 for F/M employment ratios). Clearly, educational equality is not sufficient for securing gender parity in employment. We report raw gender wage differentials, that is, the simple ratio of average female and male earnings. Raw wage gaps are sometimes criticized because they do not control for 'productivity' as measured by job tenure and education, for example, where the residual is a measure of gender pay discrimination originating within labour markets. However, there is a broader goal in comparing raw wage gaps. Rather than focusing only on whether employers fairly pay employees, raw wage gaps offer an estimate of the structural barriers to gender equality in paid labour, via pre-market discrimination in education and training, as well as within labour markets via job segregation and wage discrimination. Weischelbaumer and Winter Ebmer (2007) conducted a meta-analysis of gender wage gaps in 60 countries, based on more than 260 studies, which control for worker productivity characteristics in order to isolate the unexplained or discriminatory portion of wage gaps. They find that most of the decline over time in gender wage gaps is due to better labour market characteristics of workers and that, in some countries, the discriminatory portion of wage gaps is rising. The reason behind wage gap is still unknown.

Table 3.7: Country Wise Gender Wage Gaps

Place	*Year*	*Gender Wage Differentials (percent)*	*Measure*	*Sources*
Argentina	2009	22.0	Average monthly earnings	ILO, ILOSTAT
Armenia	2009	39.2	Average monthly earnings	ILO, ILOSTAT
Australia	2010	14.2	Median wages, full-time workers	OECD Earnings Database
Austria	2009	19.4	Median wages, full-time workers	OECD Earnings Database
Azerbaijan	2009	41.4	Average monthly earnings	ILO, ILOSTAT
Belgium	2008	8.9	Median wages, full-time workers	OECD Earnings Database
Botswana	2005-06	19.0	Average monthly earnings	Tijdens and van Klaveren (2012)
Brazil	2007	21,8	Average hourly earnings	Tijdens and van Klaveren (2012)
Bulgaria	2009	19.2	Average monthly earnings	ILO, ILOSTAT
Canada	2010	18.8	Median wages, full-time workers	OECD Earnings Database
Costa Rica	2009	8.7	Average monthly earnings	ILO, ILOSTAT
Croatia	2009	10.6	Average monthly earnings	ILO, ILOSTAT
Cyprus	2009	18.8	Average monthly earnings	ILO, ILOSTAT
Czech Republic	2009	18.1	Median wages, full-time workers	OECD Earnings Database

(*Contd...*)

Denark	2009	12.1	Median wages, full-time workers	OECD Earnings Database
Egypt	2007	25.1	Average hourly earnings	Tijdens and van Klaveren (2012)
Ethiopia	2009	43.7	Average monthly earnings	ILO, ILOSTAT
Finland	2010	19.7	Median wages, full-time workers	OECD Earnings Database
France	2009	13.1	Median wages, full-time workers	OECD Earnings Database
Germany	2010	21.6	Median wages, full-time workers	OECD Earnings Database
Greece	2008	9.6	Median wages, full-time workers	OECD Earnings Database
Hong Kong SAR, China	2009	29.2	Average monthly earnings	ILO, ILOSTAT
Hungary	2010	6.4	Median wages, full-time workers	OECD Earnings Database
Iceland	2008	13.5	Median wages, full-time workers	OECD Earnings Database
Indonesia	2008	13.7	Average hourly earnings	Tijdens and van Klaveren (2012)
Ireland	2009	10.4	Median wages, full-time workers	OECD Earnings Database
Italy	2008	11.8	Median wages, full-time workers	OECD Earnings Database
Japan	2010	28.7	Median wages, full-time workers	OECD Earnings Database
Kazakhstan	2009	33.8	Average monthly earnings	ILO, ILOSTAT
Korea	2009	38.9	Median wages, full-time workers	OECD Earnings Database
Latvia	2009	15.9	Average monthly earnings	ILO, ILOSTAT
Luxembourg	2009	13.3	Average monthly earnings	ILO, ILOSTAT
Malta	2009	24.5	Average monthly earnings	ILO, ILOSTAT
Mexico	2008	17.4	Average monthly earnings	Tijdens and van Klaveren (2012)
Netherlands	2005	16.7	Median wages, full-time workers	OECD Earnings Database
New Zealand	2010	6.8	Median wages, full-time workers	OECD Earnings Database
Norway	2009	8.1	Average monthly earnings	ILO, ILOSTAT
Paraguay	2008	5.3	Average monthly earnings	Tijdens and van Klaveren (2012)
Peru 19.4% 2009	2009	19.4	Average monthly earnings	ILO, ILOSTAT
Philippines	2008	16.8	Average hourly earnings	Tijdens and van Klaveren (2012)
Poland	2008	10.0	Median wages, full-time workers	OECD Earnings Database
Portugal	2008	15.6	Average monthly earnings	ILO, ILOSTAT
Romania	2009	6.9	Average monthly earnings	ILO, ILOSTAT
Singapore	2009	26.8	Average monthly earnings	ILO, ILOSTAT
Slovakia	2009	22.7	Average monthly earnings	ILO, ILOSTAT
Slovenia	2009	2.9	Average monthly earnings	ILO, ILOSTAT
Spain	2008	11.8	Median wages, full-time workers	OECD Earnings Database
Sweden	2009	14.9	Median wages, full-time workers	OECD Earnings Database
Switzerland	2008	19.5	Median wages, full-time workers	OECD Earnings Database
UAE	2009	29.9	Average monthly earnings	ILO, ILOSTAT
United Kingdom	2010	18.4	Median wages, full-time workers	OECD Earnings Database
United States	2010	18.8	Median wages, full-time workers	OECD Earnings Database
Venezuela	2009	5.6	Average monthly earnings	ILO, ILOSTAT
Zambia	2005	45.6	Average monthly earnings	Tijdens and van Klaveren (2012)

3.6 Wage Differential between Men and Women in India

Table 3.8 stated the wage differences between male and female workers where it is clearly noted that female are getting lesser amount of money for work rather than male. In 2010 male worker was getting Rs. 325 in a day while women worker was getting Rs. 260.31 for same work in a day.

Table 3.8: Nominal average Daily Wage by Gender and average Wage differential, across NSS rounds

Statistics	*Year*		
	1999-2000	**2004-2005**	**2009-2010**
Daily wage men (Rs./Day)	151.42	176.90	325.00
Daily wage women (Rs./Day)	116.93	131.89	260.31
Avg. gender wage differential (%)	29.50	34.13	24.85

Source: NSSO, 2000, 2005 & 2010.

3.6.1 Women's and Men's Employment Status in India

India has a gender participation gap that is higher than all Group of Twenty (G-20) nations other than Saudi Arabia. The gender participation gap is the difference between the labour force participation ratios for males and females in a country. An Indian male of working age is almost thrice more likely to have a paid job than an Indian woman of working age. And the gap in urban India is wider than in rural India because there is less distress employment in the cities than there is in the villages. There is a gender participation gap of around 60 percentage points in urban India while there is a gap of around 45 percentage points in rural India. Very large majority of the tribals (almost 90 percent) are engaged in agriculture; their other economic activities being food gathering (including hunting and fishing), pastoral, handicrafts, trade and commerce, and industrial labour. Rarely are they engaged in only one occupation. The employment status of tribal women may be considered in terms of their work participation, agriculture, forests, non-agricultural activities and impact of development programmes.

There are two main situations where women are always in vulnerably treated. First, while the fact that India has one of the lowest levels of female labour force participation among emerging markets could be because of structural problems, it is not at all clear why women have withdrawn from the labour force after 2005 despite the rise in incomes. India is unique in this respect: most other emerging market economies have seen more women enter the kitchen. This in turn means that women are pushed into the labour force during times of economic distress rather than pulled into it by attractive employment opportunities.

Second, the trends in female labour force participation across states are also worth a closer look. The general picture is on expected lines. Indian states in the southern and eastern parts of the country do better than the northern states. Bihar has the worst record. But then, Uttar Pradesh does better than Punjab. Chhattisgarh does better than Maharashtra. Kerala has only a middling record. These puzzles suggest that untangling the role of social and economic factors is a worthwhile task: how much of the low female labour force participation in various states can be explained by economic factors and how much by social factors?

IMF's economists have provided some useful statistical insights into what affects female labour force participation in various states. Their regression analysis suggests that the probability of a woman being in the workforce goes up when she is highly educated but drops depending on the number of children she has. States that have more flexible labour markets tend to have more women in their workforce. A flexible labour market also increases the chances of a woman getting work in the formal rather than the informal sector.

The standard models of economic growth show that the size of the labour force is an important driver of any economy. That is the root of all the intense debates about the demographic dividend. Several economists have shown through their empirical work that low female labour force participation ratios hold back economic growth.

It is seemed that less than a third of Indian women of working age are in the labour force. The female labour force participation ratio in East Asia at a similar stage of development was perhaps twice as high. Only Sikkim, Himachal Pradesh and Meghalaya come anywhere close to those levels right now.

The diversity of our states also means that much depends on what is happening at the sub national level. The IMF analysis suggests that the pace of change will be linked to what happens on several fronts, from education levels to road access to labour market reforms. IMF's economists have not explicitly considered violence against women as an explanatory variable in their statistical analysis. All this leads to one final point: the tragic story of the girl who was brutally raped in a moving New Delhi bus in 2012. Clearly, millions of girls like her face immense obstacles in their quest to build a new life. A large majority of them succeed. But it is not easy going: everything from social pressure to harassment outside college gates to unlit streets are challenges. The problems they battle humanize the dry academic discussions about the abysmally low female labour force participation ratios in India.

3.6.2 Correlation between Gender, Employment and Marital Status

Since women are much more likely to be constrained by marriage and child bearing and rearing than men. Table 3.9 provides information on women's and men's employment within each marital category. Among women, employment varies greatly by marital status. Women who are divorced, separated, deserted, or widowed are much more likely to be employed than currently married women; never married women are least likely to be employed. For men, employment varies little between those who are currently married and those who were formerly married; however, never married men are, as expected, less likely than ever married men to be employed. Nonetheless, the proportion of never married men who are employed is almost twice as high, at 66 percent, as the proportion of never married women who are employed, at 37 percent.

Table 3.9: Work Status and Type of Payment (from 15 to 49 year women)

Status of Work	*Marital Status*				
	Married	*Divorced/ separated/ deserted*	*Widowed*	*Never married*	*Total*
For whom work is done					
Works for a family member	46.8	26.4	31.9	40.5	44.4
Works for a someone else	38.7	59.8	50.9	43.6	40.7
Self employed	14.5	13.9	16.9	15.8	14.8
Where work is done					
Home	19.7	17.1	16.7	27.5	20.8
Away from home	80.2	82.9	83.0	72.3	79.0
Continuity of work					
Work throughout the year	58.5	72.4	70.1	58.5	59.5
Work seasonally/part of the year	37.0	24.8	26.5	32.5	35.4
Work only once in a while	4.4	2.8	3.2	8.9	5.1
Type of payment received					
Cash only	51.0	77.5	68.9	62.6	54.6
Cash and in kind	13.2	11.9	15.7	7.4 12.3	
In kind only	11.7	3.1	5.8	8.6	10.6
Not paid	24.1	7.5	9.5	21.2	22.4
Total	**100**	**100**	**100**	**100**	**100**

Source: National Sample Survey Report, 2005.

3.6.3 Correlation between Gender, Employment and Residence

Women's employment is likely to be affected by residence, since agricultural work, which accounts for most employment in rural areas, is typically more compatible with women's other responsibilities as well as with low levels of education and skill development. In fact, NFHS-3 finds

Table 3.10: Percentage of Women and Men Age 15-49 Employed in the past 12 Months by Marital Status, according to Background Characteristics in India

Vatiables		*Women*					*Men*				
		Married	*Divorced/ separated/ deserted*	*Widowed*	*Never Married*	*Total*	*Married*	*Divorced/ separated/ deserted*	*Widowed*	*Never married*	*Total*
Residence	Urban	27.1	66.4	63.4	29.0	29.3	98.8	94.8	97.7	63.9	84.0
	Rural	49.8	71.5	70.9	42.1	49.4	98.8	94.2	98.5	68.1	88.7
Age	15-19	31.4	60.4	56.8	34.0	33.4	33.4	87.6	100.0	49.3	50.4
	20-29	37.0	64.4	68.6	42.2	38.5	98.5	98.8	100.0	82.0	90.3
	30-39	48.8	76.0	75.8	58.7	50.6	99.3	93.8	98.7	95.6	99.0
	40-49	47.7	70.0	64.0	58.3	49.7	98.8	91.2	97.7	85.3	98.5
Education	None	55.4	77.5	75.2	58.6	57.0	99.2	94.2	98.7	95.5	98.6
	0-4	45.7	68.6	71.5	55.7	48.8	99.2	88.2	97.5	92.6	97.6
	5-9	30.9	61.9	51.8	37.3	33.6	99.0	96.6	97.4	70.4	87.2
	10-11	21.5	44.1	47.1	22.3	22.3	99.1	98.8	100.0	50.2	74.7
	12+	29.8	60.4	67.8	31.3	31.0	97.5	92.8	100.0	56.3	79.7
Wealth Quintile	Lowest	61.5	83.8	82.3	58.4	62.4	99.1	89.1	99.9	78.3	93.8
	Second	53.8	70.7	76.2	50.6	54.4	98.9	93.9	96.5	74.5	91.2
	Middle	47.0	71.8	69.8	42.2	47.3	98.8	96.6	98.3	70.4	88.5
	Fourth	32.7	60.9	60.9	30.8	33.5	98.8	96.7	97.3	67.1	85.9
	Highest	21.5	52.1	44.1	22.4	2.5	98.6	99.5	99.4	53.2	78.8
Total		**42.8**	**69.7**	**68.6**	**36.8**	**42.8**	**98.8**	**94.4**	**98.3**	**66.3**	**87,0**

Source: NFHS-3.

that women are about two-thirds more likely to be employed in rural than in urban areas. Table 3.10 shows that employment is higher in rural than in urban areas in every marital category, although the differential by residence is greatest, at approximately 23 percentage points, among currently married and never married women. Among men, the differential by residence in employment is negligible across marital categories, with the highest variation, at only 4 percentage points, being among the never married.

3.6.4 Correlation between Gender, Employment and Wealth

Employment declines sharply by wealth for women, irrespective of marital status. For example, among currently married women, the percentage employed declines from 62 percent for women in the lowest wealth quintile to 22 percent for women in the highest wealth quintile. Employment also declines by wealth for men, but only from 94 percent for those in the lowest wealth quintile to 79 percent for those in the highest wealth quintile. Among ever-married men, virtually all men are employed in most wealth and marital categories. For never married men, the proportion employed falls from 78 percent in the lowest wealth quintile to 53 percent in the highest wealth quintile. The relationship of employment and wealth for women suggests that women's employment continues to be linked closely to economic necessity, rather than being an expression of choice and self-fulfillment.

3.6.5 Inequality in Women's Occupational Distribution

In keeping with the predominantly rural nature of the Indian economy and the low average educational level of women, most women who work are employed in agriculture. There is, however, great variation by marital status in the proportions of employed women age 15-49 employed in agriculture: 64 percent of currently married employed women work in agriculture, compared with 41 percent of divorced, separated, and deserted employed women and 44 percent of never married employed women. The proportion of employed women working in professional, technical, or managerial occupations is highest, at 12 percent, for never married women and is about 5 percent for all categories of ever married women. The second highest occupational category for women is skilled and unskilled labour, which accounts for 20 percent of currently married women's employment and 31 percent of never married women's employment.

Table 3.11 shows that among the regular wage salaried workers, a greater percentage of men in the sample belong to the category of "Others" and Other Backward Castes (OBCs), whereas a greater percentage of women belong to Scheduled Castes (SCs) and Scheduled Tribes (STs). The gender difference between the proportions is significant at the 1 percent level for SCs and at the 10 percent level for Others. Thus, in the high wage social group of Others, we find a significant difference between the proportion of men and women in favour of men, whereas for the Scheduled Castes, the social group with the lowest average wages we find the reverse is true. Note that the average gender wage differential is greatest for the SCs at 66 percent, and it is less than 9 percent for Others. At the bottom of the distribution, therefore SCs, STs and OBCs face higher gender wage gaps, whereas at the top end of the distribution, dominated by Others category, gender wage gaps are lower. The fall in the log wage gap is the sharper for the general category (Others) than SCs, STs or OBCs. This steep fall means that the gender gap falls to zero just above the median for Others category.

Table 3.11: Summary Statistics with Distribution and average Daily Wages, by Gender, 2009-2010

Dependent Variables	*Share (%)*			*Avg. Daily wages (Rs.)*			*Average gender wage differential (%)*
	Men	*Women*	*Pooled*	*Men*	*Women*	*Pooled*	
Sector - Rural/Urban							
Rural	34.8	36.2	35	251	162.78	234.99	54.19
Urban	65.2	63.8	65	364.49	315.74	356.09	15.44
Sector - Public/ Private							
Private	68.14	60	66.72	248.61	196.84	240.49	26.3
Public	31.86	40	33.28	508.21	373.61	480.02	36.03
Education Level							
Illiterates	6.23	14.69	7.72	146.51	87.12	126.67	68.16
Primary & Below	14.07	12.22	13.74	157.71	96.65	148.18	63.17
Middle	16.48	10.71	15.47	188.02	108.79	178.39	72.84
Secondary	18.24	10.58	16.9	260.1	179.29	251.22	45.08
Higher Secondary	11.66	9.38	11.26	324.12	225.1	309.64	43.99
Graduate/Diploma	25.58	29.97	26.35	496.23	395.29	476.08	25.54
Postgraduate	7.74	12.45	8.57	652.84	526.03	620.48	24.11
Occupations							
Managers/Legislators	4.52	1.57	4	734.7	764.87	736.78	-4.1
Professionals	9.78	16.57	10.97	617.72	450.32	573.36	37.2
Technicians/Assoc. Pr	11.61	27.43	14.39	467.54	284.37	406.26	64.4
Clerical	11.55	10.45	11.36	392.32	366.78	388.2	7
Service/Sales	16.59	13.03	15.96	222.05	190.96	217.6	16.3
Craft/Skilled Agr.	18.42	8.36	16.66	212.59	102.88	202.93	106.6
Plant/Machine Opera	15	2.09	12.73	228.52	165.7	226.7	37.9
Elementary	12.53	20.52	13.94	172.99	100.38	154.23	72.3
Industry							
Agriculture	2.99	2.99	2.99	137.05	76.23	126.39	79.78
Manufacturing/Mining	27.12	13.56	24.74	254.23	160.82	245.24	58.08
Elec., Gas, Water/Constr.	4.72	1.62	4.18	362.79	468.04	369.96	-29.01
Retail/Hotels	13.77	4.83	12.2	169.46	142.95	167.61	18.54

(Contd...)

Transport/Comm.	13.46	2.23	11.49	287.22	404.87	291.24	-40.96
Fin. Intermediation	4.17	3.04	3.97	572.48	531.12	566.92	7.79
Real Estate/Renting	4.33	3.83	4.24	494.69	440.45	486.1	12.31
Public Admin. /Defence	13.69	10.4	13.11	477.66	360.3	461.32	32.57
Education	10.36	33.35	14.39	446.32	304.36	388.58	46.64
Health & Social Work	2.28	9.75	3.59	425.13	234.33	334.23	81.42
Other Services	3.11	14.39	5.09	200.4	124.01	162.5	61.59
Caste Profiles							
SC	16.41	19.7	16.99	262.19	157.93	240.96	66.02
ST	4.77	5.15	4.83	289.64	213.64	275.44	35.57
OBC	35.76	34.63	35.56	288.42	217.87	276.36	32.38
Others	43.06	40.52	42.62	383.31	352.26	378.13	8.82
Union Membership							
No Union	68.44	69.12	68.56	253.29	185.75	241.36	36.36
Union Members	31.56	30.88	31.44	479.98	426.63	470.8	12.5
Permanent Job							
Temporary	32.07	31.1	31.9	173.82	126.69	165.77	37.2
Permanent	67.93	68.9	68.1	396.37	321.74	383.14	23.2
Written job contract							
No Contract	63.75	60.1	63.11	245.2	195.39	236.94	25.49
Contract	36.25	39.9	36.89	484.18	375.5	463.71	28.94

Source: NSSO, 2009-2010.

3.6.6 Discrimination Trends in Employment for Ever Married Women

There has been a slow but steady increase in ever-married women's employment over time from NFHS-1 to NFHS-3. In the 13 years between these two surveys, ever-married women's employment has risen from 33 percent to 44 percent an increase of less than one percentage point per annum. There has also been a slow increase in the proportion employed for cash (including those getting only part payment in cash) and an even slower increase in the proportion employed in agriculture. Employment of ever-married women in professional, technical or managerial occupations has also risen, but only marginally from 1 percent in NFHS-1 to 2 percent in NFHS-3.

3.7 Disparity in Female Household Headship: Levels and Trends

Information on the household head is collected in the household schedule of the household questionnaire. Any usual member of the household can be the respondent for the household questionnaire and it is she or he who specifies which usual member of the household should be designated as the household head. The proportion of females designated as household heads has been rising over time. In the 13 years between NFHS-1 and NFHS-3, the proportion of households with a woman designated as the head has risen by more than half, from 9 percent to 14 percent.

3.7.1 Comparative Work Participation

Through the work participation rate among tribal women has been increasing over a period of time (2001-2011), it is lesser than that for the tribal males, but higher than that for the general female (table 3.12). Though the work participation among tribals is greater than among the general population, within the tribals it is again the males who have a higher work participation rate than the females, as in the general population.

Table 3.12:Work Participation Rates in India and Chhattisgarh

Sex	*India*		*Chhattisgarh*	
	2001	**2011**	**2001**	**2011**
Man	58.72	69.28	54.29	67.52
Women	41.28	30.72	45.71	32.48

Source: NSS, 2001 & 2011.

3.7.2 Women in Agriculture

Through an overwhelming majority of tribal men (85 percent) and women (91 percent) were involved in agriculture, there were more cultivators among tribal males while more tribal women were agricultural labourers (table 3.13).

Table 3.13: Industrial Classification of Tribal Workers

Variables	*Year*			
	2001		*2011*	
	Male	*Female*	*Male*	*Female*
Cultivators	45.32	54.80	43.73	56.27
Ag. Labourers	47.63	52.37	48.68	51.32
Livestock, forestry,etc	39.87	60.13	49.31	50.69
Mining and quarrying	52.14	47.86	41.57	58.43
Manufacturing Processing, servicing and repairs				
Household Industry	43.57	56.43	40.37	59.63
Other than Household	36.98	63.02	47.82	52.18
Industry				
Construction	59.78	40.22	57.86	42.14
Trade & Commerce	68.75	31.25	70.57	29.43
Transport, Shortage and Communication	72.96	27.04	71.04	28.96
Other services	63.89	36.11	56.31	43.69

Source: NSS, 2001 & 2011.

As compared to general females, the tribal females were engaged more as cultivators but less in occupations other than agriculture (table 3.14). The major role that women play in agricultural operations has been discussed by Roy Burman (1998). In the slash and burn cultivation, women join in felling and burning trees, making holes with digging stick, sowing seeds, weeding and harvesting. In plough based cultivation, transportation, weeding, winnowing and dehusking is done entirely by women while harvesting and threshing are done by both men and women. Generally the ploughing is done by men but in some tribal societies, women do the ploughing too.

Table 3.14: Classification of Female/Tribal Workers (1981-2011)

Categories	*Year*							
	1981		*1991*		*2001*		*2011*	
	GF	*TF*	*GF*	*TF*	*GF*	*TF*	*GF*	*TF*
Cultivators	33.09	43.86	34.22	47.04	42.15	54.80	43.96	56.27
Wage Labour	46.34	46.16	44.93	44.28	36.78	52.37	38.78	51.32
Manufacturing Processing, Servicing and repairs								
Household Industry	4.57	1.75	3.53	1.29	52.33	56.43	29.78	59.63
Other works	19.00	8.23	17.72	70.36	19.63	36.11	31.26	43.69

Source: Census Reports: 1981, 1991, 2001, 2011.

3.7.3 Correlation between Women and Forests

Minor forest produce forms a major source of income in many tribal communities, especially those having less than five acres of land. Women and children are almost exclusively involved in collection of minor forest produce, its storage, processing and marketing (Singh, B., 1993; Roy Burman, 1988). Increased government control of forests has distributed tribal economy adversely affecting tribals lives, particularly that of women. Appointing of agents from outside for collecting forest produce has not only affected their livelihood, but has also made the work of women more difficult. Collection of fuel wood has become more difficult since it is less accessible and more time-consuming. The result has been less income combined with less fuel wood available for themselves and lesser nutrition. It also leaves them little time for earning wages. Government control over forests has also reduced hunting to a ritual.

3.7.4 Women in Non-agricultural Activities

Only less than 10 percent of the tribal women are involved in activities other than agriculture. This is less than half the percentage of females in the general population in similar occupations. This category includes livestock, forestry mining/ quarrying, manufacturing/ processing/ servicing and repairs in household as well as non-household industries, trade/ commerce and services.

3.7.4.1 Entrepreneurship and Women

According to Hartman (1959) "Entrepreneurship is the process whereby people, money markets, production facilities and knowledge are brought together to create a commercial enterprise which did not exist before. These definitions have been used in many studies to study the characteristics of those who have started business ventures. Pareek and Nadkarni (1978) stated that entrepreneur-ship refers to the general trend of selling up new enterprises in a society and is a dynamic function of individual, socio-cultural factors, support systems and the environment. However, the contributions of these to the understanding of concept of entrepreneurship are not substantial because they have not tried to focus on the critical function of the entrepreneur and so the concept remains elusive. Entrepreneurship currently is riding the crest of a tidal wave of popularity and it has captured attention of the Government and Non-Government Organisations (NGOs) as it has become the need of the day.

Drucker (1986) illustrates entrepreneurship and intrapreneurship with numerous examples of innovations. Timmons (1986) stated entrepreneurship to be an ability to create and build something from practically. On the other hand women form almost half of the population, and expansion of women's employment is essential for accelerating economic growth. Deolankar (2003) observes that entrepreneurship among the weaker section tribal women who constitute a large section of the Indian masses needs to be brought into the main stream of development. Upper caste women, on the other hand, have enjoyed relative material prosperity in comparison, but have been subject to greater immurement and constraints on public visibility, with the taboos being sharper, the higher the caste in the hierarchy (Deshpande, 2007; Liddle and Joshi, 1986). These differences confirm findings from other literature. Das (2003) deals specifically with non-farm household enterprises in India and finds that women continue to operate trades traditionally considered the domain of women. Experimental evidence also suggests that women are more likely to be risk averse than men (Eckel and Grossman, 2008; Niederle and Vesterlund, 2007), but we cannot say if this explains the gender differences in propensities to be engaged with certain activities or if business objectives tend to be different for men and women.

It has been increasingly realized that the women entrepreneurs have vast entrepreneurial talents which could be harnessed to create employment opportunities. However like any other occupation, it has its own sphere of problems of women. Sugumar (1996) refers to entrepreneurship as the qualities which are required to innovate and start a new enterprise accept the challenge and bear the risk. Research on female entrepreneurs in developing countries shows that female lead enterprises are typically smaller, and experience slower growth than male enterprises (Mc Pherson, 1996; Mead and Liedholm, 1998). The strong positive effect of female ownership and management on growth is noteworthy. This can be explained by self selection since our study is based on only the registered sector. Registration is voluntary and it is the more enterprising and motivated owners/ managers that are more likely to take the initiative to register their firms. Therefore, it is possible, on average, that the women owners and managers in registered firms represent a group with much higher innate abilities than male managers in registered firms. Bardasi et al (2011) also cite self selection as a possible reason for their finding that in Eastern Europe, central Asia and sub-Saharan Africa, gender gaps in firm growth are much smaller. Also, while large proportions of Indian women have either no or low education, in the segment of the population with higher education, women outperform men, suggesting that those who are able to cross early hurdles have the abilities necessary for success (Khanna, 2012).

By above background women entrepreneurs can make their units economically viable if significant strategic measures can be incorporated and communicated to women folk through various media. Thus women must be encouraged to adopt such an entrepreneurial activity to earn money which will enhance their economic status.

3.7.5 Development Programmes and Tribals Women

The impact of development programmes has been different on different sections of tribal women. A small number of tribal women have taken advantage of education, new opportunities for employment and self-fulfillment. In sericulture project for tribal women in Udaipur (Brandon & Dixit, 1983) a remarkable change in the quality of life of the tribal women was reported. Besides economic benefits they had more leisure, self reliance, innovativeness, adaptability and a more aware social outlook. However, there have been negative effects of development Programmes also, such as:

- The workload of women has increased,
- With modem agricultural implements, unemployment of women has increased and they have been migrating to other areas as labourers,
- Restrictions regarding exploitation of forests have marginalised women.

3.7.6 Exploitation of Women

With introduction of Rural Land Ceiling Act, Tribal Land Transfer act, etc., the non-tribal men often marry tribal women to purchase land from tribal poor to avoid legal complications, or derive financial benefits received from Govt. but deny tribal women their position as wives;

- Lands are taken away by mine owners in the name of development and no land is given in lieu of it nor is any rehabilitation programme sponsored; when vacancies occur, jobs are given to men folk who are inheritors/owners of land;
- Women are prohibited from working in nationalised mines in evening and night shifts; they are permitted in private mines but these don't employ women to avoid maternity benefits, equal remuneration, rest shelters and creches;
- Indirect retrenchment is done by introducing voluntary retirement programme for women: a woman may retire after 36 years and offer her job to any male member who continues with her Provident Fund number and gets all her PF benefits;
- Tribal women are used for immoral trafficking in collieries and mines and by labour contractors;
- Women labourers (rejas) are exploited socially and sexually. Almost half of them are unmarried and parents don't get them married fearing loss of substantial income. On the other hand, tribal men prefer to marry non-rejas and even wires are deserted for doing this job.

In summary, the data on tribal women indicate that tribal women are working women almost without any exception. Working women in all social groups work harder than men. This is more so for the tribal women. They are overworked: they rise in the morning and go to the forest to collect fuel, fetch water, help in agricultural activities, cook for the family, look after the children, do the washing etc. Overall we can say that women are lower paid than men, they have been adversely affected to deforestation and development projects, new strategies have been devised to remove women from work, non-tribal men are marrying tribal women to get land and jobs, they are sexually exploited by non-tribal men.

Much has been written about the sexual permissiveness in the tribal society, without understanding and even with an attitude of 'holier than thou'. But the permissive sexual behaviour in the tribal society is controlled by strong social customs such as Bithla in the Santals, and it is very different than the permissiveness of the contemporary Indian elite imitating the Westerners. Tribal women are denied property rights. In their study of Gonds in Madhya Pradesh found that most tribal women were illiterate and tied to a primitive economy. Their income level can be increased by raising their literacy level, and giving them training fir income generating activities (Mawar, et al., 1993).

3.7.7 Status of Tribal Woman

The overall picture of the tribal woman that emerges from the existing materials has the following features:

- The literature on tribal women is substantially romantic and grim economic realities have been completely ignored.
- The tribal woman is a working woman and works harder than tribal men and women in any of the social groups.
- The tribal woman is illiterate.
- The tribal woman is not healthy.
- There is high fertility and greater incidence of malnutrition among them. *Haria* drinking is almost hundred percent.
- The status of the tribal women is characterised by over-work, invasion of sexually exploitative market forces in tribal society, illiteracy, sub-human physical living conditions, high fertility, high malnutrition and near absence of modern health care facilities.
- The low health and educational status adversely affects the economic status.

Adivasi women are central to the economy of their society. They take part in agricultural production, gather forest produce, do wage labour where available (from government or forest department works, *tendu* leaf and road contractors etc) and almost single handedly bear the whole burden of domestic work, child-rearing, rearing of cattle/ livestock, going to markets to sell their produce, do the marketing for their families etc. In one word, except those tasks which are a taboo for them, they do all the work. There may be variations in what they do in various areas but their central role is undeniable. In many Adivasi communities, the men even marry more than

one woman so that they can sit comfortably (doing the minimal work) while their wives toil away day and night.

Poor Adivasi women commonly referred to as head loaders, walk miles through different conditions, collecting wood. Gathering fodder, picking leaves, brewing liquor and selling them, the typical items of work of Adivasi women are all characterized by monotony, hard physical labour, harassment and exploitation. The activities they predominantly engage in are such as trade in 'minor' forest produce and manufacture and sale of products based on minor forest produce. These activities are typically low income, seasonal activities, and marginal to the economy.

The liquor trade in tribal areas finds a predominance of Adivasi women. This may seem a sharp contradiction when viewed in terms of the problems faced by Adivasi women on account of male alcoholism. But when viewed in context of the limited availability of economic options and issues of survival, it is perhaps less surprising that such trade is taken up by women. In the few cases that employment is available to Adivasi women, gender based discrimination in wages both by government and contractors reinforces their economic marginalization. The government and its departments itself pays lesser wages to women than men.

Chapter - IV

Gender Inequality in Education

Underinvestment in female education, for example, contributes to stereotypes about women's relative intelligence and skills, regardless of those possessed by the individual woman. A large time series of global data is available to examine trends in three variables in the capabilities domain: 1) total years of education of those 15 and older, 2) gross secondary school enrolment rates, and 3) life expectancy (relative to the maximum achievable by gender) (Blackden, M., S. Canagarajah, S. Klasen, and D. Lawson, 2006). Average total years of education are a stock variable that captures the cumulative societal effect of gender inequality in education. There is both greater gender equality in secondary school enrolment rates within countries and a global convergence of gender equality in secondary school enrolment rates of 0.99 in 2010, up from 0.93 in 1990.

4.1 Gender Differences in Educational Attainment and Training

While there are still significant differences in educational attainment by gender, a number of countries have recently attained not only complete parity in primary education, but have even moved to the point where women in the younger cohorts appear to be receiving both more secondary education and now even more tertiary education than are men (World Bank, 2010).

For instance, the 2009 ratio of female to male primary enrollment ranges from a low of 67 females per hundred males in Afghanistan to 108 females per hundred males in Mauritania, with parity achieved in all high income countries. Nonetheless, in a number of countries women lag significantly behind men in literacy rates, enrollment rates, and degree attainment rates. In addition, women lag behind men in all countries where studies have been performed in terms of receiving on-the-job training and apprenticeships (Jacobsen, 2007).

King, et al. (2009) spend a large part of their report discussing the importance of closing the education gap in order to reach gender equality. This closing represents both a necessary condition for women's achieving full parity in paid work participation and earnings, but also a significant cost as national governments would need to expand their spending on education in order to ensure that the genders receive equal education at each level, assuming that equality would be achieved through bringing up the group with lower attainment rather than reallocating the same level of resources so that the group with higher attainment were brought down. In addition, employers would need to spend more on training to accommodate the larger formal sector work force. These costs may be viewed either as a necessary opportunity cost for society to achieve the higher level of social output, and thus should be an offset against the gains from these increases in training, or viewed as a separate issue from the total gains from bringing women into full equality with men.

4.2 Gender Differences in Education

Eliminating gender differences in access to education and educational attainment are key elements on the path to attaining gender equality and reducing the disempowerment of women. In recognition of the pivotal role of education in development and of persistent gender inequalities in access to education, the elimination of gender disparity in primary education is one of the Millennium Development Goals. The achievement of universal primary education has been a key goal of Indian planning since Independence. However, increasing access to primary schooling still leaves the twin questions of educational quality and school retention unanswered. Continued economic development cannot be sustained with a population that has merely completed primary school; it needs a dependable supply of highly educated and skilled human capital for which a high level of educational attainment of both women and men is necessary. However, ensuring a continued supply of skilled human capital to sustain economic growth is only one objective of reducing gender inequalities in educational attainment: the other is that education, particularly

higher education of women, is a key enabler of demographic change, family welfare, and better health and nutrition of women and their families. Higher education has the potential to empower women with knowledge and ways of understanding and manipulating the world around them. Education of women has been shown to be associated with lower fertility, infant mortality, and better child health and nutrition.

Table 4.1: Percentage of Boys and Girls Attending School

Age	*Urban*		*Rural*	
	Male	*Female*	*Male*	*Female*
6-10 years	88	83	84	79
11-14 years	52	88	47	79
15-17 years	81	51	66	28

Source: NFHS III, 2005-06.

Table 4.2: Percentage of Boys and Girls Attending School

Age	*Boys*	*Girls*
6-17 years	75	85
6-10 years	80	49
11-14 years	66	81
15-17 years	70	34

Source: NFHS III, 2005-06.

4.3 Disparity in School Attendance

In the school year 2005-06, 71 percent of children age 6-17 attended school 77 percent in urban areas and 69 percent in rural areas (IIPS and Macro International, 2007). As table 4.3 shows, 66 percent of girls age 6-17 attended school, compared with 75 percent of boys in the same age group. The sex ratio of children 6-17 attending school in the 2005-06 school year is 889 girls per 1,000 boys. While gender differentials in school attendance are minimal among children age 6-10, they increase with age. In fact, the sex ratio of girls attending school per 1,000 boys attending school declines from 957 in the age-group 6-10, to 884 in the age group 11-14, and then to a low of only 717 in the age group 15-17. In addition to the gender differential in school attendance among children age 15-17, the low absolute levels of school attendance for both girls and boys in this age group is also of concern. Less than half of boys and about one-third of girls age 15-17 attend school.

Table 4.3: Percentage of Boys and Girls Attending School

Sex	*Age Groups (in Year)*			
	6-17	**6-10**	**11-14**	**15-17**
Boys	75	85	80	49
Girls	66	81	70	34

Source: *NFHS III,* 2005-06

An examination of the data on school attendance by age, however, reveals that gender disparity in school attendance is largely a rural phenomenon (table 4.4 and 4.5). In urban areas, about equal proportions of boys and girls attend school at each age; however, in rural areas, gender inequality in attendance is evident in every age group and increases with age.

Table 4.4: Percentage of Boys and Girls Attending School in the Urban

Sex	*Age Groups (in Year)*		
	6-10	**11-14**	**15-17**
Boys	88	83	52
Girls	88	81	51

Source: NFHS III, 2005-06.

Table 4.5: Percentage of Boys and Girls Attending School in the Rural

Sex	*Age Groups (in Year)*		
	6-10	**11-14**	**15-17**
Boys	84	79	47
Girls	79	66	28

Source: NFHS III, 2005-06.

Notably, even in urban areas, only about half the children age 15-17 attend school. Both supply and demand-side factors play a role in whether children attend school or not. Key supply side factors include the availability, accessibility, and quality of schools factors for which no information is available in NFHS-3. The demand-side factors include the level of education of household members and household wealth factors whose influence can be examined using NFHS-3 data. Adults who are educated are more likely to ensure that their children are educated. Wealth enables access to education by providing the resources needed to buy quality education and by reducing the opportunity cost of children's time. For poorer households, children's time spent in school is time not spent in contributing to the economic sustainability of the household.

4.3.1 Correlation between School Attendance and Education of Household Head

As shown in table 4.6 school attendance at all ages and for both boys and girls increases with the education level of the household head. Among all children age 6-17, only 53 percent of girls and 65 percent of boys attended school in 2005-06 if they belonged to a household with an uneducated head of household. By contrast, 9 out of 10 boys and girls attended school if they belonged to a household where the head had 12 or more years of education. It is also notable that belonging to a household which the household head has a high level of education is associated with higher educational attainment for the next generation: almost three out of four children age 15-17 in households where the household head has 12 or more years of education were attending school, compared with the national average of 35 percent for girls and 48 percent for boys age 15-17. Gender differentials in school attendance decline sharply as the educational level of the household head increases (table 4.7). The differentials are particularly notable for the age group 15-17: in this age group, the sex ratio of children (females per 1,000 males) attending school increases from a low of 546 in households with an uneducated household head to 900 in households with a household head who has at least 12 years of education.

Table 4.6: Percentage of Male and Female Children Attending School by Education of the Household Head and Wealth Quintile of the Household in India

Variables	*Sex*	*Current age in years*			
		6-10	**11-14**	**15-17**	***Total***
Education of household Head					
None	*Female*	69.5	53.9	18.6	52.9
	Male	76.0	68.0	34.0	64.9
0-4 years	*Female*	87.1	70.6	28.2	67.0
	Male	87.6	77.1	40.7	73.4
5-9 years	*Female*	88.4	78.6	38.7	73.4
	Male	90.3	86.0	50.7	79.9
10-11 years	*Female*	91.2	90.2	55.9	82.2
	Male	93.2	93.7	68.5	87.7
12+ years	*Female*	94.4	94.2	71.6	88.8
	Male	94.6	96.4	79.6	91.8

(Contd...)

Wealth quintile					
Lowest	*Female*	65.3	46.9	12.8	49.7
	Male	72.8	63.8	30.0	62.6
Second	*Female*	78.3	62.3	20.2	60.3
	Male	83.4	74.2	38.8	71.4
Middle	*Female*	85.8	71.7	28.0	66.6
	Male	88.0	81.7	43.9	75.9
Fourth	*Female*	92.2	84.7	45.4	77.6
	Male	91.1	86.7	53.8	80.6
Highest	*Female*	95.4	93.9	68.8	87.4
	Male	84.7	79.5	48.3	75.1
Total	***Female***	**81.0**	**70.3**	**34.6**	**66.6**
	Male	**84.7**	**79.5**	**48.3**	**75.1**

Source: NFHS III, 2005-06.

Table 4.7: Sex Ratio of Children Age 6-17 who Attended School by Education of Household Head

Year	***Year***				
	None	**>4**	**5-9**	**10-11**	**12+**
6-10	914	994	980	978	998
11-14	792	916	914	963	977
15-17	546	692	763	817	900

Source: NFHS III, 2005-06.

4.3.2 Correlation between School Attendance and Household Wealth

School attendance also increases sharply by the wealth status of households (table 4.6). The data suggest that belonging to a household in the lowest wealth quintile is associated with even lower rates of school attendance at every age than belonging to a household where the household head is uneducated. In addition, gender inequality in school attendance also varies more sharply by wealth in every age group than it does by education of the household head. The greatest variation in the sex ratio (females per 1,000 males) of children attending school by wealth is for the age-group 15-17: in this age group, the sex ratio of those attending school increases from a low of 426 in households belonging to the lowest wealth quintile to 936 in households belonging to the highest wealth quintile.

4.3.3 School Attendance by State

The sex ratio (girls per 1,000 boys) of children age 6-17 who attended school in the 2005-06 school year ranges from 745 in Rajasthan and Bihar to 1,081 in Meghalaya. There are nine states where the sex ratio of children attending school is less than 900, 16 states where the ratio is 900-999 and four states where the proportion of girls attending school is more than the proportion of boys attending school.

4.3.4 Age and School Attendance Rate

Examining school attendance of children by age does not tell us whether children are beginning school at the right age (considered to be age 6 years in India) and are progressing from class to class in an age-appropriate manner. The net attendance rate (NAR) and the gross attendance rate (GAR) are measures of age-appropriate school attendance. These rates are defined separately for the primary and secondary levels of education as follows:

Table 4.8: Attendance Rate for Primary and Secondary School

Attendance Rate	*For primary school*	*For secondary school*
NAR (net attendance rate)	Children age 6-10 years in classes 1-5 as a proportion of all children age 6-10 years	Children age 11-17 years in classes 6-12 as a proportion of children age 11-17 years
GAR (gross attendance rate)	All children in classes 1-5 as a proportion of all children age 6-10 years	All children in classes 6-12 as a proportion of all children age 11-17 years.

Table 4.9 shows the net attendance rates for all boys and girls by residence. Age-appropriate primary level school attendance, at about 7 out of 10 children, is considerably lower than school attendance by children age 6-10 discussed earlier (more than 8 out of 10). This suggests that a large number of children are not starting school at the recommended age. Even at the primary level, gender inequalities are evident in rural areas. The NAR at the secondary level also reveals large gender disparities in rural areas and a high dropout rate for girls as well as for boys. Girls and boys are also about equally likely to be in an age-inappropriate grade. The proportion of girls age 11-17 attending school is 55 percent, 9 percentage points lower than the secondary school NAR for girls (46 percent). For boys the corresponding difference between the proportion in this age group attending school (67 percent) and the NAR (57 percent) is 10 percentage points (not all data shown). Gender disparities are much greater in rural areas and at the secondary school level; and age inappropriate school attendance is more common at the secondary school level than at the primary school level for both boys and girls.

Table 4.9: Net Attendance Rate (NAR) for Children Age 6-17 in the School

Sex	*For Primary School*			*For Secondary School*		
	Total	*Urban*	*Rural*	*Total*	*Urban*	*Rural*
Male	73	74	73	57	61	55
Female	71	74	69	46	60	40

Source: NFHS III, 2005-06.

4.3.5 Educational Attainment among Adults: Levels and Trends

Table 21 and 22 depict the educational attainment of women and men age 15-49 in two different ways. Table 4.10 shows the percentage of boys and girls with years of education greater than the number of years. Only 59 percent of women and 82 percent of men age 15-49 years have ever been to school and only 22 percent of women and 35 percent of men have 10 or more years of schooling. While this figure clearly shows that educational attainment at each level of education is lower for women than for men, the pattern of gender differentials is easier to see in table 4.11 which shows the percentage of women and men with a specified number of years of education.

Table 4.10: Percentage of Women and Men Age 15-49 by Cumulative Number of Years of Education Completed

Sex	*Year*				
	Any Number	5+	8+	10+	12+
Boys	82	72	55	35	20
Girls	59	51	36	22	12

Source: NFHS III, 2005-06.

Table 4.11: Percentage of Women and Men Age 15-49 with Specified Number of Years of Education Completed

Sex	Year				
	<5	5-7	8-9	10-11	12+
Boys	10	17	21	15	20
Girls	8	15	14	10	12

Source: NFHS III, 2005-06.

Gender differentials in favour of men are very small at low levels of education (<5 and 5-7 completed years of education): 23 percent of women, compared with 27 percent of men who have 0-7 complete years of education. Beyond seven completed years of education, gender differentials widen dramatically and remain wide. Among the age-group 40-49, only 14 percent of women and 28 percent of men had 10 or more years of education. By contrast, among the 20-29 year-old population, 27 percent of women and 39 percent of men have 10 or more years of education. Despite the continuing absolute low level of educational attainment even in the 20-29 age group, the proportion who have 10 or more years of education has increased at a faster rate for women than for men. Specifically, the proportion of women with at least 10 years of education has nearly doubled between the youngest and the oldest age cohort; whereas, for men, it has increased by only 40 percent. There is also a slight decline in the gender differential in the proportions that have 10 or more years of education.

Table 4.12: Percentage of Women and Men Age 20-49 who have Completed at least 10 Years of Education by Age

Sex	*Year*		
	20-29	**30-39**	**40-49**
Male	39	34	28
Female	27	18	14

Source: NFHS III, 2005-06.

Although educational attainment is very low among both women and men age 15-49, it is higher among the younger age groups than among the older age groups (table 4.13). But overall analysis shows that men populations are more literate than women. Table shows, the majority of the women population (15-49 years) are illiterate in rural areas rather than urban habitant of women.

Table 4.13: Percentage Literate among Women and Men Age 15-49 by Age in India

Age in years	*Women*	*Men*
15-19	74	89
20-24	64	84
25-29	55	81
30-34	48	76
35-39	43	70
40-44	40	69
45-49	38	68

Source: NFHS III, 2005-06.

Table 4.14: Percentage of Women and Men Age 15-49 who are Literate by Residence in India

Status	*Women*	*Men*
Urban	75	88
Rural	46	72
Total	**55**	**78**

Source: NFHS III, 2005-06.

Table 4.15 shows that educational attainment increases rapidly with household wealth for both women and men, although, at every level of wealth, women are much less likely than men to have 10 or more years of education. Further, the percentage point change with each unit increase in the wealth quintile is greater for men than for women, except between the fourth and the highest quintiles. Consequently, the gender differential in absolute terms increases from 6 percentage points in the lowest wealth quintile to 19 in the fourth wealth quintile, and then narrows to 13 in the highest wealth quintile. It is also worth noting that negligibly small proportions of women and men have 10 or more years of education in the lowest wealth quintile.

Table 4.15: Percentage of Women and Men Age 20-49 who have Completed at least 10 years of Education by Wealth Quintile

Sex	*Lowest*	*Second*	*Middle*	*Fourth*	*Highest*
Men	6	14	25	41	72
Women	1	3	9	22	59

Source: NFHS III, 2005-06.

4.4 Relation between Age, Educational and Household Heads

Female household heads are older, on average, than male household heads as the age distribution of household heads by sex. In particular, 29 percent of female household heads are at least 60 years old, compared with 20 percent of male household heads. This suggests that a substantial proportion of household heads may be so designated due to social or cultural reasons (for example, the oldest household member is reported as the household head out of respect) rather than because they are the main breadwinners.

Nonetheless, it is notable that the proportion of female heads of household who are less than 40 years of age is quite similar to the proportion of male heads of household in that age group 32 percent of female heads of household vs. 36 percent of male heads of household. The proportion of female household heads who have no education, in keeping with gender inequality in access to education in the population as a whole, is about twice the proportion of male household heads who have no education. Also, the proportion of female household heads with no education, at 67 percent, is much higher than the national average of 42 percent for uneducated women age 6 or older (IIPS and Macro International, 2007). Only 9 percent of female household heads have at least 10 years of education, compared with the national average for all women age 6 years or older of 14 percent. By contrast, the proportion of male household heads with 10 or more years of education, at 26 percent, is slightly higher than the proportion of all men age 6 and over with 10 or more years of education (24 percent).

Table 4.16: Percent Distribution of Male and Female Heads of Household by Age and Education in India

Variables	*Sex of Household Head*	
	Female	*Male*
Age		
<20	0.8	0.5
20-29	9.7	10.4
30-39	21.6	25.3
40-49	19.9	25.6
50-59	18.7	17.9
60+	29.2	20.2
Education		
None	67.0	32.6
0-4 years	8.7	11.2
5-9 years	15.6	29.1
10-11 years	3.9	11.7
12+ years	4.6	14.7
Don't know/missing	0.2	0.2
Total	**100.0**	**100.0**

Source: NFHS III, 2005-06.

4.5 Wealth Profile of Households by Sex

One-fourth of households headed by females are in the lowest wealth quintile, compared with one fifth of households headed by males. Female headed households are also under represented in the higher two quintiles. Whereas 41 percent of male-headed households belong to the top two quintiles, these quintiles account for only 34 percent of female headed households.

4.5.1 Female Household Headship by State

Female household headship ranges from a low of 8 percent in Madhya Pradesh, Jammu and Kashmir, Gujarat, and Rajasthan, to a high of 25 percent in Kerala, Bihar and Goa. Notably, most of the states where female household headship is very low are in the north, west, or central parts of the country and most of the states where female household headship is relatively high are either in the south or northeast. Nonetheless, there is great variation even between adjoining states in the percentage of households headed by females.

Table 4.17: Percentage of Households that are Headed by Females in Various States of India

Region/ State	*Percentage of householdsthat are headed by females*
North	
Delhi	9.5
Haryana	11.1
Himachal Pradesh	18.6
Jammu & Kashmir	8.2
Punjab	10.9
Rajasthan	8.7
Uttarakhand	15.7
Central	
Chhattisgarh	11.6
Madhya Pradesh	7.5
Uttar Pradesh	13.9
East	
Bihar	25.0
Jharkhand	11.2
Orissa	13.0
West Bengal	15.0
Arunachal Pradesh	11.2
Assam	13.4
Manipur	17.3
Meghalaya	22.1
Mizoram	15.9

(*Contd...*)

Nagaland	14.9
Sikkim	14.3
Tripura	13.4
West	
Goa	25.3
Gujarat	8.4
Maharashtra	12.4
South	
Andhra Pradesh	14.9
Karnataka	15.8
Kerala	24.6
Tamil Nadu	20.2

Source: NFHS III, 2005-06.

4.5.2 Trends in the Age and Educational Profile of Female Household Heads

An examination of data on women who were designated household heads in NFHS-1, NFHS-2, and NFHS-3 provides some evidence that, on average, female heads of household are younger in NFHS-3 than they were in NFHS-1. Female heads of household age 39 or less accounted for 27 percent of all female household heads in NFHS-1, this proportion fell to 25 percent in NFHS-2, but then rose to 32 percent in NFHS-3. In keeping with the spread of education in India over time, the proportion of female household heads with no education has fallen slightly from 71 percent in NFHS-1 to 67 percent in NFHS-3. There has also been an increase in the proportions who have 10 or more years of education over the same time period, from 6 percent in NFHS-1 to 7 percent in NFHS-2 to 9 percent in NFHS-3. Nonetheless, all three surveys show that uneducated females are substantially overrepresented among female heads of household, compared with uneducated females in the population as a whole.

Table 4.18: Trends in Percent Distribution of Female Heads of Household by Age and Education in India

Variables	*NFHS-1*	*NFHS-2*	*NFHS-3*
Age			
<20	1.0	0.7	0.8
20-29	7.0	5.8	9.7
30-39	19.4	18.5	21.6
40-49	23.5	22.6	19.9
50-59	20.6	19.5	18.7

(*Contd...*)

60+	28.4	32.9	29.2
Don't know/missing	0.1	0.0	0.0
Education			
None	70 .8	66 .4	67 .0
0-4 years	9.5	11.9	8.7
5-9 years	12.7	14.8	15.6
10-11 years	3.4	3.7	3.9
12+ years	2.9	3.2	4.6
Don't know/missing	0.7	0.1	0.2
Total	**100.0**	**100.0**	**100.0**

4.5.3 Educational Status of Tribal Women

Table 4.19 depicts that literacy rate is increasing year by year but after comparing between tribals male and female, female literacy is lower than male literacy. It can be seen amongst all states of India whether it is metropolitan city or rural state. Andhra Pradesh, Rajasthan, Jammu and Kashmir shows that there are very low levels of female literacy with 39.2, 38.0 and 18.9 respectively (table 4.20). Despite government efforts to promote education among the Scheduled Tribes (STs), their literacy rates as compared to the national average have remained low, a Parliamentary Committee has said this week. The literacy rate as per Census 2011 is 73 percent but for STs is 59 percent only.

Table 4.19: Literacy Rates of Scheduled Tribe Persons Sex wise All India Rural

Years	*Scheduled Tribes*		
	Male	*Female*	*Average*
1951	7.93	24.95	-
1961	13.37	2.90	8.16
1971	16.92	4.36	10.68
1981	22.94	6.81	14.92
1991	38.45	16.02	27.38
2001	57.39	32.44	45.02
2009-10	70.7	52.1	61.6

Education is regarded as a key instrument for the empowerment of women. Education changes their worldview, improves their chances of employment, facilitates their participation in public life, and also influences their fertility. Several studies indicate that educated women have, on an average, fewer children and they take good care of their socialization. Although considerable progress has been made with regard to literacy and education, the overall picture still remains unfavorable to women. At the beginning of the 20th century, the country as a whole was largely illiterate with just 5.3 per cent of the population counted as literate. Only 0.60 per cent women were then literate. In 1951, the first Census taken four years after independence, the picture was not much better. The female literacy rate stood at 7.93 percent, as compared to 24.95 per cent for men. The 2001 Census suggests a 65.38 per cent literacy rate for India (including all categories), with 75.85 per cent for males, and 54.16 per cent for females. Literacy is not evenly spread throughout India. There are 25 states with Union territories that are below the national average for female literacy. These data suggest that nearly half of India's female population is still illiterate. This is not a small number. A massive programme is needed to make nearly 240 million women literate. It is also to be noted that most of these women are located in rural and tribal areas. Another point to remember is that most of the women included in the literate category have not had education beyond the primary level.

The number of women goes down as we move to higher levels of education. However, women are to be found in all professions, including medicine and engineering. An idea can, however, be had by knowing the percentage of females by number of years of schooling.

Table 4.20: Literacy Rates* of Scheduled Tribe Persons in Rural Areas (2009-10)

States/UT	*ST*		
	Male	*Female*	*Average*
Andhra Pradesh	56.9	39.2	48.3
Arunachal Pradesh	76.4	67.4	72.1
Assam	84.3	76.6	80.5
Bihar	67.9	45.0	57.0
Chhattisgarh	75.0	58.5	66.9
Goa	98.8	60.0	78.6
Gujarat	74.2	52.7	63.5
Haryana	77.4	42.2	58.9
Himachal Pradesh	81.8	61.4	71.7

(*Contd...*)

Jharkhand	64.4	43.0	54.6
Jammu & Kashmir	51.9	18.9	36.5
Karnataka	65.4	40.6	52.8
Kerala	94.3	82.0	87.0
Madhya Pradesh	65.6	47.8	56.9
Maharashtra	76.3	56.1	66.1
Manipur	90.5	78.8	84.9
Meghalaya	95.4	94.4	94.9
Mizoram	97.8	95.6	96.8
Nagaland	93.8	90.6	92.2
Odisha	62.3	42.5	52.2
Punjab	90.5	84.9	88.0
Rajasthan	66.0	38.0	52.4
Sikkim	89.9	81.9	86.3
Tamil Nadu	55.8	39.2	48.8
Tripura	85.6	70.6	78.5
Uttar Pradesh	49.9	38.6	44.3
Uttaranchal	75.8	64.2	69.7
West Bengal	74.4	57.7	65.8
A & N Islands	76.9	85.2	80.6
Chandigarh	—	—	—
D & N Haveli	78.4	49.8	65.3
Daman & Diu	99.2	83.9	93.4
Delhi	100.0	—	100.0
Lakshadweep	97.1	88.1	92.5
Puducherry	—	—	—
India	70.7	52.1	61.6

Note: Age 7 years and above persons.

Source: GOI, NSSO, Primary Data (2009-10).

The low educational status of tribal women is reflected in their lower literacy rate, lower enrolment rate and higher dropouts in the school. The literacy rate of the tribal population as well as Scheduled Castes and general population are given in table 4.21.The following major trends can be seen from tables 4.21 which are the literacy rate of tribals is lower than that of general as well as SC population; the literacy rate of the rural tribal female is the lowest of all groups; there is gender bias in the literacy of tribal population as in other groups, the female literacy being lower than the male literacy. Through there has been five-fold increase in the literacy of tribal females it still is much lower than the national average for the females.

Table 4.21: Literacy Rates among General, Scheduled Caste and Scheduled Tribe population

Population	*Census, 2001*		
	General	*Scheduled Caste*	*Tribe Scheduled*
Total	65.38	54.64	43.40
Male	75.85	66.64	57.38
Female	54.16	41.90	29.15

Source: Primary Census Abstract General Population, Scheduled Casters and Scheduled Tribes, 2001.

Any one above age 7 who can read and write in any language with an ability to understand was considered a literate. In censuses before 1991, children below the age 5 were treated as illiterates. The literacy rate taking the entire population into account is termed as "crude literacy rate" and taking the population from age 7 and above into account is termed as "effective literacy rate". Effective literacy rate increased to a total of 74.04 percent with 82.14 percent of the males and 65.46 percent of the females being literate but when it is compared separately between male and female, female literacy is lower than the male.

Table 4.22: Year wise Literacy Rate from 1901 to 2011

Year	*Population*		
	Total	*Male*	*Female*
1901	5.35	9.83	0.60
1911	5.92	10.56	1.05
1921	7.16	12.21	1.81
1931	9.50	15.59	2.93
1941	16.10	24.90	7.30
1951	16.67	24.95	9.45
1961	24.02	34.44	12.95
1971	29.45	39.45	18.69
1981	36.23	46.89	24.82
1991	42.84	52.74	32.17
2001	64.83	75.26	53.67
2011	74.04	82.14	65.46

Source: Census of India, 1901 to 2011.

Table 4.23 and 4.24 depict the level of education by sex where literacy level and education level, both are inclined but female literacy and education level are lower than male. It has been calculated that from 2004 to 2005, only 45.8 percent ST males were not literate while in the case of female the frequency was 71.5 percent of illiteracy. And from 2009 to 2010, 58.3 percent population of female were illiterate while large number of males were literate by good level of education.

Table 4.23: Level of General Education Rural Males (Persons of Age 15 years and above) (2004-05 & 2009-10)

Level of General Education	*ST*	
	2004-5	**2009-10**
Not literate	45.8	35.8
Literate & up to primary	29.3	26.4
Middle	14.5	18.3
Secondary	5.5	11.1
Higher Secondary	2.8	5.7
Diploma/Certificate	0.4	0.6
Graduate & above	1.7	2.2
Overall	100.0	100.0

Source: Primary Census Abstract General Population, Scheduled Casters and Scheduled Tribes, 2001.

The table 4.24 reveals that the level of women's education is not good. Only few number of women are attained good level of higher education. The women education in ancient India was quite good but in the middle age it was deteriorated because of many restrictions against women. In terms of population, India is the second largest country of the world due to the low level women education. If a woman is uneducated, the future of country would also be uneducated. Women education is very important for the country to fully develop. It is like an effective medicine to cure a patient completely and provide health back. Women education is a big opportunity for India to be developed socially and economically. Educated women are the weapon who yield positive impact on the Indian society through their contribution at home and professional fields. They are the reason of improved economy in the country as well as society. An educated woman has capability to handle her home and professional life. They can effectively contribute in controlling the population of India as they would like to marry at a later age in comparison to the uneducated woman.

Table 4.24: Level of General Education Rural Females (Persons of Age 15 Years and above)

Level of General Education	*ST*	
	2004-05	**2009-10**
Not literate	71.5	58.3
Literate & up to primary	16.4	21.8
Middle	7.7	10.3
Secondary	2.5	5.7
Higher Secondary	1.3	2.7
Diploma/Certificate	0.1	0.3
Graduate & above	0.5	0.9
Overall	100.0	100.0

Source: GOI, NSSO, Report No. 516, Employment & Unemployment Situation among Social Groups in India, 61st Round, (July 2004 – June 2005), October 2006 and NSSO, Primary Data (2009-10).

Table 4.25 stated the school gross enrolment ratios of ST children where enrolment rate is increasing for both boys and girls but girls enrolment is lower than boys in every years. From 1986 to 1987, boys were enrolled by 111 point while girls were enrolled with 68 point. It is increased by 2008 for every class but enrolment rate and dropout rate for girls were low as compare to boy's enrolment. The dropout rates for girls are higher than those for boys in tribal as well as general population. The drop-out rate for tribals at the secondary level is as high as 87 percent and for the girls it is almost 90 percent. Consequently, there is a negligible percent (0.06 percent) of tribal women in institutions of higher education.

Table 4.25: School Gross Enrolment Ratios of ST Children

Category/Class	*Enrolment Ratio, Class I-V* (**6-11** *years*)		
	ST		
	Boys	*Girls*	*Total*
1986-87	111.0	68.0	90.1
1990-91	125.4	81.4	104.0
2000-01	116.9	85.5	101.1
2002-03	104.8	92.3	98.7
2003-04	94.7	87.8	91.4
2004-05	128.1	115.5	121.9
2005-06	131.45	120.02	125.84
2007-08	136.42	130.60	133.57

(*Contd...*)

Class VI-VIII (11-14 Years)			
1986-87	45.6	21.8	34.1
1990-91	53.9	26.7	40.7
2000-01	72.5	47.7	60.2
2002-03	55.0	40.8	48.2
2003-04	84.0	66.6	75.8
2004-05	73.9	59.5	67.0
2005-06	77.54	64.94	71.48
2007-08	81.09	70.16	75.81
Class I- VIII (6-14 Years)			
1986-87	87.1	51.1	69.6
1990-91	99.6	60.2	80.4
2000-01	102.5	73.5	88.0
2002-03	86.7	73.9	80.5
2003-04	90.6	81.1	86.1
2004-05	108.5	95.8	102.4
2005-06	111.93	100.57	106.40
2007-08	116.26	108.94	112.70

Source: GOI, Educationforallindia.com, Selected Educational Statistics, 2007-08.

There is a wide gender disparity in the dropout rate in India. India spends 1.8 percent of the national budget on its children, who form nearly 25 percent of its population. This explains why we are a country of 330 million illiterates, why 50 to 60 percent of children do not go beyond their primary schooling and why more than 50 millions become drop outs. The Right to Education Act covers children in the 6 to 14 years age group, precisely for these classes in school. Table 4.26 shows that girls average dropout rate is higher than the boys at all schooling level. So, the dropouts need to be the biggest focus of the implementation mechanism being set up. Since the benefits that accrue to a country by having a literate population are multidimensional it becomes imperative to study the determinants of school drop outs. There is a need to analyze the primary reasons for drop-outs among rural/urban girl children and to identify the age group of rural/urban girls with high dropout rate.

Table 4.26: School Dropout Rates STs (Rural + Urban)

Stage	*Drop out Rates (%)*		
	ST		
	Boys	*Girls*	*Total*
Primary (I – V)			
1990-91	60.3	66.1	62.5
1995-96	55.0	58.9	56.6
2001-02	51.0	54.1	52.3
2002-03	50.8	52.1	51.4
2003-04	49.1	48.7	48.9
2004-05	42.6	42.0	42.3
2005-06	40.2	39.3	39.8
2007-08			
Elementary (I – VIII)			
1990-91	75.7	82.2	78.6
1995-96	62.3	71.2	66.0
2001-02	67.3	72.7	69.5
2002-03	66.9	71.2	68.7
2003-04	69.0	71.4	70.1
2004-05	65.0	67.1	65.9
2005-06	62.9	62.9	62.9
2007-08			
Secondary (I – X)			
1990-91	83.3	87.7	85.0
1995-96	—	—	—
2001-02	79.9	82.9	81.2
2002-03	78.4	83.0	80.3
2003-04	77.9	81.2	79.3
2004-05	77.8	80.7	79.0
2005-06	78.0	79.2	78.5
2007-08			

Source: GOI, Educationforallindia.com, Selected Educational Statistics, 2007-08.

Table 4.27 shows the girls' dropout rate is higher in maximum states rather than the boys in ST communities. A comparison of the traditional and modern system and tribal higher education was made by Narmadeswer Prased (1991) who found that the tribe's men desire an education which may enables them to fit in to the modern world. Most of the students are dropping their education because of lack of suitability of present education with the tribal culture. Bairathi (1991) has examined the role of education for tribal upliftment has said that the condition of school particularly in the interior parts of tribal settlements is worse. These are not well managed and there is shortage of teachers in most of the schools at all time. Primary level schools are managed by a single teacher. The teacher has to take care of not only the management of school, but also to teach many classes simultaneously in one big room. In such a condition a good standard of education cannot be attained. Shortage of teachers, lack of basic amenities as sitting arrangements, drinking water facilities, and high distance from home to school leads them to loose the interest in education and this force them to drop their study. Gadgil and Dandekar (1991) has studied about the problem of wastages in tribal education by taking a batch of students in first standard in a given year following up in the subsequent years till the last grade are reached. i.e, fifth Dropouts from school before completing the final grading of primary education constitutes wastes; and the incidence of wastage is computed from the proportion of Dropout to the initial enrolment in the first grade.

The National Council of educational Research and training made substantial contribution to the area of tribal education. A seminar on tribal education in India (1993) organized by the National council of educational research and Training discussed the various aspects of tribal education like the facilities available, coverage, wastage and stagnation, utilization of financial assistance, basic problem of tribal education, socio-economic problems, curriculum, methods and text books and the relative roles of Government and voluntary agencies in the education of tribal people.

Tribal parents are mostly illiterate. They always show a very indifferent attitude towards the education of their children. They are interested in providing household responsibilities to their children a very early stage of their education. "The parents of these students do not have any relationship with the society outside and are unaware of the importance of education. All teachers are talented. Teaching such children is a herculean task". Teachers do not take much effort to improve the educational level of the tribal students. Lack of communication, high level of absenteeism in the class, bad result in study, lack of attention in classroom by the tribals are some of the factors that has increased the indifferent attitude of the teachers towards the tribal students.

Table 4.27: Dropout Rates in Classes I-V, I-VIII, I-X- 2007-08 - ST Students

State/UT	*Classes I- V*			*Classes I- VIII*			*Classes I- X*		
	Boys	***Girls***	***Total***	***Boys***	***Girls***	***Total***	***Boys***	***Girls***	***Total***
Andhra Pradesh	43.56	49.07	46.26	70.19	74.73	72.40	81.08	83.61	82.26
Arunachal Pradesh	45.05	42.89	44.06	51.08	50.02	50.60	66.11	64.94	65.57
Assam	0.00	0.00	0.00	78.89	74.64	77.11	86.99	85.49	86.36
Bihar	39.05	26.85	34.67	97.50	97.88	97.66	98.72	98.94	98.80
Chhattisgarh*	20.97	30.50	25.62	-	-	-	-	-	-
Goa	-	-	-	-	-	-	-	-	-
Gujarat	53.21	51.79	52.57	62.68	64.35	63.43	72.21	75.32	73.64
Haryana	-	-	-	-	-	-	-	-	-
Himachal Pradesh	0.00	0.00	0.00	-27.22	-11.59	-19.43	24.91	34.43	29.63
J & K	38.05	30.67	34.80	40.05	33.45	37.55	69.86	57.82	65.30
Jharkhand*	27.29	16.34	22.63	-	-	-	-	-	-
Karnataka	14.62	15.96	15.27	35.80	40.89	38.22	54.02	59.43	56.63
Kerala	0.43	5.63	3.00	-1.12	-3.83	-2.44	42.80	34.71	38.91
Madhya Pradesh	0.00	0.00	0.00	69.76	67.78	68.91	82.18	87.39	84.43
Maharashtra	27.24	31.37	29.20	40.65	45.05	42.72	67.79	76.83	72.07
Manipur	63.77	69.90	66.70	62.64	65.37	63.95	67.61	73.56	70.61
Meghalaya	49.86	46.19	48.02	62.74	57.74	60.26	78.67	75.75	77.22
Mizoram	48.47	47.09	47.82	64.68	61.46	63.16	71.85	67.94	70.00
Nagaland	34.46	30.89	32.82	39.18	35.50	37.47	68.24	64.03	66.28
Odisha	38.38	39.92	39.11	82.68	83.41	82.99	85.55	83.58	84.79
Punjab	-	-	-	-	-	-	-	-	-
Rajasthan	47.53	53.63	50.44	60.40	67.15	63.31	63.84	73.36	67.65
Sikkim	34.63	21.11	28.04	52.33	37.54	45.03	66.27	53.96	60.41
Tamil Nadu	0.00	0.00	0.00	27.39	15.04	22.21	72.83	73.04	72.93
Tripura	35.88	40.84	38.26	65.23	67.50	66.30	80.38	82.78	81.51
Uttar Pradesh	0.00	0.00	0.00	25.57	-25.31	8.05	48.07	61.69	53.93
Uttarakhand*	11.74	8.69	10.23	-	-	-	-	-	-

(Contd...)

West Bengal	45.09	48.53	46.76	80.54	74.97	78.39	87.94	84.18	86.70
A & N Islands	19.48	24.05	21.61	31.64	21.55	27.16	42.69	37.17	40.24
Chandigarh	-	-	-	-	-	-	-	-	-
D & N Haveli	19.14	32.40	25.82	30.67	56.30	42.74	61.16	73.13	66.66
Daman & Diu	6.88	16.11	11.42	27.87	40.66	33.71	59.00	50.23	55.06
Delhi	0.00	0.00	0.00	-34.28	-53.63	-42.78	20.27	8.81	14.92
Lakshadweep	-5.04	8.05	1.24	-11.80	-11.59	-11.70	25.62	34.88	30.03
Puducherry	-	-	-	-	-	-	-	-	-
INDIA	**31.04**	**31.68**	**31.34**	**62.62**	**62.31**	**62.48**	**76.02**	**77.97**	**76.85**

Note: Zero indicates that there is no Drop-Out.

Source: GOI, Educationforallindia.com, Selected Educational Statistics, 2007-08.

In spite of the much publicised Sarva Shikshan Abhiyans, Ashram schools, mid day meal schemes the number of Adivasi children going to school and finishing at least primary school is low. The number of ST girls in school is even lower. The female literacy rate among tribals in 1991 was far lower (18.2 percent) as compared to overall female literacy for the country (39.2 percent). According to the latest 2001 Census figures female literacy among Scheduled Tribes went up to 28.36 percent. Though there was an increase in total as well as female literacy among tribals, it is still at a slower pace as compared to the overall population, and to the general female literacy in the country. In 136 identified districts of erstwhile 11 states (now 13) tribal female literacy was below 10 percent as per the 1991 census. But the total figures may not give the actual picture in particular areas. On the one side the ST female literacy rate in north eastern states is very high while on the other side there are states where their literacy rate is abysmally low.

Chapter - V

Gender Disparity in Health Status

In many parts of the world, women receive less attention and health care than man do and particularly girls often receive very less support than boys. As a result of this gender bias, the mortality rates of females often exceed those of males in these countries (Sen, A., 2001). This is an important issue because gender discrimination that contributes to poorer health status for girls than for boys is likely to be the main pathway for excess female child mortality. Such discrimination occurs in (a girl) receives less attention than would be bestowed upon a son. She is less warmly clad, she is probably not so well fed as a boy would be and when ill, and her parents are not likely to make the same strenuous efforts to ensure her recovery (Census of India 2011). Girls in India are discriminated against in other ways as well fewer months of breastfeeding, less nurturing and play, less medical treatment if they fall ill, less special food, less prenatal attention. As a result, girls are far more susceptible than boys to disease and infections, leading to poor health and a shorter lifespan. It is this lifelong discrimination in nurturing and care that is the real killer of girls, less visible and less dramatic, but as unequivocally lethal as female foeticide and infanticide (UNICEF, 1998).

In India most of the women are still not receiving health facilities. According to NFHS-3 almost one out of every five women in India did not receive any antenatal care for their last birth in the five years preceding the survey. There is wide variation in the use of antenatal care services among the states. Utilization of antenatal care is almost universal in Kerala, Tamil Nadu and Goa. In addition, more than 90 percent of women received anti natal care (ANC) in Andhra Pradesh, Maharashtra, West Bengal, Karnataka, Delhi and Punjab. The percentage of women receiving antenatal care was lowest in Bihar. In India there is broad North- South contrast between areas of low female autonomy and unfavorable demographic performance on the one hand and comparatively high female autonomy and relative favorable demographic performance on the other. The particularly high birth and death rates that continue to prevail throughout most of Northern India must be seen within the context of local kingship arrangements (Bhat, P. N. Mari and. A. J. Francis Zavier, 2003).

Poor condition of women can be seen in availing nutritious food, prevalence of anemia and nutritional status of women. Women's autonomy has been determined by three areas- control over finance, decision making power and freedom of movement. Women with greater freedom of movement obtained higher level of antenatal care and were more likely to use safe delivery care. The influence of women's autonomy on the use of health care appears to be as important as other determinant such as education (Shelah S. Bloom, David Wypij, Monica Das. Gupta, 2001).

Sex preference is mainly manifested in the form of excessive mortality of female child. The poor health status of female relatively to males is found to be due to the discrimination against females in the allocation of food and health care within household. There is gender discrimination in childhood feeding, immunization coverage, treatment seeking and nutritional status (Pandey, P. Rohini, 2003). According to NFHS-3, women consume less nutritious food than man.

5.1 Access to Health Care

Factors that limit women's access to health care at the household level can be gender related, purely economic, or supply driven. For example, the need for permission and concern that there may not be a female provider are both hurdles to seeking health care that women face because they are women. Others, such as getting money needed for treatment, having to take transport, or distance to the health facility, can be hurdles for both men or women because they are likely to be related, at least in part, to the household's economic condition and to the supply of health care. However, these hurdles are also likely to have a gender component, because, being female, women have limited freedom of movement and access to income. Finally, others such as unavailability of health care providers or drugs are supply driven, but likely to be more of a problem for women than for men since it may be more difficult for women, largely for gendered reasons, to revisit the health facility if services are not received the first time.

Table 5.1 shows that women face a number of hurdles in accessing health care for themselves. The most common hurdle among the eight asked about is the distance to a health facility and the least common is getting permission to go. Notably, almost one fifth of women report that not having a female provider is a concern and for one tenth of women, finding someone to go with them is a problem. Each potential hurdle is much more common among poorer women than among the wealthier ones. Further, poorer women face many more hurdles than do richer women: about one in four women belonging to the lowest wealth quintile face five or more of the listed hurdles, compared with 6 percent of women in the fourth quintile and 3 percent in the highest quintile. Notably, however, even in the highest wealth quintile, over one-fifth of women face one or more hurdles in accessing health care for themselves.

Table 5.1: Percentage of Women Age 15-49 Specified Hurdle by Wealth Quintile in India

Variables	*Wealth quintile*					
	Lowest	*Second*	*Middle*	*Fourth*	*Highest*	*All women*
Hurdles to health care:						
Getting permission to go	10 .9	8. 6	7. 5	5. 5	2. 3	6. 7
Getting money needed for treatment	34.8	24.3	18.5	10.4	3.0	17.3
Distance to the health facility	47.4	36.1	26.3	16.6	5.9	25.3
Having to take transport	45.4	33.1	23.3	13.9	4.5	22.9
Finding someone to go with you	21.4	15.9	12.2	8.2	3.3	11.7
Concern that there may not be a female health provider	30.1	24.0	19.4	14.9	8.2	18.7
Concern that there may not be any health provider	35.4	28.7	23.8	18.6	10.8	22.7
Concern that there may be no drugs available	36.8	29.7	23.5	18.3	9.9	22.9
Women who face:						
0 hurdles	28.5	40.0	50.3	61.5	79.5	53.4
1-2 hurdles	24.8	24.9	23.4	20.9	13.0	21.1
3-4 hurdles	23.3	19.2	15.1	11.4	5.7	14.4
5+ hurdles	23.4	15.9	11.3	6.2	2.8	11.1

5.2 Cultural Context and Women's Health

Accounts of women's lives often do not adequately take into account the extent to which gender is not simply an individual characteristic but also a contextual characteristic that is bound up in gender-related cultural beliefs and practices widely shared in a community context (Hirschman, 1985). Women, especially in more patriarchal countries, are often situated within broad social networks and cultural contexts that can shape a variety of life experiences, including illness (Dodoo and Frost, 2008). The cultural contexts in which individuals live their lives can directly as well as indirectly influence health through mental and emotional pathways that vary for men and women (Macintyre and Ellaway, 2003; Read and Gorman, 2010).

Cultural contexts can condition the unfolding of women's health in multifaceted ways. Following the lead of others (Giddens, 1984; Johnson Hanks, et al., 2011; Sewell, 1992), this study views social structure as made up of a material schema interplay. This interplay makes up what we think of as "culture" and the repeated patterns we refer to as "structure." The schematic side of social structure refers to mental frameworks such as beliefs, heuristics, or worldviews that individuals or groups of people use to construe reality and organize behavior. Schemas are always present in concrete objects or actions. For example, a schema that goes along with dowry practice is one that construes women as burdensome, since giving a daughter and her dowry is financially burdensome.

The *material* side of the material schema duality of social structure refers to any *perceivable* things such as physical objects, outward practices, or spoken words. The perceivable materials of dowry include such things as dowry-related gossip, songs sung about dowry, verbal and non-verbal communication at the time of dowry negotiations, and the physical acts of giving and receiving dowry related objects such as cash, jewelry, and electronics. Perceivable actions and objects are all examples of "materials," but it is important to keep in mind that materials always instantiate one or more schemas. Dowry related materials may carry the schema that the burden of an additional female household member is being offset by receiving a dowry. Taken together, such material schema interplays work to pattern the world's social structures (Giddens, 1984; Johnson Hanks, et al., 2011; Sewell, 2005). Given this understanding, material schema duality of social structures can constrain and support individuals' health in several ways. Material-schema structures shape the conditions of social interactions, stressors, and opportunities available to individuals as they experience the world around them. Shared local understandings, behaviors, and social interactions surrounding gender are sustained by the ongoing presence of material-schema structures. In these ways, health is best understood as a function not just of the material-schema characteristics of individuals and their interactions, but of the material schema elements of broader community contexts in which health and health disparity unfold.

Since materials may directly influence health "without the mediation of schemas" (Johnson Hanks, et al., 2011:40), communities with high frequency of dowry could shape individuals' health *directly*. Dowry has a direct effect on the comparative costs of sons and daughters and hence on differential resources and opportunities available to males and females. As a brief illustration, if a parent in a community with high frequency of dowry wants to buy high quality shoes for a daughter, such shoes may be unavailable or difficult to find. Merchants might explain: "We only have that kind of shoe for boys. Customers simply don't spend that much money on girls' shoes and so we don't carry those kinds of shoes for girls". Because there are no or few high quality girls' shoes locally available, girls will be less likely to receive this resource regardless of whether a parent shopping for a daughter's shoes has internalized a schema that devalues females. Here, female access to an orthopedic health resource is constrained. Other health related resources and opportunities may be constrained in a similarly direct way by cultural context, affecting the overall maintenance of health.

Community schemas may also shape health. For instance, high levels of women's immobility in a community reinforces local schemas holding that a woman's place is not in public spaces, and so when women go into male dominated public spaces, they are subject to scrutiny, sustained gazes, sexual harassment, and a variety of stressors (Derne, 2000:155–56, 2008:177). Experiencing such sustained threat and adversity is associated with consequences for health (Hawkley, et al., 2005).

To take another example, male first eating serves as a "reservoir of meaning," carrying and instantiating schemas in a community, including schemas of gender difference and male superiority. As schemas tied to male first eating are *transposed* onto other spheres of life, these schemas influence community members' social interactions with women in a variety of domains and social settings (Appadurai, 1981). That is, people carry schemas into a range of life situations as they interact with women, including women outside of their family (e.g., servants, laborers, women in the bazaar, clients, etc.). The transposition of schemas may be deliberate; it may also be taken-for-granted, unconscious, and automatic (Tinkler, Li. and Mollborn, 2007). Women and girls living their lives in communities with such shared schemas will experience greater daily wear and tear worse treatment at the hands of community members, greater hassles, and less cooperation in securing basic needs and accomplishing goals. Unabating insults, threats, and experiences increase the likelihood of chronic stress and lower thresholds for a variety of acute and chronic health conditions (Hawkley, et al., 2005; Hertzman and Frank, 2005).

One of the main psychosocial pathways through which social interactions and experiences lead to health problems is through physiological response to stress. While the body's stress response is helpful in the short term (e.g., providing energy in order to flee danger), repeated and extended activations of the body's stress response (allostatic load) can increase the likelihood of a variety of health problems (Mc Ewen, 2002). Repeated activation of the stress response may take place due to an individual's anticipation of danger or threats, revisiting stressful memories, or even imagining stressful scenarios. The pernicious health effects of repeated and extended stress response activation exist in part because the body is not given adequate time to recover from its stress response before another response occurs. A number of the bodys long term maintenance tasks (e.g., digestion and growth) are repeatedly set aside for extended periods of time in favor of responding to stress. Regardless of whether women are members of households that engage in practices such as male first eating, women residing in communities where a culture of gender discrimination holds sway will tend to experience greater subordination, less cooperation, and more chronic stress than women elsewhere, resulting in a greater likelihood of having poor health.

5.3 Health Status of Tribal Women

A comprehensive review of the health status of tribal women has been prepared by Basu (1993). His paper discusses, inter alia, the following dimensions: sex ratio, age at marriage, fertility and mortality, life expectancy, nutritional status, maternal mortality, mother and child health care practices, family welfare programmes and sexually transmitted diseases. The main conclusions of the paper are:

5.3.1 Anemia

Anemia is one of the most common diseases complicating antenatal women worldwide, particularly in the developing countries (Ministry of Palestinian Health, 2006). Anemia is more common during pregnancy; hence pregnant women are at higher risk than non-pregnant women (March of dimes, 2010). It is a major public health problem and one of the most common nutritional disorders worldwide has major consequences for human health, economic and social development (Dorothy, et al., 2006; WHO, 2002). In India, anemia affects an estimated 50 percent of the population (Florentino, R.F., 2003). More than half of women (55 percent) and almost one quarter of men (24 percent) are anemic, out of these 39 percent of women have mild anemia, 15 percent have moderate anemia and 2 percent have severe anemia. And in men, 13 percent have mild anemia, 10 percent have moderate anemia and 1 percent have severe anemia (National Family Health Survey, 2005-06). The prevalence of anemia for ever married women has increased from 52 percent in NFHS-2 to 56 percent in NFHS-3. It is estimated that about 20 percent 40 percent of maternal deaths in India are due to anemia and one in every two Indian women (56 percent) suffers from some form of anemia (National Family Health Survey-3, 2005-06).

5.3.2 Higher Fertility with Inclining Female Infant Mortality

Higher fertility rate in tribal women compared to the national women compared to the national average (Basu S., 1993; Chatterjee, 1993) has reported increase in the incidence of diseases with increase in so-called "development". He has compared this incidence of diseases in the tribal population living in three different environments:

- Forest based
- Denuded Forest Area, and
- Industrially polluted area. The incidence of disease is lowest in the first and the highest in the third.

Kar (1993) has reported that the reproductive behaviour of tribal woman in Arunachal Pradesh is intimately related to her value system and cultural traditions. She is considered to be healthy if she can give birth to four or five children and also work in the fields. The health status of the tribals have been discussed in Status of the Tribals in India, (Basu, 1993). The factors which influence the health status of the tribal population in general, are also applicable to the tribal women, in fact, more so. For example, it has been found that

illiteracy, in tribal, as also in non-tribal population, is positively correlated with ill health. The tribal women, as women in all social groups, are more illiterate than men. The tribal women share, with women of other social groups, problems related to reproductive health.

Health is an important indicator of the well being of any group. Most health related studies are limited, they do not cover the various dimensions of health affecting the status of tribal women like (i) sex-ratio, (ii) Female literacy, (iii) Marriage practices, (iv) Age at marriage, (v) Age of mother at first conception (vi) Life expectancy at birth, etc. In Andhra Pradesh, for example, more than 50 per cent of the tribal people do not have access to drinking water, 70 per cent do not have power connections and more than 75 per cent do not have access to roads. Although Rs.50 crore was allocated to private contractors for tribal education and health, thousands of tribal people were affected by malnutrition, hunger and disease. In Orissa, Rs.680 crores allocated for tribal development had not been spent.

Poverty, deprivation and now the reduction of government expenditure on basic medical health facilities is reflected in the absolutely poor health condition of adivasi women and children. Child bearing is in this 21st century still a risk to the life of the woman. Anaemia is the normal condition for women, and malnutrition is rampant. Thus, the uproar in Maharashtra in 2005 over malnutrition deaths exposed the fact that the infant mortality rate (IMR) in tribal areas was 80 per 1000 births and over 50 percent of these deaths were of newly born children. Further the report revealed that 23,500 children died every year in tribal areas in the state alone. In AP too, in the ITDA areas 80 percent of the deliveries

are conducted at home. The IMR rate is 165 per 1000 births while that for the general population is 92/1000 births. 55 percent of children in the ITDA areas are underweight. Even in the so called advanced state of Kerala the IMR in a tribal block of Palakad dist. was 66 per thousand births. In Uttapradesh's Sonabhadra dist. in one month alone 19 ST children died of malnutrition, which actually means due to lack of food. The plight of the women who are bearing these children can easily be understood. While these facts have been highlighted by a section of the urban media what we want to highlight is that it is that it is the policies of the government which have led to this state of affairs. Some piecemeal solutions like serving nutritious khichdi in anganwadis cannot change the basic conditions of the advasi population.

The scanty data and information available on the health status of the Adivasi population clearly show that the maternal mortality (between 8 to 25 per 1000) is more than double the rates than in the more advanced regions. Maternal mortality was reported to be high among various tribal groups but no exact data is available. The main causes of maternal mortality were found to be unhygenic and primitive practices for parturition. The crude death rates are also very high. These adverse health indicators are largely due to inadequate access to the nutritious foods and lack of access to health care services.

High levels of Hepatitis B infection among sections of the already minuscule tribal population of the Andaman and Nicobar Islands raise medical and social concerns. Compared to the average 4 to 5 per cent rate in the general population of mainland India, the prevalence rate in these tribal populations is over 20 per cent. The lack of purchasing power to buy food even at the public distribution system (PDS) rates and the distress sale of whatever food surpluses exist are the main reasons for the starvation deaths in the Kalahandi, Bolangir, Koraput (KBK) region. The coal mafia in West Bengal is employing poor Santhali adivasi men and women to extract coal illegally from abandoned open cast mines. This is posing serious health hazards. Accidents and deaths are common here.

The lack of food supply through the TPDS is compounded by the fact that Adivasis have no rights in forests that used to provide them with a variety of food. A ban on hunting has meant reduced supply of healthy meat while a switch over to cash crops has led to reduced availability of food. Due to the depletion of forests due to excessive felling by vested interests adivasi women have to walk much longer distances to collect fuel wood and minor forest produce. Even in advanced stages of pregnancy women have to work hard and go long distances. Thus their workload has increased. The problem of hunger and malnutrition in Adivasi areas is clearly linked to the inequalities and threats to livelihood security in these regions. The solution of providing food for work or free food would only take care of the immediate needs of the Adivasis, but will not provide a long term solution. There could be several factors responsible for this, but there is no denying that malaria is a major cause of the deaths. Even if one survives an illness, it only leaves him or her more vulnerable to another, with the body's defences dwindling because of poverty and malnourishment.

Poverty stops them from visiting the doctor when they fall ill. The maternal mortality rate is nearly 25 per cent and the infant mortality rate is around 165 for every 1,000, compared to 95 for every 1,000 at the State level. The under five mortality rate is also very high, nearly 50 per cent. Eighty per cent of the children are anaemic and 55 per cent under weight. Almost all the tribal girls get married by the time they attain puberty and become mothers at a very young age.

Maternal and child health care practices were found to be largely neglected in various tribal group (i.e. Baster tribal groups, Kutia Kondhs of Orissa, Santals, Jaunsaris, Kharias etc.) From the inception of pregnancy to its termination, no specific nutritious diet was consumed by women. On the other hand, some pregnant tribal women (i.e. Dudh Kharias, Santals) reduced their food intake because of the fear of recurrent vomiting and also to ensure that the baby may remain small and the delivery may be easier. Vaccination and immunization of infants and children were inadequate among tribal groups. There were two genetic disorders namely sickle cell anaemia which were found to occur in rather high frequencies in Schedule Tribes and Scheduled Caste populations, both male and female were equally affected.

Chapter - VI

Methodology

Gender describes socially constructed differences between men and women, boys and girls etc. Gender is defined on the basis of social norms, behaviors, activities, relationship, responsibilities which are assigned by the society as appropriate for male and female (WHO, 2010). Understanding of gender varies in different races, nations, castes, ethnic groups, religions. The dimension and degree of discrimination against women manifests itself in different culture, politics, race, region, countries, and economies differently. However, gender discrimination is considered as a tremendous constraint towards the development process and it is found as a causal factor of violence against women. (Jannatul Ferdaush, K. M., Mustafizur Rahman, 2011*Gender Inequality in Bangladesh, Unnayan Onneshan-The Innovators*). In this regard, we would try to search for the answers of the question. *"Do the socio-cultural norms influence gender gap against women in the society?"*

6.1 Tools of Data Collection

Statistical data for research investigations may either by primary or secondary. So, the method of data collection is based on by examining records (secondary data analysis); by using self report measures (primary data analysis). The first method of data collection requires extensive literature review by the existing records. These might include books, journal, census report etc. A second data collection method involves asking key programme and observation to respondents or key participants.

6.1.1 Secondary Data Collection

The effective research is based upon the past knowledge, a survey of past literature helps to eliminate the duplication of what has been done and sometimes provides hypothesis. Thus, the secondary analysis is based on extensive literature review; State Sample Registration Report, NFHS- 2 and 3 and DLHS-3 were used to examine the association between induced abortion and prevalent status among the districts in Chhattisgarh as well as consequences of induced abortion on women's reproductive health. The research for related literature has been completed before proceeding with the actual conduct of the study (table 6.1)

Table 6.1: Framework for Secondary Data

Type	*Methods*	*Techniques*
Library Research	Analysis of historical records	Recording of notes, Content analysis, Type and Film listening and analysis.
	Analysis of documents	Statistical compilations and manipulation, reference and abstract guides, contents analysis.
Laboratory Research	Small group study of random behaviour, play and role analysis	Use of audio- visual recording devices, use of observers, etc.

6.1.2 Primary Data Collection

Primary data collection is based on field researches where many needful tools had been used which are given in table 6.2.

Table 6.2: Tools of Primary Data Collection

Field Research	Non- participant direct observation	Observational behavioural scales, use of score cards, etc.
	Participant observation	Interactional recording, possible use of tape recorders, photo graphic techniques.
	Mass observation	Recording mass behaviour, interview using independent observes in public places.
	Mail questionnaire	Identification of social and economic background of respondents.
	Opinionnaire	Use of attitude scales, projective techniques, use of sociometric scales.
	Personal interview	Interviewer uses a detailed schedule with open and closed questions.
	Focused interview by FGDs	Interviewer focuses attention upon a given experience and its effects.
	Group interview	Small groups of respondents are interviewed simultaneously.
	Telephone survey	Used as a survey technique for information and for discerning opinion; may also be used as a follow up a questionnaire.
	Case study and life history	Cross sectional collection of data for intensive analysis, longitudinal collection of data of intensive character.

6.1.2.1 Use of Standardised Questions by Schedule/Questionnaire

Standardized questionnaires are used in the field to collect information about various aspects of women respondents and others. The main way of collecting this information is by asking people questions by self-administered questionnaires. Among the types of information that can be collected by means of a questionnaire are facts, activities, level of knowledge, opinions, expectations and aspirations, membership of various groups, and attitudes and perceptions. Thus questionnaire is based on closed and open ended question.

Closed questions ask the respondent to choose, among a possible set of answers, the response that most closely represents his/her viewpoint. The respondent is usually asked to tick or circle the chosen answer. Questions of this kind may offer simple alternatives such as 'Yes' or 'No'. They may also require that the respondent chooses among several answer categories, or that he/she uses a frequency scale, an importance scale, or an agreement scale. The possibility of format effects or response bias for this type of question can be reduced by changing the sequence of response categories and values. Some closed questions may have a dichotomous response format, which means only two mutually exclusive responses are provided.

Open-ended or free-response questions are not followed by any choices and the respondent must answer by supplying a response, usually by entering a number, a word, or a short text. Answers are recorded in full, either by the interviewer or, in the case of a self-administered survey, the respondent records his or her own. There is always the possibility with open-ended questions that responses may come in very different forms, and these may lead to answers that cannot be systematically coded for analysis. If the survey is administered by an interviewer, appropriate probing helps clarify such answers. In the case of a self-administered survey, guidance by writing specific instructions on how to answer the question can often minimize the number of responses that have very different dimensions.

Care is taken in writing open-ended questions so as to avoid formats that elicit a dichotomous yes/no. In addition, the wording of questions should seek to reduce the possibility of eliciting responses that are aligned along very different dimensions and therefore cannot be systematically coded. In self-administered surveys, it is useful to provide instructions on the format of the response that is required so as to minimize opportunities for the respondents to answer the question according to very different dimensions.

A contingency question is a special case of a closed ended question because it applies only to a subgroup of respondents. The relevance of the question for a subgroup is determined by asking a filter question. The filter question directs the subgroup to answer a relevant set of specialized questions and instructs other respondents to skip to a later section of the questionnaire. The advantage of contingency questions is that detailed data may be obtained from a specific subgroup of the population. Some questions may apply only to females and not to males; others may apply only to people in school, and not to those who are employed. At the base of good contingency questions are clear and specific instructions to respondents. The formats for filter and contingency questions are vary. One option is to write directions next to the response category of the filter question.

6.1.2.1.1 Likert Scaling

Likert scaling is the most frequently applied attitude scaling technique in educational research. It consists 5 but we had taken 2 main steps.

6.1.2.1.2 Determining the Attitude to be Measured

In some important areas, attitude measurement includes pupil attitudes towards family members, society and cultural practices. In addition, given the importance of retaining value within family and social systems, there is a great interest in measuring the sources of satisfaction with, and attitudes towards, their family as well as society.

6.1.2.1.3 Listing Possible Scale Items

An attitude is often defined as a state of readiness, or a tendency to respond in a certain manner when confronted with particular stimuli. Social psychologists consider that attitudes arise from deeply rooted personality characteristics and value systems within individuals, and that they become manifest in the form of opinions. The main difficulties in measuring attitudes are that (a) the object of an attitude can range from the very specific to the very general, (b) attitudes are not static, and (c) attitudes are both shaped and changed by socio-demographic circumstances and life experiences.

In the field of educational research, the measurement of attitudes has become an important issue in attempts to monitor the 'affective' (that is non-cognitive) outcomes of schooling. The most popular approach to attitude measurement has been via the use of attitude scales.

Attitude scales usually consist of a number of attitude statements which are presented to respondents with a request that they should indicate whether they agree or disagree. Scaling techniques are deployed to order respondents along some underlying attitudinal continuum. Here, a set of statements, or a series of items, are devised that express a wide range of attitudes, from extremely positive to extremely negative. The statements are designed to reflect favorably or unfavorably on the object of the attitude. One common approach for constructing these statements is to organize a discussion focussed on the stimulus for the attitude (for example, the self status of women respondent) with individuals or small groups representative of the target population to whom the scale has administered. The various negative and positive comments and statements made during this discussion has been selected and edited for use as stimuli in the attitude scale. Another approach is to ask a sample of respondents to respond to a set of open ended statements related to the attitude being investigated. These responses are then used to construct attitude statements. Each statement is followed by an agreement scale on which respondents are requested to indicate the degree to which they agree or disagree with each statement. Although the scale may have only two choices (yes/no), more choices may sometimes permit a finer distinction in the intensity of the attitude.

6.1.2.1.4 Recall Period

Questions asking someone to describe their own behaviour can be unreliable if badly worded such that the answers relate more to how people think they should behave within their society and culture, than to how they actually are behaving. In addition, people often give an answer which they think is more popular or socially acceptable and sometimes give false answer in order to preserve their self image in the presence of the interviewer. A common problem with behaviour questions is that of memory recall which depends on the length and recency of the time period and the importance of the topic.

6.1.2.1.5 Aided Recall

Aided recall is effective methods for helping respondents recall vital events like violence, birth and death. In this method a moral support is established for respondents, by researchers. Alternatively, interviewers recorded the associated major happenings which are mentioned by respondents and the numerical year is assigned later.

6.1.2.1.6 Hidden Cross Checks

Another method which is commonly used during survey research is the use of hidden cross check in the questionnaire. This involves asking for the same information in different ways in different parts of the survey so that the responses become valid.

6.1.2.1.7 Threatening Questions about Behaviour

Regarding the issues of family welfare, some of the topics which may be perceived as threatening to the respondents are women's status and role of decision making. Carefully designed question formats and wording is substantially improved response accuracy to queries on that topic.

6.2 Data Analysis

After data collection, analysis is closely related of the establishment of categories of the data, the application of the categories to raw data through coding, tabulation and then drawn statistical inferences. The unwieldy data is necessarily be condensed into a few manageable groups and tables for further analysis. Thus researchers had classified the raw data into some purposeful and usable categories. Coding operation is usually done at this stage through which the categories of data are transformed into symbols that is tabulated and counted. Editing is the procedure that improves the quality of data for coding. After coding tabulation is a part of technical procedure wherein the classified data are put in the form of tables. The mechanical devices are used at this juncture. Analysis work after tabulation is generally based on the computation of various percentages by applying statistical formulae.

Chapter - VII

Study Area

In India, the Protection of Women from Domestic Violence Act (PWDVA) was introduced in 2005 but poor implementation and important socio-cultural factors leads to increased violence against women and gender inequality. In light of this deplorable situation, Oxfam launched the Asian Circle project in Chhattisgarh and Odisha, with particular focus on tribal communities within those states. It has been found that gender gap is not only seen in the urban population but it is also prevalent amongst tribals' communities. It is pertinent that the disparity of gender is occure in different ways in different societies. To know the actual fact about gender, socio-demograhich data of Chhattisgarh is mentioned below because in many places gender gaps are interlinked with regional areas, cultural norms, socioeconomic status and religions.

7.1 Chhattisgarh at a Glance

Chhattisgarh is a young and a new state but the reference of this state can be traced in ancient texts, and inscriptions. In ancient times Chhattisgarh was known as Dakshin Kosala and it is said that Lord Rama has spent some time here when he was on his was on his 14 years exile. A major part of the Chhattisgarh as we know today was known as Dandakaranya in the ancient times. Other parts were known as Dakshina Koshal. In the medieval period, the region, which falls south of the *Vindhyas*, came to be known as Gondwana.

Earliest human settlements were established in this region much before they came into existence in any other part of the country. Historians and anthropologists are trying to establish the exact date for the earliest human settlement in this region. Right from the beginning, Chhattisgarh has been swarmed with migrants from nearby places, who now constitute a major part of the population. Right from the days of great Magadha Empire,

Chhattisgarh remained part of every empire that ruled the country from north to south, but their dominance was political only.

Table 7.1: Chhattisgarh Figure at Glance

Total Population	*Absolute*			*Percentage*		
	Total	*Rural*	*Urban*	*Total*	*Rural*	*Urban*
Persons	25545198	19607961	5937237	100.00	76.76	23.24
Males	12832895	9797426	3035469	100.00	76.35	23.65
Females	12712303	9810535	2901768	100.00	77.17	22.83
Decadal Changes 2001-11						
Persons	4711395	2959905	1751490	22.61	17.78	41.84
Males	2358677	1489983	868694	22.52	17.93	40.09
Females	2352718	1469922	882796	22.71	17.62	43.72
Sex Ratio	991	1001	956			
Child Population (0-6 years)						
Persons	3661689	2924941	736748	14.33	14.92	12.41
Males	1859935	1479586	380349	14.49	15.10	12.53
Females	1801754	1445355	356399	14.17	14.73	12.28
Child Sex Ratio	969	977	937			
Literates						
Persons	15379922	11008956	4370966	70.28	66.00	84.05
Males	8807893	6403012	2404881	80.27	77.00	90.57
Females	6572029	4605944	1966085	60.23	55.06	77.24
Schedule Caste Population						
Persons	3274269	2511949	762320	12.82	12.81	12.84
Males	1641738	128559	383179	12.80	12.84	12.64
Females	1632531	1253390	379741	12.84	12.78	13.07
Schedule Tribe Population						
Persons	7822902	7231082	591820	30.62	36.88	9.97
Males	3873191	3577134	296057	30.18	36.51	9.75
Females	3949711	3653948	295763	31.07	37.24	10.19

Source: Census of India, 2011.

As the region was extremely inaccessible, not much interference could be made in the lifestyle of the tribes.Kalchuris were the first rulers who ruled clearly over this region till 19th century.After the fall of kalchuris, it was time for the Bhonsles of Nagpur to dominate over this region for a brief period in the 19th century.However with the decline of the Marathas, there prevailed complete lawlessness throughout the region and many tribal chieftains established rule over small tracts throughout the region,which marked the beginning of a heterogeneous mix of races from all over the country working together to create a prosperous Chhattisgarh.Chhattisgarh the 26th state of India, was carved out of Madhya Pradesh on November 1,2000.Located in central India it covers an area of 135,133 sq km. Raipur is the capital of Chhattisgarh is bordered by Bihar, Jharkhand and Uttar

Pradesh in the north, Andhra Pradesh in the south, Orissa in the east and Madhya Pradesh in the west. The state lies at 17 46' n 24 '5'N latitude and 80 15 'E longitude. Chhattisgarh has 18 districts- Bastar, Bilaspur, Dantewada (South Bastar), Dhamtari, Durg, Janjgir-champa, Jaspur, Kanker (North Bastar), Kabeerdham, Korba, Koriya, Mahasamund, Raigarh, Rajnandgaon and Surguja.

Table 7.2: District Wise Population in Chhattisgarh

S.No.	*District*	*Population*		
		Males	*Females*	*Total*
1.	Koriya	341440	322667	664107
2.	Surguja	1255688	1223488	2479176
3.	Jashpur	420169	422074	842243
4.	Raigarh	757627	730196	1487823
5.	Korba	616262	594120	1210382
6.	Janjgir- Champa	757792	759939	1517731
7.	Bilaspur	1180144	1148361	2328505
8.	Kabeerdham	327960	330548	658508
9.	Rajnandgaon	738055	758406	1496461
10.	Durg	1640952	1613635	3254587
11.	Raipur	1771384	1739357	3510741
12.	Mahasamund	442411	455039	897450
13.	Dhamtari	207711	641226	848937
14.	Kanker	345302	348688	693990
15.	Bastar	759865	771593	1531458
16.	Narayanpur	70189	70017	140206
17.	Dantewada	409135	418701	827836
18.	Bijapur	128761	126419	255180
	Total	**12170847**	**12474474**	**24645321**

Source: Census of India, 2011.

According to census report, 2001 female tribal population is almost equal to male tribal population which is numerically 50.32 percent in Chhattisgarh. The data of equality shows that amongst tribal community, there is no differentiation and disparity in the preference of female or girl child. The tribal equally accepted the birth of both girls and boys.

Table 7.3: Sex Wise Schedules Tribes Population (2001)

District	*Male*	*Female*	*Total*	*Percentage of Female to total Population*
Koriya	131957	128083	260040	49.26
Surguja	541949	534720	1076669	49.66
Jashpur	233166	236787	469953	50.39
Raigarh	222470	225233	447703	50.31
Korba	210373	209516	419889	49.90
Janjgir-Champa	75454	77615	153069	50.71
Bilaspur	197984	199120	397104	50.14
Kawardha	60510	61447	121957	50.38
Rajnandgaon	166587	175101	341688	51.25
Durg	172038	176763	348801	50.68
Raipur	181409	183864	365273	50.34
Mahasamund	114221	118264	232485	50.87
Dhamtari	91748	93767	185515	50.54
Kanker	180825	184206	365031	50.46
Bastar	428973	437515	866488	50.49
Dantewada	277670	287261	564931	50.85
Chhattisgarh	3287334	3329262	6616596	50.32

Source: Censes of India, 2001.

The separate sex ratio is observed in the district level of Chhattisgarh where it is significantly noted that ST female sex ratio is highest in the State and also greater than the sex ratio of General population and Schedule Caste Communities. The average ST female sex ratio in Chhattisgarh was 1013 while it was 975 in General population and 994 in Schedule Caste population.

Table 7.4: Female per thousand of General, Schedule Caste., Schedule Tribe Population

District	*Total*	*Gen*	*SC*	*ST*
Koriya	946	922	959	971
Surguja	972	952	979	987
Jashpur	999	969	992	1016
Raigarh	994	977	1011	1012
Korba	964	938	962	996
Janjgir-Champa	998	992	1000	1029
Bilaspur	971	962	965	1005
Kawardha	1002	1000	994	1015
Rajnandgaon	1023	1011	1028	1051

(Contd...)

Durg	982	973	994	1027
Raipur	980	970	996	1014
Mahasamund	1018	1009	1027	1035
Dhamtari	1004	996	1021	1022
Kanker	1005	982	1043	1019
Bastar	1011	992	1012	1020
Dantewada	1016	943	989	1035
Chhattisgarh	989	975	994	1013

Source: Censes of India, 2001.

It can be observed from table 7.5 that, in urban population as well as where Schedule Caste and General population are abundantly residing which has female population is low and gender gap is higher than other areas. In Chhattisgarh, Bilaspur, Raipur and Korba are Industrial zones as well urban city whereas Jnjgir Champa, Kawardha are the place where SC and General population are huge in number. In above mentioned areas, female population is lower and gender gap is higher in both urban and rural part of the city rather than tribal areas of Chhattisgarh.

Table 7.5: District wise Gender Gap in Chhattisgarh

States	***Urban***				***Rural***			
	Persons	***Male***	***Female***	***Gender Gap***	***Persons***	***Male***	***Female***	***Gender Gap***
Koriya	77.2	86.3	66.8	19.50	56.80	70.70	42.40	28.30
Surguja	84.7	91.6	77.1	14.50	52.40	65.60	38.80	26.80
Jashpur	83.4	90.6	75.6	15.00	62.80	74.40	51.30	23.10
Raigarh	80.3	89.8	70.2	19.60	68.60	81.50	55.70	25.80
Korba	79.0	89.0	68.0	21.00	51.50	67.80	35.00	32.80
Janjgir-Champa	78.5	90	66.4	23.60	64.30	80.70	48.10	32.60
Bilaspur	80.8	89.7	71.3	18.40	57.60	74.50	40.50	34.00
Kawardha	75.1	86.8	62.5	24.30	53.40	69.60	37.50	32.10
Rajnandgaon	82.4	90.9	73.7	17.20	76.00	86.30	66.20	20.10
Durg	82.3	90.5	73.5	17.00	71.30	83.70	59.30	24.40
Raipur	79.6	88.2	70.3	17.90	63.50	79.00	48.10	30.90
Mahasamund	77.6	87.9	67.0	20.90	65.60	80.20	51.60	28.60
Dhamtari	79.4	89.3	69.5	19.80	74.20	86.10	62.43	23.67
Kanker	85.3	92.7	77.6	15.10	72.30	82.20	62.43	19.77
Bastar	80.5	88.5	72.1	16.40	39.60	52.40	26.98	25.42
Dantewada	77.9	86.8	67.9	18.90	26.20	35.50	17.10	18.40
Chhattisgarh	80.6	89.4	71.1	18.3	60.50	74.10	46.99	27.11

Source: Censes of India, 2001.

Infant mortality rate is a key indicator of health in any population of any place/areas. Table 7.6 stated that state has high infant mortality rate (total: 63; rural: 65; urban: 52) and pre natal mortality rate (total: 53; rural: 55; urban: 44) which shows that poor health status of the state.

Table 7.6: Child (Aged 0-4 Years) and Infant Mortality Indicator

Indicators	*Total*	*Rural*	*Urban*
Infant Mortality Rate	63	65	52
Neonatal Mortality Rate	45	46	36
Early Neo Natal Mortality Rate	36	38	25
Late Neo Natal Mortality Rate	8	8	10
Pre Natal Mortality Rate	53	55	44
Still Birth	18	17	19
Child Mortality	20	22	13

Source: Census of India-2011.

The life span of female is higher than the male but data shows that female mortality is higher under four aged group, from 20 to 24 year and 55 to 59 year aged group which indicates the depriviation for women health and status.

Table 7.7: Percentage Distribution of Deaths to Total Deaths by Residence, Sex and Age Group

Age Group	*Total*			*Rural*			*Urban*		
	Total	*Male*	*Female*	*Total*	*Male*	*Female*	*Total*	*Male*	*Female*
Below 1	21.3	20.7	22.0	22.6	22.5	22.6	14.9	12.6	18.5
1-4	8.3	5.5	11.5	9.3	6.0	12.9	3.4	3.6	3.1
>4	29.6	26.2	33.5	31.8	28.5	35.5	18.3	16.2	21.6
5-9	2.9	3.3	2.4	3.1	3.9	2.3	1.5	0.8	2.5
10-14	1.8	2.5	1.0	2.0	2.8	1.2	0.7	1.2	0.0
15-19	3.5	1.3	6.2	3.9	1.1	7.0	1.9	2.3	1.2
20-24	2.7	2.7	2.6	2.6	2.8	2.3	3.2	2.4	4.3
25-29	1.3	1.0	1.6	1.1	0.7	1.6	2.2	2.4	1.9
30-34	3.4	2.8	4.0	3.1	2.5	3.9	4.6	4.5	4.8
35-39	1.8	1.4	2.2	1.3	0.7	2.0	4.0	4.3	3.6
40-44	3.3	4.4	2.2	3.1	3.9	2.3	4.4	6.4	1.2
45-49	3.1	4.0	2.0	2.6	3.5	1.6	5.4	6.1	4.4
50-54	3.0	3.1	2.9	2.8	2.8	2.7	4.1	4.4	3.7
55-59	5.6	6.2	5.0	5.7	6.7	4.7	5.1	4.2	6.6
60-64	7.6	10.0	4.8	6.9	9.5	3.9	11.2	12.0	9.9
65-69	9.8	11.1	8.3	10.0	11.6	8.2	8.8	8.9	8.9
70-74	8.4	10.4	6.1	8.0	9.9	5.9	10.8	12.9	7.5
75-79	6.0	5.5	6.7	6.3	6.0	6.6	4.6	3.2	6.8
80-84	4.0	2.7	5.5	3.7	2.1	5.5	5.4	5.3	5.5
85+	2.2	1.3	3.2	1.9	1.1	2.7	3.8	2.4	6.0

Source: Census of India, 2011.

Comparatively sex wise infant mortality rate is declining year by year from 2001 to 2008 but when it is compared between sex wise than it has been observed that female infant mortality rate is higher than the male infant mortality.

Table 7.8: Comparative Sex Wise Infant Mortality Rates

Year	*Chhattisgarh*		*India*	
	Males	*Females*	*Males*	*Females*
2001	-	-	64	68
2002	61	66	62	65
2003	68	71	57	64
2004	78	42	56	61
2005	63	64	56	61
2006	59	62	56	59
2007	58	61	55	56
2008	57	58	52	55

Source: Sample Registration Survey Report, 2009.

In 2001 male literacy rate was 77.4 percent out of 64.7 percent literacy rate of Chhattisgarh while the female literacy rate was 51.9 percent with 25.5 percent male and female literacy gender gap.It is pertinent to note that where the sex ratio gap was higher, there were also male and female literacy gap was greater than other areas like Korba, Janjgir- Champa, Bilashpur and Kawardha.

Table 7.9: Literacy Gap between Male and Female in Chhattisgarh

District	*Persons*	*Male*	*Femele*	*Male and Female Literacy Gap*
Koriya	63.1	75.7	49.7	26.0
Surguja	54.8	67.6	41.6	26.0
Jashpur	63.8	75.2	52.4	22.8
Raigarh	70.2	82.7	57.6	25.1
Korba	61.7	75.9	46.9	28.9
Janjgir-Champa	65.9	81.8	50.1	31.7
Bilaspur	63.5	78.4	48.2	30.2
Kawardha	55.2	71.0	39.5	31.5
Rajnandgaon	77.2	87.2	67.6	19.6
Durg	75.6	86.4	64.6	21.8
Raipur	68.5	81.9	54.8	27.2
Mahasamund	67.0	81.1	53.3	27.8
Dhamtari	74.9	86.5	63.4	23.1
Kanker	72.9	82.7	63.3	19.4
Bastar	43.9	56.3	31.6	24.7
Dantewada	30.2	39.8	20.7	19.1
Chhattisgarh	64.7	77.4	51.9	25.5

Source: Census of India, 2001.

According to economic census 2005, of Chhattisgarh, it has been reveals from table 7.10 that percentage of female participation was less in number. Activity wise 27.90 percent female were employees in rareing of animals, 30.25 percent women employees in agriculture services, and 12.68 percent women were earning from fishing.Very less percentage of women were working in the mining and quarrying, construction, sale, maintenance and repaire of motor vehicles,transport and storage as compare to other activities.

Table 7.10: Activity Wise Female Employment

District	*Persons*	*Male*	*Femele*	*Male and Female Literacy Gap*
Koriya	63.1	75.7	49.7	26.0
Surguja	54.8	67.6	41.6	26.0
Jashpur	63.8	75.2	52.4	22.8
Raigarh	70.2	82.7	57.6	25.1
Korba	61.7	75.9	46.9	28.9
Janjgir-Champa	65.9	81.8	50.1	31.7
Bilaspur	63.5	78.4	48.2	30.2
Kawardha	55.2	71.0	39.5	31.5
Rajnandgaon	77.2	87.2	67.6	19.6
Durg	75.6	86.4	64.6	21.8
Raipur	68.5	81.9	54.8	27.2
Mahasamund	67.0	81.1	53.3	27.8
Dhamtari	74.9	86.5	63.4	23.1
Kanker	72.9	82.7	63.3	19.4
Bastar	43.9	56.3	31.6	24.7
Dantewada	30.2	39.8	20.7	19.1
Chhattisgarh	**64.7**	**77.4**	**51.9**	**25.5**

Source: Economic Census, 2005.

It is significantly observed that the number of female employees were greater rather than the female employees in urban areas. In all the districts of Chhattisgarh, except Dhamtari, female employees were greater in rural areas. The average number of female employees amongst all districts, were 42.86 in rural areas while it is 10.42 in urban areas.

Table 7.11: District Wise Female Employment

Activity	*Urban*			*Rural*		
	Total Employment		*Percentage of Female*	*Total Employment*		*Percentage of Female*
	All	*Female*		*All*	*Female*	
Rareing of Animal	15445	4122	26.69	2928	817	27.90
Agricultural Service	141229	63544	44.99	324	98	30.25
Fishing etc	2390	505	21.13	410	52	12.68
All Agricultural activity	159064	68171	42.86	3662	967	26.41
Mining & Quarrying	1457	420	28.83	221	12	5.43

(Contd...)

Manufacturing	73878	18188	24.62	21925	4088	18.65
Electricity, Gas& Water	69	2	2.90	60	2	3.33
Construction	1522	99	6.50	835	15	1.80
Sale, Maintenance & Repair M/V & M/C	2627	100	3.81	3581	40	1.12
Wholesale Trade	1536	118	7.68	1745	51	2.92
Retail Trade	141499	23430	16.56	66801	5790	8.67
Restaurants & Hotel	9687	2502	25.83	4391	741	16.88
Transport &Storage	2590	105	4.05	6543	59	0.90
Posts and Telecommunication	1355	51	3.76	3038	156	5.13
Financial Intermediation	316	50	15.82	621	84	13.53
Real Estat Banking and Service	3006	113	3.76	4579	140	3.06
Pub Admin Defence Social Sectors	459	79	17.21	223	14	6.28
Education	930	276	29.68	982	238	24.24
Health and Social Work	8827	4808	54.47	2110	171	8.10
Other Community Services	15073	2255	14.96	8549	969	11.33
Other Activities	8	0	0.00	0	0	0.00
Non-Agriculture Activities	264839	52596	19.86	126204	12570	9.96
Agri and Non Agricultural work	423903	120767	28.49	129866	13537	10.42

Source: Economic Census, 2005.

7.1.1 Physiographic Profile

State of Chhattisgarh has a shape of Sea horse. Main physiographic components are the plains of Mahandi Basin, embanked by high plateaus and hills of Dandakaranya and Northern hills. Overall the area looks like a very broad Valley running west to east with a very gently eastwardly slope.

Table 7.12: The Mainland of Chhattisgarh Comprises of Three Main Physiographic Regions

Physiographic Profile	*Approximate % of Geographical Area*	*Dividend Part*
Mountains	27.50	• Maikal Range (Rajnandgaon, Kawardha and Bilaspur districts) • Chhuri Udaipur Hills (Korba and Raigarh districts) • Changbhakhar Devgarh Hills (Koriya and Surguja districts) • Abujhmad Hills (Narayanpur, Bijapur, Bhopalpattnam and Pakhanjur tehsils)

(*Contd...*)

Plateau and Regions	29.29	• Pat regions (Surguja and Jashpur districts) • Pendra-Lormi Plateau (Lormi, Pendra Road, Kota, and Pandaria tehsils) • Dhamtari-Mahasamund Uplands (Saraipali, Mahasamund, Kasdol, Nagri • Gariyabandh, Devbhog, Kurud and Dhamtari tehsils.) • Durg Uplands (Rajnandgaon and Durg districts) • Bastar Plateau/ Dandakaranya Plateau (Kanker, Bastar and Dantewara distt.)
Plains/Rivers Basins	43.21	• Kanhar Basin • Rihand Basin • Surguja Basin • Hasdo Rampura Basin • Korba Basin • Raigarh Basin • Bilaspur-Raigarh Plains • Sarangarh Plains • Durg- Raipur Plains • Kotri Basin • Bastar Plains

7.1.2 Minerals

Chhattisgarh is a land of opportunities. It is the richest state in mineral resources with all major minerals including diamonds available in abundance about 20 percent of the country's steel and cement are produced here. Major industries in steel, aluminum and cement are present in the state. Chhattisgarh contributes substantially to the economy and human resources of the country.

Table 7.13: Production of Major Mineral in Chhattisgarh and India: Year 2013-14

Major Minerals	*Chhattisgarh*	*India*	*Share (%)*
Coal	127093	56308	22.6
Iron Ore	30156	15243	19.8
Limestone	21061	27872	7.6
Dolomite	2595	7108	36.5
Bauxite	1314	21666	6.1
Tin	34851	34851	100.0

Source: District Statistical Hand Book, 2013.

Table 7.14: District wise Availability of Various Minerals

District	*Minerals*	*Source Area*
Korea	Coal	Sonhat, Chirmiri, Jilmili
Sarguja	Coal	Tatapani, Ramcola, Lakhanpur, Vishrampur
	Bauxite	Mainpat, Samripat
Jashpur	Bauxite	Jashpur (Bagicha and Jashpur Tahshil)
	Gypsum	Jashpur Tahshil
	Gold	Kunkuri and Patthal
Raigarh	Coal	Karsiya, Dharmjaygarh, Garhghora, Raigarh
	Limestone	(Area of Madh River Coal) Saranggarh and Karsiya
Korba	Coal	Gavra, Deepika, Kushmunda, Korba, Hasdo
	Bauxite	Rampur, Balgi, Bankimongra Phutkapahadh, Pawankherapahadh, Kamselapahadh, Korba
Janjgir- Champa	Limestone Dolomite	Agartala, Pamgarh Tahshil Champadhabra, Akartala
Bilaspur	Dolomite	Bilha, Kota
	Limestone	Bilha
	Manganese	Kota
	Bauxite	Pendra and Lormi
	Iron Alloys	Pendra
	Gypsum	Pendra
Kawardha	Bauxite	Kawardha and Pandariya
	Chuhi	Kawardha
	Limestone	Kawardha
Rajnandgoan	Limestone	Khairagarh, Chhikhadan and Rajnandgoan
	Iron Alloys	Khairagarh, Chhikhadan and Mohla
	Gold	Rajnandgoan
	Silver	Rajnandgoan and Mohla
	Quartzite	Dongargarh Mohla
Durg	Uranium	Dalirajhara, Dondi Lohara
	Iron Alloys	Durg, Gunderdahi, Gurur, Dhamdha
	Limestone	Manpur and Devbhog
Raipur	Diamond,Granit	Manpur and Devbhog
	Corrundum & Gold	Navapara, Rajim and Navagaon
	Limestone	Raipur,Bhatapara,Tilda and Bhilaigarh
Mahasamund	Limestone	Saraipalli,Mahasamund
Dhamtari	Khadiya	Dhamtari
Kanker	Bauxite	Antagarh
	Iron Alloys	Bhanupratappur
	Gold	Pankhajur
Bastar	Iron Alloys	Narayanpur
	Gold	Narayanpur
	Bauxite	Narayanpur

(*Contd...*)

	Limestone	Jagdalpur
	Copper	Narayanpur
	Dolomite	Jagdalpur
Dantewada	Iron Alloys	Bailadilla and Raoghat
	Copper	Bijapur, Bhopalpatnam and Dantewada
	Limestone	Konta, Dantewada
	Quartzite	Dantewada
	Dolomite	Konta
	Gold	Konta
	Tin Alloys	Konta and Dantewada
	GraniteKorandam	BhopalpatnamBhopalpatnam and Konta
	Alexandrite	Dantewada

Source: District Statistical Hand Book, 2013.

7.1.3 Agriculture

Chhattisgarh is known as the *"rice bowl"* of central India. Chhattisgarh used to produce over seventy percent of the total paddy production in the state. Apart from paddy, cereals like maize, kodo-kutki and other small millets, pulses like tur and kulthi and oilseeds like groundnut, soyabean, niger and sunflower are also grown. Chhattisgarh produced nearly half of all food grains, and one third of all major craps were grown in the undivided Madhya Pradesh during the kharif season. The main rabi crops of Chhattisgarh are jower, gram, urad, mong and moth. Chhattisgarh produced 45 percent of the jower and over eighty percent of the gram which was produced in undivided Madhya Pradesh. Chhattisgarh produced very little wheat. A quarter of all produce of pulses in Madhya Pradesh during the rabi season comes from Chhattisgarh. There are very few cash crops grown in Chhattisgarh and there is a need to diversify the agriculture produce towards oilseeds and other cash crops.

Table 7.15: Climatic Zones

Agro-climatic Zone	*Districts*
Chhattisgarh Plains	Raipur, Gariyaband, Baloda Bazaar, Mahasamind, Dhamtari, Durg, Bemetara, balod, Rajnandgaon, Kabirdham, Bilaspur, Mungeli, Korba, Janjgr and part of Kanker district (Narayanpur and Kanker block) along with part of Raigarh district.
Bastar Plateau	Jagdalpur, Kondagaon, Dantewada, Bijapur, Narayanpur and remaining part of Kanker district
Northern Hills	Surguja, Surajpur, Balrampur, Korea, Jaspur and Dharamjagarh tehsil of Raigarh district.

Table 7.16: Area Under Major Crops (In Thousand Hectares)

Crop	*Year*			
	2010-11	*2011-12*	*2012-13*	*2013-14*
Cereal	3937.8	3939.9	3982.2	3987.7
Paddy	103.7	104.8	102.2	105.0
Wheat	5.7	5.3	6.2	5.2
Jowar	104.9	107.4	116.8	123.4
Maize	127.9	121.6	111.1	102.4
Kodo-Kutki	2.3	2.9	2.8	2.7
Small Millet	39.2	37.7	34.5	33.0
Pulses				
Gram	250.5	260.2	267.9	289.7
Tuar	54.5	52.9	51.9	52.8
Urad	107.1	102	98.7	96.9
Moong	16.3	15.4	15.5	15.2
Kulthi	50.9	48.7	47.6	45.9
Lakh (Tiwda)	359.2	347.6	331.8	315.2
Sugarcane	15.4	17.5	23	23.9
Oilseed				
Groundnut	29.6	28.7	29.4	29.2
Ram Till	69.4	66.5	66.2	63.6
Till	20.5	19.7	19.7	17.0
Soyabean	95.8	103.2	101.5	107.8
Linseed	37	35.3	32.2	31.2
Mustard	50.2	49.2	47	47.5

Source: District Statistical Hand Book, 2013.

The climate of the state is sub-humid and it receives about 1200-1600 mm of average annual rainfall. Of this, 90 percent is received during the south west monsoon season. The monsoon sets in June in the southernmost tip of Bastar district and by 25th June it covers all parts of Chhattisgarh. The main crops of Northern hills are rice, jowar, maize, tuar, groundnut, alsi, sugarcan etc. The average productivity of some important crops in the three agro-climatic zones is shown in given table:

Table 7.17: Productivity of Crops (unit: kg/ha)

Crop	*Chhattisgarh Plain*	*Bastar Plateau*	*Northern Hills*
Rice (rainfed)	1107	1016	1019
Rice (irrigated)	1649	1797	1894
Total Rice	1314	1041	1019
Lathyrus	494	-	-
Maize	-	1586	1142
Rape-Mustard	-	637	566
Wheat	1475	-	1521
Gram	662	624	533

Source: District Statistical Hand Book, 2013.

According to government estimate, net sown area of the state is 4.828 million hectare and the gross sown area is 5.786 million hectare. About 80 percent of the population of the state is rural and the main livelihood of the villagers is agriculture and agriculture based small industry.

Table 7.18: Land Use Pattern of Chhattisgarh

Land Use	*Area (in hectare)*	*Percentage*
Total Geographical Area	13789836	100
Area Under Forest	6331274	45.91
Land Not Available For cultivation	1027061	7.45
Other Cultivated Land Excluding Fallow Land	1231871	8.93
Fallow Land	513907	3.72
Total Cultivated Land with Fallow Land	1745778	12.66
Net Sown Area	4685723	33.98
Area Sown More Than Once	1011984	7.34
Gross Area Sown	5697707	41.31

Source: District Statistical Hand Book, 2013.

7.1.4 Flora and Fauna

Chhattisgarh state has almost subtropical humid climate, a climate good to support a rich biodiversity. The state has teak, sal and mixed forests as climax communities. Further, more than 40 percent of its land area is covered with forests. However, only a fragmentary knowledge of biodiversity of the state is there. In the animal kingdom, richness component of almost all the mammals is known. Some listing of amphibia and fishes are also available, but for other groups of animals, very little or almost no record is available. Similarly among plants Botanical Survey of India has published Flora for some of the districts of the state. There are several publications on the medicinal plants and some publications on the edible mushrooms of the state, but, for other groups of plants, although, some research work has been done in the universities but there are no published records of their wealth.

Some distinct varieties of common birds are also found in Bastar. For instance, the Jungle Crow is pitch dark and slightly larger than the domestic crow. It has a heavy duty bill and a deep and hoarse "caw". It is more audacious in attacking the nests of gentler birds and even the pups of smaller animals. Its movement in the forest often leads to tiger or panther kills. Other species of avifauna include partridges (which nest in shrubs outside villages and run almost as fast as they fly), cattle egret, pond heron, babblers, parrots and parakeets, blue jay, wagtails, quails (both black and grey varieties), bulbul, koel, fly catchers, woodpeckers, sun bird and weaver bird. Major wildlife species include blue bull, Chinkara, black buck, Sambhar, Barking Deer, wild dog, wild boar, jackals, hyena, and crocodiles. Tigers are in the Kurandi reserve forest and in the Kanger Valley National Park. Panthers are distributed almost all over Bastar, especially in the Northern plains. Indian sloth bears are in the Northern plains around Kanker and in the Southern part around Bailadila. Bison are in the Kutru National Park. Crocodiles are in the riverine ponds in the Kanger Valley National Park at Bhaisadarha.

7.1.4.1 Flora

The forest products that are produced are Teak *(Tectona grandis)*, Sal *(Shorea robusta)*, Bamboo, Sheesham, Mahua, Tamarind, Haldu, Saja, Sheesham *(Dalbergia sissoo)* and various herbs. Tiger, Leopard, Cheetal, Sambhar, Nilgai, Gaur *(Bison)* and Wild Buffalos.

Table 7.19: List of Endangered Taxa of the State

Scientific Name	*Family*
Alstonia venneta R.Br.	Apocynaceae
Balospermum montanum Muell – Arg	Euphorbiaceae
Barleria lupulina Lindl	Acnathaceae
Begonia picta Sm.	Begoniaceae

(*Contd...*)

Berberis asiatica Roxb. ex DC.	Berberidaceae
Butea monosperma var. Lutea	Papilionaceae
Celastrus paniculata Willd.	Celastraceae
Chlorophytum arundinaceum Baker	Liliaceae
Chlorophytum tuberosum Baker	Liliaceae
Clerodendrum serratum (l) Moon	Verbenaceae
Cordia rothii Roem & Schult	Boraginaceae
Costus speciosus (Koen.)	Zingiberaceae
Crateriostigma plantaagineum Hochst	Scrophulariaceae
Curculigo orchioides Gaertn.	Amaryllidaceae
Curculigo angustifolia Roxb.	Zingiberaceae
Curcuma aromatica Salish	Zingiberaceae
Curcuma caesia Roxb.	Zingiberaceae
Cymbidium aloifolium Sw.	Orchidaceae
Embelia tsjerian-cottam A.Dc.	Myrsinaceae
Entada phaseoloides Merrill.	Mimosaceae
Eryngium foeditum L.	Apiaceae
Euphorbia fusiformis Buch-Ham.	Euphorbiaceae
Geodorum dialatatum R.Br.	Orchidaceae
Gloriosa superba L.	Liliaceae
Grewia rothii DC.	Tiliaceae
Gymnema sylvestre R.Br.	Asclepiadaceae
Hedyschium cronarium Koenig ex Retz	Zingiberaceae
Marsdenia tencissima (Roxb) Moon	Asclepiadaceae
Neolitsia chinensis (Lamk.) Chun	Lauraceae
Operculina turpethum	Convolvulaceae
Oryza meyeriana Mailli ssp. graulata Tateoka	Poaceae
Peucedaman dhana Buch-Ham.ex Clarke	Apiaceae
Phrynium imbricatum Roxb.	Zingiberaceae
Plumbago zeylanica L.	Plumbaginaceae
Pterocarpus marsupium Roxb.	Fabaceae
Pygmaeopremna herbacea (Roxb) Moldenke	Verbenaceae
Rauvolfia serpentina Benth. ex. Kurz.	Apocynaceae
Spilanthus calva DC.	Asteraceae
Strychnous potatorum L.f.	Loganiaceae
Swertia angustifolia Buch-Ham.ex D.Don	Gentianaceae
Tacca leontopetaloides (L.)Kuntze	Taccaceae
Trachyspermum sytctocarpum (Clarke)Wolff	Apiaceae
Tylophora indica (Burm.f.)Merr.	Asclepiadaceae
Urginea indica (Kunth.) Roxb.	Liliaceae
Zanthoxylum rhesta (Roxb.) DC.	Rutaceae

Table 7.20: Endemic and Rare Flora of Chhattisgarh State

Name of the Flora	***Location/ Remarks***
Sophora bakeri	Restricted to the cooler parts of Jashpur
Crotalaria trifoliastrum	Recorded from Raigarh
Uraria prunellaefolia	Collected from Bastar forests in 1952 and believed to be extinct.
Mucuna imbricata, Vigna pisosa	Rare species collected from marshes of Bhudeopur (Raigarh)
Nogra and Lespideza sps.	Recorded from Jashpur division
Hoya wrighitii	Large perennial climber, totally epiphytic, Found in Bailadilla hills
Desmodium tortosum	Endemic in the State
Erythrina resupinata	Getting rare and found only in a few marshy Places in the State.

7.1.4.2 Fauna

Biogeographically, the State is under Deccan Bioregion comprising of the representative fauna of Central India. The Tiger *(Panthera tigris)*, Leopard *(Panthera pardus)*, Gaur *(Bos gaurus)*, Sambhar *(Cervus unicolor)*, Chital *(Axis axis)*, Nilgai *(Boselaphus tragocamelus)* and Wild Boar *(Sus scrofa)* are specific fauna. The State is a proud possessor of rare wildlife like the Wild Buffalo *(Bubalus bubalis)* and Hill Myna *(Gracula religiosa)*, which have been declared as rare and endangered.

7.1.5 Arts and Culture of Chhattisgarh

Majority of the population in Chhattisgarh comprises of the local tribal groups. *Gonds* form the largest group among these natural residents of the land followed by *Oraon, Kanwar, Birhar Saura*, Role and so many other tribes. It also has a good percentage of schedule castes and other backward classes. This apart, it also has a sizable migrant population with migrations taking place from all over the country through centuries. Now these migrant groups are a part of the cultural milieu that the cultural milieu that the state present. Religiously, majority of the people are Hindus, Christians and Muslims comprise only a small part.

Table 7.21:Paintings and Crafts of Chhattisgarh

Traditional Paintings	***Handicrafts***
Pithora Painting	Wrought Iron
Rangoli	Wood Craft
Savnahi	Clay Art (Terracotta Art)

(Contd...)

Athekanhaiya	Carpet Weaving
Hartalika	Kosa Silk
Govardhan Painting	Stone Craft
Gharsingar	Tumba
Nohdora	Doll and Toy Making
Tatoo Making	Bamboo Craft

7.1.6 Dance & Music of Chhattisgarh

Chhattisgarh often resounds and reverberates with the beats of the drum. Country dances are the chief source of amusement. Dance and music forms of this state have very close relation to its tribal heritage and culture that they are practicing from the time immemorial. Major music forms of the state are Pandwani singing, Chandeni, and Bhathari. Some of the popular dance forms of the state are Panthi Dance, Nacha, Gond and Muria.

Ghotul is a better known event in tribal life and they have aroused considerable interest from anthropologists to study the tradition. Both boys and girls are allowed to spend a night out in the ghotul (kind of rest house), every week. Ghotuls are regarded as a shrine, built by Lingo Pen, a Gond (a tribe) cult hero. Here, the unmarried boys of the village learn songs and dance from their leader. Besides, every week, there is a dance carnival as well in which the girls also take part. Moreover, it is treated like a pilgrimage.

Table 7.22: Folk Dances and Songs of Chhattisgarh

Dances
• Gaur Maria Nritya
• *Pandwani* Gayan
• Bhartari Gayan
• Lok Natya Nacha
• Gammat
• Karma
• Kaksar
• Soowa Dance
• Raut Dance
• Panthi

(Contd...)

Folk Songs
• Sohar
• Bihav
• Pathoni
• Bhadoni
• Sawnahi
• Cher Chera
• Sua songs
• Mata Seva: Gaura
• Dohe Songs, Danda Song
• Janvara, Dewar Song
• Bhojali
• Dhankul
• Nagpanchami
• Loriya
• Fugdi, Kau Mau, Khuduwa, Dandi Pouha

Table 7.23: Musical Instruments and Their Uses

Dhol	It is made up of wood, this is fully covered with animal skin (goat). This is generally used in *Shaila* and *Faag* dances.
Nagada	On several occasions, this is used by the yamars and dholakias in tribal regions. This is especially used for *Faag.* Nagadas are beaten with sticks of wood or iron.
Algoja	This resembles a flute with three or four holes and is used by herders or in fairs.
Khanjedi	When three or four pairs of bells are attached with *dholak*, it takes the form of *Khanjedi.* This is played with hands.
Dholak	This is another form of dhol. Made up of wood, it is fully covered with leather on both sides. It is used during *Faag* and *Bhajan,Pandwani etc.*
Tasha	It is made up of soil, this too is covered with animal skin and is played with thin wood stick. This is used along with *Nagada* during *Faag.*
Flute	Generally used by the people of Rawat caste, this instrument is used on the occasion of Bharthari and Pandwani.
Karthal	Made up of long round wood sticks, it has two parts and is played with both hands. Again, this is used for Pandwani and bhajans.
Jhanjh	It is made up of iron into two pieces, with a hole in between. The pieces are held in both hands and then played.
Manjira	A small *Jhanjh* is often called *Manjira.* It is made up of metal and is used during *Bhajans, Faag* etc.
Monhari	Like flute, it is made up of wood and has six holes. At one end, it is covered with bronze.
Sing Baaja	This is the main instrument of *gadwa baja.* The horns of singa animal are attached to it; therefore, it is called *Sing Baaja* by the tribals.

7.1.7 Festivals and Fairs of Chhattisgarh

Chhattisgarh is one the most fascinating and colorful states of India. Known for its exceptional scenic beauty and the unique tribal populations, Chhattisgarh has a number of vivid and colorful festivals, held all round the year. The famous and widely celebrated festivals of Chhattisgarh include the Dusshera, Deepavali, Holi, Govardhan Pooja, Pola, Nawakhai and many others are celebrated with great vividness and festivity.

Dusshera is the most famous festivals of Chhattisgarh and is celebrated with great fanfare in Bastar region. Madai festival is another famous festival of Bastar region held in the different villages extending from Mandla of Bastar. It's quite popular among Gond tribes of Bastar and thousands of devotees gather under the shade of a sacred tree to sacrifice a goat to the mother goddess and the whole nights is spent in dancing, eating and making merry. Hariyali, Kora, Navakhani and Cherta Festivals are the most important agricultural festivals of Chhattisgarh. Chhattisgarh also organizes many colorful fairs in different towns and cities of the state, all round the year. Chakradhar Festival (September or October), Goncha Festival (July), Narayanpur Mela (last week of February) and Sheorinarayan Fair (February) are other widely celebrated and most enjoyed fair and festivals of Chhattisgarh.

Table 7.24: Major Festivals and Fairs of the State

Festivals	*Fairs*
Bastar Lokotsav	Champaran Mela
Madai Festival	Rajiv Lochan Mahotsav
Bhoramdeo Festival	The Bhagoriya Fair
Goncha Festival	The Chakradhar Fair
The Earth Festival	The Narayanpur Mela
First Fruit Festival	
Chakradhar Samaroh	
Hareli	
Teeja Pola Festival	
Fagun Madai	

7.2 Bastar

Traditionally the area is mentioned as Dandakaranya in the epic *Ramayana*, and part of the Kosala Kingdom in the *Mahabharata*. Around 450 AD, Bastar state was ruled by Nala King, Bhavadatta Varman, who is mentioned to have invaded the neighboring Vakataka kingdom, during the reign of its King, Narendrasena (440-460). The princely state of Bastar was established around 1324 AD, when Annama Deva, brother of the last Kakatiya King, Pratapa Rudra Deva (1290-1325), left Warangal and established his kingdom at Bastar under the tutelage of local goddess, 'Dantheshwari', who still is the tutelary deity of Bastar region, her famous Dantheshwari Temple stands today at Danthewada, also named after her. Annama Deva ruled till 1369 when he was followed successively by Hamir Deva (r. 1369-1410), Bhaitai Deva (1410–1468), Purushottama Deva (1468–1534) and Pratapa Raja Deva (1602–1625) after which the Bastar branch of the dynasty became extinct in the third generation with Dikpala Deva (1680–1709), after which a descendant of the younger brother of Prataparaja Deva, Rajapala Deva became the next King in 1709. Rajapala Deva had two wives, first a Baghela Princess, married, who had a son, Dakhin Singh, secondly, a Chandela Princess, who has two sons, Dalapati Deva and Pratap.Trouble however struck again when after the death of Rajapala Deva in 1721, the elder queen ousted other claimants and placed her brother on the throne of Bastar, Dalapati Deva took refuge in the neighboring kingdom of Jeypore and finally regained his throne a decade later in 1731. Its capital was Jagdalpur, where Bastar royal palace built by its ruler, when its capital was shifted here from old capital Bastar.

Later at some point in the 15th century Bastar was divided into two kingdoms, one based in Kanker and the other ruled from Jagdalpur. The present Halba Tribe claims to descend from the military class of these kingdoms. Until the rise of the Marathas, the state remained fairly independent until 18th century. In 1861, Bastar became part of the newly formed Central Provinces and Barer, and in 1863, after years of feud, over the Kotapad region; it was given over to the neighboring Jeypore state in 1863, on the condition of payment of tribute of Rs. 3,000, two thirds of which sum was remitted from the amount payable by Bastar. By virtue of this arrangement the tribute of Bastar was, reduced to a nominal amount. Pravir Chandra Bhanj Deo (1929–1966), the 20th and the last ruling head of the Bastar state, ascended the throne in 1936, before it acceded to India in 1948 during the political integration of India.Maharaja pravir Chandra Bhanj Deo was immensely popular among the tribal.

7.2.1 Demographics

According to the 2011 census Bastar district has a population of 1,411,644, roughly equal to the nation of Swaziland or the US state of Hawaii. This gives it a ranking of 348th in India (out of a total of 640). The district has a population density of 140 inhabitants per square kilometre (360/sq mi). Its population growth rate over the decade 2001-2011 was 17.83 percent. Bastar has a sex ratio of 1024 females for every 1000 males, and a literacy rate of 54.94 percent.

In 1981 Bastar had a population of 1,842,854 with 1,249,197 of the residents being members of scheduled tribes. This also represented about 70 percent of the population. However these figures are for the pre 1999 Bastar District which had the same boundaries as the modern Bastar Division.

Table 7.25: Demographics of Bastar

Description	***Year***	
	2011	**2001**
Actual Population	1,411,644	1,198,067
Male	697,359	595,779
Female	714,285	602,288
Population Growth	17.83%	18.18%
Area Sq. Km	10,083	10,083
Density/km2	140	119
Proportion to Chhattisgarh Population	5.53%	5.75%
Sex Ratio (Per 1000)	1024	1011
Child Sex Ratio (0-6 Age)	991	1009
Average Literacy	54.94	44.27
Male Literacy	65.70	56.75
Female Literacy	44.49	31.93
Total Child Population (0-6 Age)	212,819	210,110
Male Population (0-6 Age)	106,904	104,572
Female Population (0-6 Age)	105,915	105,538
Literates	658,587	437,362
Male Literates	387,907	278,762
Female Literates	270,680	158,600
Child Proportion (0-6 Age)	15.08%	17.54%
Boys Proportion (0-6 Age)	15.33%	17.55%
Girls Proportion (0-6 Age)	14.83%	17.52%

Source: Census of India, 2001 & 2011.

7.2.2 Languages

Languages spoken include Halbi, Gondi, even Chhattisgari Bhatri, which falls within the Odia language group but only shares about 60 percent lexical similarity with Oriya, spoken by about 600 000.

7.2.3 Economy

Rice is grown predominantly during kharif season as rain fed crop having 2.38.9 million hectare area but the productivity of this crop is low 08.53 qt/ha in Bastar region of Chhattisgarh. The irrigated area (1.67 percent) and fertilizer use (4.6 kg/ha.) in the Bastar district are very less, which is insufficient to supply adequate nutrient to the crop.

The pattern of livelihood in Bastar continues to be dictated by tradition. Even today, agricultural practices are traditional. Use of wooden ploughs is overwhelming while the number of iron ploughs is negligible. The same is true of bullock carts. The number of tractors is negligible while the bullock carts are all pervasive.

The usage of traditional agricultural implements has lowered the production of agriculture. The kharif crops grown here are paddy, urad, arhar, jowar and maize. The rabi crops include til, alsi, moong, mustard and gram. Collection and sale of forest produce and other forest related work supplements meager agricultural incomes.

Most people do not find employment all year round. The cycle of floods and droughts makes livelihoods extremely vulnerable. The people are often forced to resort to moneylenders in times of crisis, which usually means a life of continued indebtedness. The absence of alternate employment opportunities is responsible for the high incidence of poverty in the area. In the Bastar plateau, irrigation coverage is only 1.2 percent. Exceptionally fortunate in its water resources, the region has good rainfall and rapid run off due to the undulating terrain. There is potential for rainwater harvesting. Forty percent of livelihoods are forest based, 30 percent are agriculture based and 15 percent of livelihoods are dependent on animal husbandry. Another 15 percent of the income of people comes from wage labour.

Table 7.26: Occupation

Tahsil	*Farmers*		*Labors*		*Family Industries*		*Other Working*		*Main Working*	
	Male	*Female*	*Male*	*Female*	*Male*	*Female*	*Male*	*Female*	*Male*	*Female*
Jagdalpur	9735	2150	5834	3160	768	245	31692	7054	12609	5575
Bastar	20668	4003	6178	2556	590	159	4120	852	7570	7855
Bakawand	16745	2248	6016	1656	577	153	4947	866	4923	8368
Lohandiguda	12710	3420	1828	1242	173	67	1022	345	5074	3081
Tokapal	9365	2535	2375	1516	284	144	2902	769	4964	5134
Bastanar	10340	3653	196	128	105	18	593	207	4006	1588
Darbha	14242	7062	1810	1229	409	164	1322	463	8918	3088

Source: Jila Vyapar Avum Udyog Kendra Bastar.

7.2.4 Agriculturists

People with land, who depend almost entirely on cultivation, either on their own holdings or on the holdings of others. They supplement their income and consumption with animal husbandry and sundry labour at times. Some of them have also diversified into small services or small manufacturing activities.

7.2.5 Labourers

People without their own land or with very little land. They survive by working as farm and casual labour. They also work in the nonfarm sector, in mines, small shops, on construction sites and as part of the urban work force.

7.2.6 Agriculturists and Forest Gatherers

Those with some land, and living in the vicinity of forests. In areas adjacent to the forests, most people (including those who own some land) gather minor forest produce. A major part of the household consumption and income is based on forest gathering, with agricultural activities providing supplementary income.

7.2.7 Forest Gatherers and Labourers

People living close to the forests with very little land or without their own land. They are primarily dependent on forest produce, which they gather and sell or directly consume. Occasional labour on fields or in the forest supplements their income. Sometimes they migrate to other places to sell their labour. Forests play an important role in the lives of the people, providing food security and livelihood through the collection of minor forest produce, and employment (as casual labour) in the Forest Department. The forests provide for people's consumption needs– fuel and firewood, medicines, food and drink, implements and housing materials

7.2.8 Manufacturers

These are traditional occupation based producers. These include the weavers, the blacksmiths, carpenters, chattai (woven mats of bamboo or other grasses) weavers and tailors, bamboo craftsmen and the potters. They operate in the cottage or household sectors, in tiny units, which may be family, owned and worked, or may even have some contracted workers. Some people have taken to modern manufacturing, operating electrical repair or lathe shops. These are located in the big villages or along main roads.

Table 7.27: Industries And Investments

Year	*Through Jila Udhyog Kendra*			*Through Khadi Gramodyog*			*Total*		
	Units	*Employment*	*Average Invest-ments [in lakhs]*	*Units*	*Employment*	*Avg Invest-ments [in Lakhs]*	*Units*	*Employment*	*Avg Invest-ments [in Lakhs]*
2006-07	40	260	7	157	554	4	197	814	4
2007-08	24	238	10	160	586	4	184	824	4
2008-09	20	120	6	157	373	2	177	493	3
2009-10	16	148	9	210	758	4	226	906	4
2010-11	15	96	6	-	-	-	75	96	6

7.2.9 Service Persons

These include traditional as well as modern service providers. This group is bridging traditional livelihoods and new opportunities, sometimes replacing but often merging with each other. It is a growing segment, its expansion fuelled by the need for manufacturers and users to establish common ground. It tends to be based on simple and easily understood transactions.

Entry barriers and requirements are few. Even as the demand for some services is declining for those offered by cobblers, for example, there are newer trades that are springing up car and tractor mechanics, for instance, based on apprenticeship and 'on the job training' systems. The processes of skill acquisition tend to break social and cultural barriers, as people work together at dhabas, (food stalls) workshops and construction sites.

7.2.10 Organised Sector

People with jobs in the public/ private organised sector typically requiring formal education, this segment includes public sector service and employment in offices, industries and educational institutions and in development related services.

7.2.11 Major Industries

There are some major industries in Chhattisgarh which are playing their vital role for the development of local people:

7.2.11.1 Nagarnar Steel Plant

National Mineral Development Corporation (NMDC) is setting up a 3 MTPA capacity Greenfield Integrated Steel Plant in Nagarnar, located 16 km from Jagdalpur, with an estimated outlay of Rs 210 billion. The land for the plant has already been acquired as of August 2010 and as of February 2012, five major packages of the steel plant have already been awarded to internationally acclaimed companies at a cost of around Rs. 65 billion.

7.2.11.2 Tata Steel Plant

Tata Steel had inked the deal with the Chhattisgarh Government in June 2005 to set up a green field integrated steel plant at Lohandiguda, about 20 km from Jagdalpur. The proposed 5.5-million tonne per annum plant has an estimated outlay of Rs 195 billion. An environment ministry panel has recommended the diversion of forest land for the steel plant in a decision that was taken in the meeting of a Forest Advisory Committee (FAC) of the Ministry of Environment and Forests (MoEF), Government of India.

7.2.11.3 Lambodhar Cement Products

LCP is situated in Kasturi near Nagarnar. The owner of these factories is Chavi Narayan Sethiya. It is 20 km from jagdalpur.

7.2.12 Tribals of Bastar

Bastar, the land of tribes and about 70 percent of the total population of Bastar comprises tribals, which is 26.76 percent of the total tribal population of Chhattisgarh. The major tribes of the Bastar region are the Gond, Abhuj Maria, Bhatra Bhatra are divided into Sub Cast San Bhatra, Pit Bhatra, Amnit Bhatra Amnit Hold Highest Status, Halbaa, Dhurvaa, Muria and Bison Horn Maria. The Gonds of Bastar are one of the most famous tribes in India, known for their unique Ghotul system of marriages. Gonds are also the largest tribal group of central India in terms of population.

The tribes of Bastar region are known for their unique and distinctive tribal culture and heritage in all over the world. Each tribal group in Bastar has their own distinct culture and enjoys their own unique traditional living styles. Each tribe has developed its own dialects and differs from each other in their costume, eating habits, customs, and traditions and even worships different form of god and goddess. A large number of Bastar tribals are still living in deep forests and avoid mixing with outsiders in order to protect their own unique culture. The tribes of Bastar are also known for their colorful festivals and arts and crafts. The Bastar Dussehra is the most famous festival of the region. The tribals of Bastar were also amongst the earliest to work with metal and have expertise in making beautiful figurines of tribal gods, votive animals, oil lamps, carts and animals.

7.2.13 Arts and Crafts

An area where Handicraft is most widely practiced in Bastar is Kondagaon. Many products are made from such art such as vessels, jewellery and the images of the local deities and some decorative. The method of preparation of the products is quite simple and also called as the lost wax technique that happens to be perfect for the tribal settings.

The Bastar district specializes in the preparation of items from the Dhokra Handicraft. This process calls for a great deal of precision and skill. The artifacts prepared from Dhokra technique of this art use the cow dung, paddy husk and red soil in the preparation, beeswax being the most important one. Apart from contouring, wax wires are also used for decoration purpose and for giving a finishing touch to artifacts. From the Bell Metal Handicraft of Chhattisgarh in India, the real genius and creative faculty of the artisans come into picture and thus make for some of the most wonderful pieces of art.

The Dhokra and Bell Metal Handicraft can be found all over the world but the way in which the artisans of Chhattisgarh carve the things by the impression of their sheer dexterity is worth watching. Some of the handicraft items are so appealing that the tourists take them back as souvenirs.

7.2.14 Educational Status

The average literacy rate is not showing satisfactory because it is very below than state and national literacy rate. It can be seen that female and male literacy rate in urban areas are better than rural areas of Bastar. It has been studied from table that the total literacy rate of Jagdalpur is 64.19 percent where female literacy is very low with 14.25 percent which is higher than other blocks.

Table 7.28: Educational Status of Bastar

Literacy Status	*Census*		*Total*	
	2011	**2001**	***Rural***	***Urban***
Average Literacy	54.94 %	44.27 %	50.37 %	82.32 %
Male Literacy	65.70 %	56.75 %	61.64 %	89.42 %
Female Literacy	44.49 %	31.93 %	39.52 %	75.11 %
Literates	658,587	437,362	517,571	141,016
Male Literates	387,907	278,762	310,756	77,151
Female Literates	270,680	158,600	206,815	63,865

Source: Census of India, 2001 & 2011.

Table 7.29: Block Wise Status of Literacy in Bastar District

Blocks Name	*Total*	*Rural Population Literacy %*	
	Literacy %	*Male*	*Female*
Jagdalpur	64.19	49.94	14.25
Bastar	40.72	26.75	12.99
Bakawand	46.3	30.18	15.15
Lohandiguda	31.1	20.35	9.88
Tokpal	37.06	24.33	12.05
Bastnar	11.87	9.1	3.08
Darbha	24.42	16.02	7.5

Source: Census of India, 2001 & 2011.

7.2.15 Study Villages: An Overview

In Chhattisgarh, Bastar District is considered as the largest tribal districtand its villages are abundant with tribal population. Bastar District has over 70 percent tribal population. Around 26.76 percent of the total tribal population of the state resides in this district. For the study purpose Madpal, Nyanar and Dhurguda villages are selected.

7.2.15.1 Madpal Village

Madpal village is located in Jagdalpur Tehsil of Bastar district in Chhattisgarh, India. Jagdalpur is nearest town to Madpal village. It is a large village located in Jagdalpur of Bastar district, Chhattisgarh with total 721 families residing. The village has population of 2938 of which 1405 are males while 1533 are females as per Population Census 2011.The Halba population is dominating in this village. In population of children with age 0-6 is 410 which makes up 13.96 percent of total population of village. Average Sex Ratio of Madpal village is 1091 which is higher than Chhattisgarh state average of 991. Child Sex Ratio for the Madpal as per census is 1060, higher than Chhattisgarh average of 969. Madpal village has lower literacy rate compared to Chhattisgarh. In 2011, literacy rate of Madpal village was 59.14 percent compared to 70.28 percent of Chhattisgarh. In Male literacy stands at 71.14 percent while female literacy rate was 48.18 percent As per constitution of India and Panchyati Raaj Act, Madpal village is administrated by Sarpanch (Head of Village) who is elected representative of village.

Table 7.30: Demography of Madpal

Variables	*Total*	*Male*	*Female*
Total No. of Houses	721	-	-
Population	2,938	1,405	1,533
Child (0-6)	410	199	211
Schedule Caste	186	96	90
Schedule Tribe	1,228	593	635
Literacy	59.14 %	71.14	48.18
Total Workers	889	720	169
Main Worker	508	0	0
Marginal Worker	381	331	50

7.2.15.2 Nyanar Village

Nayanar is a medium size village located in Keskal of Bastar district, Chhattisgarh with total 143 families residing. The Nayanar village has population of 750 of which 365 are males while 385 are females as per Population Census 2011. In Nayanar village population of children with age 0-6 is 121 which makes up 16.13 percent of total population of village. Average Sex Ratio of Nayanar village is 1055 which is higher than Chhattisgarh state average of 991. Child Sex Ratio for the Nayanar as per census is 681, lower than Chhattisgarh average of 969. Nayanar village has lower literacy rate compared to Chhattisgarh. In 2011, literacy rate of

Nayanar village was 33.55 percent compared to 70.28 percent of Chhattisgarh. In Nayanar Male literacy stands at 45.05 percent while female literacy rate was 23.51 percent. As per constitution of India and Panchyati Raaj Act, Nayanar village is administrated by Sarpanch (Head of Village) who is elected representative of village.

Table 7.31: Demography of Nyanar

Variables	*Total*	*Male*	*Female*
Total No. of Houses	143	-	-
Population	750	365	385
Child (0-6)	121	72	49
Schedule Caste	-	-	-
Schedule Tribe	731	355	376
Literacy	33.55	45.05	23.51
Total Workers	468	227	241
Main Worker	187	-	-
Marginal Worker	281	80	201

Source: District Statistical Hand Book, 2013.

7.2.15.3 Dhurguda Village

This village was 58.56 percent compared to 70.28 percent of Chhattisgarh. In Dhurguda Male literacy Dhurguda is a medium size village located in Jagdalpur of Bastar district, Chhattisgarh with total 383 families residing. The village has population of 1607 of which 783 are males while 824 are females as per Population Census 2011. Dhurwa peoples are present here abundantly.In Dhurguda village population of children with age 0-6 is 217 which makes up 13.50 percent of total population of village. Average Sex Ratio is 1052 which is higher than Chhattisgarh state average of 991. Child Sex Ratio for the Dhurguda as per census is 1067, higher than Chhattisgarh average of 969. The village has lower literacy rate compared to Chhattisgarh. In 2011, literacy rate of this stands at 68.58 percent while female literacy rate was 49.02 percent.

Table 7.32: Demography of Dhurguda

Variables	*Total*	*Male*	*Female*
Total No. of Houses	383	-	-
Population	1607	783	824
Child (0-6)	217	105	112
Schedule Caste	0	0	0

(Contd...)

Schedule Tribe	1072	552	550
Literacy	58.56	68.58	49.02
Total Workers	720	457	263
Main Worker	460	0	0
Marginal Worker	260	110	150

Source: Census of India, 2011.

7.2.16 Tribals of Bastar

Bastar, the land of tribes and about 70 percent of the total population of Bastar comprises tribals, which is 26.76 percent of the total tribal population of Chhattishgarh. The major tribes of the Bastar region are the Gond, Maria, Bhatra, Muriya, Halba, Dhurwa. The tribes of Bastar region are known for their unique and distinctive tribal culture and heritage in all over the world. Each tribal group in Bastar has their own distinct culture and enjoys their own unique traditional living styles. Each tribe has developed its own dialects and differs from each other in their costume, eating habits, customs, traditions and even worships different form of god and goddess. A large number of Bastar tribals are still living in deep forests and avoid mixing with outsiders in order to protect their own unique culture. The tribes of Bastar are also known for their colorful festivals and arts and crafts. The Bastar Dussehra is the most famous festival of the region. The tribals of Bastar were also amongst the earliest to work with metal and have expertise in making beautiful figurines of tribal gods, votive animals, oil lamps, carts and animals.

7.2.16.1 Bison Horn Maria

It is one of the famous tribal groups of India. Mostly found in Chhattisgarh's Bastar region they are a major sub- caste of a tribal community called Gond. Apart from the Jagdalpur tehsil towards the south of river Indrawati in the state of Chhattisgarh, they mainly reside in the district of Garhichiroli in Maharashtra as well as some parts of Madhyapradesh. They introvert nature makes

them live in isolation in the interiors of dense forest areas of these states. Main distinct language spoken by this tribe of Chhattisgarh is Dandami Maria. Some of them even speak mutually unintelligible Gondi dialects, which is an oral language of Dravidian origin. Most of the members of this community of Bison Horn follow the tradition and customs of the Hindu religion.

7.2.16.2 Gond

The Gonds tribals, who are recognized as the koytorias are widely dispersed throughout the state. However, they meanly predominate the dense forests enclosed in Southern Chhattisgarh's Bastar district that accounts for more than 20 per cent of Chhattisgarh population. The three principal sub-castes of the aboriginal Gonds are the Dorla, Muria and Muria races. The unique and one of a kind Ghotul marriage tradition of the Gonds is renowned all across the world.

7.2.16.3 Muriya

The Murias are one of the innumerable tribes that inhabit Chhattisgarh. They are a prominent sub-caste of the Gonds, who dominant the populace of Chhattisgarh. The Muria tribesmen primary reside in the dense forest zones of Narayanpur tehsil and Kondagaon tehsil of Bastar district, the home of majority of the tribals.

The Muria economy is predominantly agrarian. They cultivate rice in plenty. Some Muria tribals also depend up on collecting forest products. The forest products are not only used to make useful products, the edible part are also consumed by the poverty ridden tribals. In case of illness and maladies, they seek the remedial powers of the Mahua plant.

The tribals are a highly superstitious a lot, who believe in worshipping the cult Gods and Goddesses. The Muria society is devoid of a caste system and the people also practice magic, dark arts and wizardry. Their society is quite progressive and although Ghotul marriages are the common practice.

7.2.16.4 Abujhmaria

The Abujhmaria race of tribal people is one of the principal sub-castes of the Gond tribals. They live in isolated and inhabit the scheduled enclaves of Narayanpur tehsil of Bastar district. The area inhabited by the

Abujhmaria tribals is a dense forest that spreads across nearly 1500 miles of lush greenery.

The Abujhmaria tribals are very much feared by mankind. They are a primitive race, whose mannerisms are rather ferocious. The savage and barbaric tribesmen are hostile to strangers and sometimes directly shoot them with their arrows. The tribal people are scantily clad and simple cover themselves with a loincloth. However, they are very fond of traditional ethnic jewellery; they adorn themselves with several iron rings strung around their neck. The women love wearing earring and sometimes pierce as many as 14 holes in their ears and hang two rings or studs from them.

7.2.16.5 Halba

The Halba tribals are widely dispersed all over Chhattisgarh, Maharashtra, Madhya Pradesh and Odisha. One of India's predominant tribes, the Halba tribe inhabits the district of Durg, Bastar and Raipur in Chhattisgarh. Three sub-clans have been integrated to from the Halba tribe. They are namely:

- Chhattisgarh
- Bastaria
- Maratia

The mannerisms and lifestyle of the Halbas, who inhabit Bastar, closely resemble that of their counterpart, who resides in Andhra pradesh's Warangal district. The Halba tribe owes its nomenclature to the term Hal that locally means ploughing or farming. This clearly implies that the Halbas were primarily farmers although now a day they are involved in a myriad of professions of their choice. Of all the tribes that occupy Chhattisgarh, the Halbas are possibly the most affluent and progressive a lot. They also enjoy the privileged status of a high local caste and hence are deeply revered in the tribal society. The unique individuality of the Halbas is evinced by their apparels, dialects and traditional customs what adds to the diversity of their dialect are the pronounced traces of Oriya, Marathi and Chhattisgarhi languages.

7.2.16.6 Bhatra

This tribe is clustered mainly around Bastar and Raipur districts of

Chhattisgarh. Although there are several conjecture and surmises regarding their origin, there is no concrete evidence that solves this mind boggling mystery. The garments worn by the Bhatra tribals are truly one of a kind and their traditions are unparalleled by any other society in the world. It is formed by the conglomeration of the Pit, Sebhatra and Amnet tribes. Live in relationships are surprisingly not an alien or taboo concept in their society. Like all other tribals, the Bhatras too love to enjoy life to the hilt and regale in food, meat, drink, mirth and merriment. The Bhatras are also deeply religious and superstitious races, who believe in the magic of dark, art and sorcery.

7.2.16.7 Dorla

Dorla, also called Dora are a tribal people community found mainly in Bastar area of central India. They are mainly found in Dantewada and Bijapur districts of present day Chhattisgarh state. They were earlier known as *Dor Koi* or *Dora Koi* and as it indicated a slightly inferior status in the society, they gradually changed the name to *Dora* or *Dorla.* They usually undertake agricultural activities and live simply in forested areas and mostly illiterate and have a strong belief in supernatural powers and witchcraft. They also worship native gods or goddess like *Mutta-lamma, Gangamma, Gaman, Kiror* etc. and follow Hindu tradition. They speak *Dorli* or *Dorla* language, which is a Dravidian language and a dialect of Koya language. Dorla people used to collect forest produces like *tendu* leaves which is used to manufacture *beedi* and harassed by forest contractors while trading *tendu* leaves and some members of tribe like Bhadranna joined Maoist groups to fight for justice to their community. Bhadranna fought with Maoists and returned to main stream after his surrender but several others still continue.

7.2.16.8 Dhurwa

The Dhurwas are possibly the most significant indigenous tribe that occupies the domicile of Chhattisgarh's Bastar district. In terms of social hierarchy, the Dhurwas rank second only after the elite Bhatra tribe. The Dhurwas are also recognised by the popular *nom de plume* parjas that locally mean the public. However the tribesmen prefer the nomenclature Dhurwas that in their native dialect means a local village chieftain. The Dhurwas depend upon agriculture for their economic subsistence. The tribal people are also talented craftsmen, whose expertise is manifested by the exquisite handicrafts that they make out of cane and other forest products. They are highly religious, pious and worship several local cult Gods and Goddesses. Mirth and merrymaking are an eminent part of all celebrations and no religious celebration is complete without animal sacrifice and coconut is also offered to mollify the deities.

We are clearly defined the gender related data and socio-demographic status of the study area at state, district and village level which helps to understand the differentials of gender that are prevalent among tribals.

Chapter - VIII

Result and Discussion

Our prehistoric forebears are often portrayed as spear wielding savages, but the earliest human societies are likely to have been founded on enlightened egalitarian principles, according to scientists. Various studies have shown that in contemporary tribals' communities, men and women tend to have equal influence on where their group lives and who they live with. The Culture of each tribe distributes equal work and rights between male and female to manage their society. But in recent trend equality is diminishing by the impact of aculturisation. The findings challenge the idea that sexual equality is a recent invention, suggesting that it has been the norm for humans for most of our evolutionary history.

Mark Dyble, an anthropologist who led the study at University College London, said: "There is still this wider perception that hunter-gatherers are more macho or male dominated. We'd argue it was only with the emergence of agriculture, when people could start to accumulate resources that inequality emerged". Dyble says the latest findings suggest that equality between the sexes may have been a survival advantage and played an important role in shaping human society and evolution. "Sexual equality is one of a important suite of changes to social organisation, including things like pair bonding, our big, social brains, and language, that distinguishes humans," he said. "It's an important one that hasn't really been highlighted before."

In countries where women are imprisoned, tortured, or even put to death for asserting their rights, they are victims of their governments, societies, and cultures. In these countries, change is difficult to accomplish, and often dangerous. In countries where extreme patriarchy exists women are stripped of their rights and dignity. Although these male driven societies revolve around the gender stereo type that men are superior, many of these attitudes stem from religious beliefs, and thousand year old culture, traditions, and rituals that even women have been slow to challenge understandably, out of fear for their own lives, but also out of respect for long-standing values. Women are beaten into submission either physically or psychologically by their societies, may simply accept "that is just the way it is." By this opinion we are trying to find out how tribal women living in their sociocultural norms with inequality.

8.1 Result

Qualitative findings about gender inequality with the analysis and result are based on the tribal's opinion, their way of living, culture and impact of surroundings. With this mindset we observed all the situation of women with different dimentions.

8.1.1 Demography and Socio- economic Position of Women

It is relevant to note that any tribal groups are at the same stage of social and cultural changes towards gender disparity. It has been pointed out regards location of the tribals' areas. There are four types of areas which are given below:

1. These are the tribal groups who are living in remote and inaccessible tribal villages.
2. The groups which have had sufficient interaction with the rural and urban population and in which dominating activity by other communities as well as money lenders and contractors have significantly changed their frame of references.
3. The group of the people who have made adjustments with the rural cum urban social environment and who are already on the way to assimilation into large complex.
4. The groups who have became part of the urban and rural complex and as such are indistinguishable from the other population.

While it is generally agreed that we must give sufficient time to the last three group to get oriented to the modern Indian social life, as a whole, there is a great deal to be said in favour of retaining some of the important form of tribal culture. It is evident that changing pattern of attitudes toward made and female status, are bound to make on roads even into the hard core of the tribal culture as a whole. It may be useful to outline criteria of cultural development as well as gender equality for four groups mentioned above.

8.1.1.1 Number of Household Studied

Out of the 100 surveyed household in the three villages, 50 percent data were collected from Dhurguda. 16 percent and 34 percent data were gathered from Niyanar and Madpal Respectively.

Table 8.1: Village Wise Number of Household Studied

Village	*Surveyed Household*	*%*
Dhurguda	50	50.00
Niyanar	16	16.00
Madpal	34	34.00
Total	**100**	**100.00**

8.1.1.2 Population Composition

Table 8.2 depicted that out of 504 respondents, there were 244 males and 260 females which were covered for the present study. The percentage of female (51.59 percent) was greater than male (48.41 percent).

Table 8.2: Population Composition

Sex	*Number*	*%*
Male	244	48.41
Female	260	51.59\
Total	**504**	**100.00**

8.1.1.3 Age Group

Age distribution table stated that less than 20 percent of the population belongs to 6-10 years for both males and females and 13.69 percent populations were below 5 years and younger population is 9.33 percent which came in 11-20 years of age group. Around 1/10th percent population come between 31- 40 years and about 1/5th of the sample representatives were between the age group of 41-50 years age group. Only 11.90 percent peoples were above 60 years old in surveyed populations. Though estimation of age is very difficult among tribals due to lack of authentic records but age has been recorded with the help of events.

Table 8.3: Age Group Distribution

Age Group	*Number*	*%*
Below 5	69	13.69
6-10	81	16.07
11-20	47	9.33
21-30	66	13.10
31- 40	48	9.52
41-50	71	14.09
51- 60	62	12.30
61and above	60	11.90
Total	**504**	**100.00**

8.1.1.4 Marital Status

Table 8.4 revels that around more than 50 percent populations were married akin 46.75 percent respondents were unmarried. It had been recorded that at the same time 1.30 percent women were widow and only 0.43 percent respondents were widower as well as divorce/separated. 0.43 percent women's conditions were more pathetic and deplorable in nature. These deserted and separated women blame themselves and their fate, when asked about whether women had been legally separated. We are surprise no respondents were in legally separated. 'Oral Desertion' is very common in this region. The marriage pattern and family ties ensure that women are not cut off from family support. In these areas (as in all other areas) women have their own perceptions of gender equality that cannot be easily quantified by standard indicators

Table 8.4: Marital Status

Marital Status	*Number*	*%*
Unmarried	216	46.75
Married	236	51.08
Widow	6	1.30
Widower	2	0.43
Divorce/ Separated	2	0.43
Total	**462**	**100.00**

8.1.1.5 Literacy Rate and Level of Education

An overwhelming majority (58.20 percent) of the respondents are literates, which hampers many of their activities, especially handling money and properties or availing the government benefits meant for them. Thus feminisation of literacy is seen in this study. It had been observed that large percentage of the population was only educated by primary level and very few percentages of respondents were highly educated.

Table 8.5: Literacy and Level of Education

Literacy	*Population (5+)*	
	Number	*%*
Illiterate	186	41.80
Literate	259	58.20
Total	445	100.00
Education Level		
Primary	111	42.86
Middle	73	28.19
High School	45	17.37
Higher Secondary	18	6.95
Graduate	4	1.54
Post graduate	8	3.09
Total	**259**	**100.00**

8.1.1.6 Occupation

Table 8.6 depicted the occupational pattern of surveyed population where majority of respondents (55.00 percent) were daily labour as a carpenter, painter, auto and truck driver and 36.00 percent respondents depend on farming and rest of the total respondents were doing work in business sectors as well as government/private job. Worldwide, women participate less in the formal or paid work, sector of the economy than do men. The International Labor Organization (2009) estimates total worldwide female participation in the paid work force at 40 percent, with generally a lower rate in the less developed countries (closer to 35 percent) and a higher rate in the more developed countries (closer to 45 percent in the OECD).

Table 8.6: Occupational Pattern

Occupation	*Number*	%
Farmer	36	36.00
Daily Labour (*Carpenter, Penter, Auto & Track Driver etc.*)	55	55.00
Business *(LIC Agent, Shopkeeper, Photographer, TV mechanics, Wood seller etc.)*	7	7.00
Job	2	2.00
Total	**100**	**100.00**

8.1.1.7 Annual Income

Economic conditions of Dhurwa people are not good. They are poor and their incomes are per annum each. They are not aware about expenditure and spend almost their whole annual income on food items and clothes as well as festivals and fairs.

Table 8.7: Annual Income Range

Income Range (in Rs.)	*Number*	%
Below 5500	4	4.00
5501- 15500	35	35.00
15501-25500	23	23.00
25501-35500	12	12.00
35501- 45500	6	6.00
45501- 55500	5	5.00
55501- 65500	2	2.00
65501-75500	3	3.00
75501- 85500	2	2.00
85501- 95500	3	3.00
95501- 105500	2	2.00
105501 & Above	3	3.00
Total	**100**	**100.00**

8.1.1.8 Business Permitted by Female Folk

Tribal women in India contribute positively to the local economy and participate along with men in subsistence activities. In reality, women do more work than men and even though business is permitted by female folk (71.00 percent). They participate in all agricultural activities (except ploughing) and other sectors of indigenous cottage industries. They share major responsibilities in the production process. In addition, they have to manage household chores, which is a stupendous task. Child rearing is also the responsibility of the women.

Married women in the study area carry out all types of work at home as well as outside that are demand of mixed agro-pastoral economy. Apart from looking after the house, children and cattle major portion of the agriculture is done by women who do weeding, hoeing, harvesting and threshing. Role of women is not only of importance in economic activities, but her role in non-economic activities is equally important.

Table 8.8: Business Permitted by Female Folk

Responses	*Number*	*%*
Yes	71	71.00
No	29	29.00
Total	**100**	**100.00**

8.1.1.9 Keep the Money by Business

When we observed of the keeping pattern of money, majority of the females (43.00%) keep money which were earned by whether male or female whilst 18.00 percent males keep money by themselves. It has been also observed that 39.00 percent respondents did not able to specify about whom kept money of earning. Married women in the study area carry out all types of work at home as well as outside that are demand of mixed agro-pastoral economy. Apart from looking after the house, children and cattle major portion of the agriculture is done by women who do weeding, hoeing, harvesting and threshing. Role of women is not only of importance in economic activities, but her role in non-economic activities is equally important.

Table 8.9: Keep the Money by Business

Sex	*No.*	*%*
Male	18	18.00
Female	43	43.00
Both	39	39.00
Total	**100**	100.00

8.1.1.10 Deviation of Wage Earn Money

Even the economic power of the women in the household is not translated into a corresponding community authority. They are not ignored at household level but are not given due credit and importance alongside. However, female labour is central to all economic activities among tribals. Women perform waged and non-waged, productive and unproductive labour. The workload that is associated with these activities most unlikely does not give women any time to indulge in community affairs. Working for wages is not necessarily an indicator of autonomy. The wage earning tribal women cannot make the decision to work on their own, nor do they have control over their earnings. Table 8.10 depicted that deviation of wage was prevalent between men and women. It is dominated by male workers and others. In the study areas 61.00 percent women respondents were sufferer. There is an enormous literature that documents the existence of and explores the causes of the gender wage gap, mainly for recent years (1970 – 2010), but also for historical periods. The gender wage gap exists at all times and places. In the calculations below first benchmark the current gender pay ratio at 60 percent in developing countries and 75 percent in developed countries (women's to men's earnings) based on my own earlier surveys of gender wage gap studies (Jacobsen, 2007).

Table 8.10: Deviation of Wage Earn Money

Responses	*Number*	*%*
Yes	61	61.00
No	39	39.00
Total	**100**	**100.00**

This lower participation of women than men in the formal sector appears in large part due to their having much greater work responsibilities in the informal, or household, sector. Whether these responsibilities are assumed by free choice, by following of social norms, by coercion, or by lack of opportunities in the formal sector (whether due to gender discrimination or general lack of opportunities) can vary by person and by society. For the developed nations, it appears that women now exhibit free choice to participate to a greater degree in the household sector (as compared to men); for less industrialized nations, particularly where women may receive less schooling or training that is useful for paid work, the matter of choice is much less clear. However, studies across a wide variety of societies and times show that when opportunities for women's work expand in the paid sector, with the concomitant rise in women's wages, that women increase their participation in paid work significantly. This is well documented for the rise of manufacturing employment, particularly in textiles, in the U.S.

and the U.K. (Goldin, 1990; Simonton, 1998; Costa, 2000). Thus rising wages and rising female participation in the labor force rise hand-in-hand, implying that there are gains to the society from women's movement into the paid work sector at these times.

8.1.1.11 Firstly Food Serve

When we observed the cultural norms of food serving to men, it has been seen that first serving of food is given to men for men honourship. When we figure out the frequency 79 percent women agreed that they serve food firstly to men then others in the family. Only 19 percent respondents considered that they take food accompanied with each others, and rest families are taken separately after given food to all family members. Women and girls habitually eat last in sixty six percent of households in India. Patterns of segregation and subordination support and are supported by symbolical enactments, of which male first eating order is an especially important form. This is in part due to its regularity and early onset in life. Between the ages of five and ten, gendered "gastronomic deference" is enforced: girls are trained to eat as future "little wives" and boys to eat as future husbands (Appadurai, 1981:498). In many cases, a wife eats her husband's leftover food, and other women in the household eat leftovers separately after male household members have eaten (Chakravarty, 1972:37; Khare, 1976 b:8; Lamb, 2000: 33–34). Even in well off peasant families, women are left to consume the food that adult male family members leave after men have had their fill (Chen, Huq. and D'Souza, 1981).

Table 8.11: Firstly Food Serve

Sex	*Number*	*%*
Male	79	79.00
Female	2	2.00
Both	19	19.00
Total	**100**	**100.00**

8.1.1.12 Main Responsibility

It has been observed that 62.00 percent female main responsible person in the family rather than male (11.00 percent) while only 27 percent respondent considered that they have mutual responsibilities. Role of tribal women in the study area is not only of importance in the economic activities, but her role in non- economic activities is equally important. Formation and continuity of family hearth and home is the domain of the women. Women's role as wives, mothers, and organizers and as basic foundation of other dimensions of social life is of extreme importance. The role of women in childbirth, funerals and fairs and festivals is an important part of village life. Here women are carriers of traditional information in absence of written records. They are crucial actors in the preservation and dissemination of such knowledge. They are not only competent food producers and house makers but are also the transmitters of rich local oral traditions. Among patrilineal communities, inheritance is in male line and sons inherit the property of their father. If sons wanted to give a share to unmarried sisters, the community did not object it to.

Table 8.12: Main Responsibility

Sex	*Number*	*%*
Male	11	11.00
Female	62	62.00
Both	27	27.00
Total	**100**	**100.00**

8.1.1.13 Main Role for Earning Money

Feminisation of poverty is very common and microcredit and finance scheme usually have no limit and restriction and other criteria that supportive system taking ahead to women. Table 8.13 reveals that 46.00 percent females had main role in families for earning money while only 35.00 percent males had responsibility to earn money. The male frequency was dominating by female because male tribals were drunker and engaged in antisocial activities. In study villages 46.00percent female were playing as a main responsible person in her family for earning money where only 35.00 percent males played main role for their families. Women play

an important role in their household economy. They work in most operations of all sectors of the local economy and for longer hours each day than men. In addition to the domestic and reproductive activities associated with household maintenance they also collect and gather free goods especially fuel, fodder and water. Tribal women operate effectively in most economic and social institutions, participating in both local and migrant labour activities. Women's autonomy in terms of decision making is highly constrained among tribals. They have little access to, and exercise limited control over resources; and few are free from threat and violence at the hands of their husbands.

Table 8.13: Main Role for Earning Money

Sex	*Number*	*%*
Male	35	35.00
Female	46	46.00
Both	19	19.00
Total	**100**	**100.00**

8.1.2 Position of Women on Religious, Fair and Festivals

Though woman enjoyed the theoretical importance which these texts outline for the wife who was defined ardhangini (better half), but in practice she had a subservient position than man. She was regarded as a 'chattle' (a corporal moveable property) with no rights. It was generally seen and believed that women had lower status with reference to power and influence than men in all spheres of life family, community, religion and politics. Till recently, it was held that up to marriage, she is protected by her parents, during married life, she is looked after by her husband, and after the death of her husband, she was used to spend remaining years of her life under the roof of her children without any will or desire and rights in the family. She was not allowed to decide how money would be spent or invested. She did not have any money at her disposal. She had to take permission to spend money from her elders father, brother or husband or any other male or female elder person in the family. In brief, she had no

personality of her own. Some scholars have explained this inferior status of women as a result of patriarchal code of living. The rigid codes of behaviour as outlined for women in Brahmanical texts were also responsible for the low status of women in India. With above societal analysis we are fascinated to tribal's women to know their status and position in their own family and society.

8.1.2.1 Propitiate to Worship for God and Goddesses

The tribal under study operate with tenets that are restrictive of women's participation in their rituals. Women are never appointed as priests, and are skillfully manipulated against themselves. Both sexes participate in ceremonies, but men shoulder major responsibilities. They are present only during festivals and certain ceremonies as spectators or at the time of earning merit for oneself. The women are deprived of public authority. Religion legitimizes gender hierarchy. The subordination of women in religious activities and their denial of access to positions of religious leadership has been a powerful tool in most world religions in supporting the patriarchal order and the exclusion of women, from the public form (Ortner, 1974; Sered, 1994; Franzmen, 2000). The religious sphere is a major field for male dominance, and a strategy to deprive women of public authority (Scott, 1988; Jones, 1993). There are a few innovations in religious sphere, and hence these changes must exist within a traditional, ritual and textual structure. Religious institutions are resistance to gender equality. In structure an explicitly male religious framework contains the tribal societies. Though the secular institutions strive to eradicate inequality but it was seen that women of these areas were lagging behind in all fields. Even the economic power of the women in the household is not translated into a corresponding community authority. They are not ignored at household level but are not given due credit and importance alongside. However, female labour is central to all economic activities among tribals. Women perform waged and non-waged, productive and unproductive labour. The workload that is associated with these activities most unlikely does not give women any time to indulge in community affairs.

Women play an important role in their household economy. They work in most operations of all sectors of the local economy and for longer hours each day than men. In addition to the domestic and reproductive activities associated with household maintenance they also collect and gather free goods especially fuel, fodder and water. Tribal women operate effectively in most economic and social institutions, participating in both local and migrant labour activities. Women's autonomy in terms of decision making is highly constrained among tribals. They have little access to, and exercise limited control over resources; and few are free from threat and violence at the hands of their husbands. Working for wages is not necessarily an indicator of autonomy. The wage earning tribal women cannot make the decision to work on their own, nor do they have control over their earnings. The marriage pattern and family ties ensure that women are not cut off from family support. In these areas (as in all other areas) women have their own perceptions of gender equality that cannot be easily quantified by standard indicators. Table 8.14 reveals that participation in worship for god and goddesses is permitted for men (76.00 percent), while females can participate in some specific worship. In Dhurwa, there is some specific worship in their communities, where both male and female can participate.

Table 8.14: Propitiate to Worship for God and Goddesses

Sex	*Number*	*%*
Male	76	76.00
Female	15	15.00
Both	9	9.00
Total	**100**	**100.00**

8.1.2.2 Both Male and Female Participation all Fair and Festivals

About fifty percent women in the study area replied in affirmative. Husbands should and do help in cooking and bringing water. There is practically no task, other than minding small children, which does not require cooperation of both sexes. The work done by women is constant, diverse and often arduous. The work of men tends to be seasonal. In the men's light working season, they may help in the work at home. There are restrictions for women in dhurwa. They cannot worship before the shrines of family and village gods. Among dhurwa women it has been observed by prohibitions during menstruation. They do not worship, cook food and bring water. All the women justified the restrictions considering them impure. In Dhurwa community, majority of the respondents (69.00 percent) considered that women cannot participate in all types of fairs and fastivals.

Table 8.15: Both Male and Female Participation all Fair and Festivals

Responses	*Number*	%
Yes	31	31.00
No	69	69.00
Total	**100**	**100.00**

8.1.3 Allowed Female at Worship Place

Table 8.17 depicted, up till now 78.00 Percent respondent opined that today women are allowed to worship the impact of education.

Table 8.16: Allowed Female at Worship Place

Responses	*Number*	%
Yes	78	78.00
No	22	22.00
Total	**100**	**100.00**

8.1.4 Allowed Female at Traditional Panchyat

One may conclude that as the whole, tribal women have had fairly high status. She had been treated as a person having her own prestige and name, and her domestic accomplishments were recognized and appreciated. Barring a few exceptions, she has had a fair amount of power in the process of decision-making, practically in all spheres of life.

Table 8.17: Allowed Female at Traditional Panchyat

Responses	*Number*	%
Yes	64	64.00
No	36	36.00
Total	**100**	**100.00**

8.1.4.1 Allowed Female at Modern Panchyat

It is interesting to note that although by convention every village Panchayat has a female member, the lady never bothers to attend the meeting or to take any active interest in the proceedings of Panchayat. However, statuary village panchayats and reservation of seats for scheduled tribes and scheduled castes have given boost to women's status. They have significant role to play in panchayats these days and many dhurwa women have been able to become pradhans of the panchayats.

Table 8.18: Allowed Female at Modern Panchyat

Response	*Number*	*%*
Yes	85	85.00
No	3	3.00
Don't Know	12	12.00
Total	**100**	**100.00**

8.1.4.2 Female Raised their Voice at Modern Panchayat Meeting

Aware and educated women who are the member of Panchayat raised their voice against any kind of decision which are taken by other members of Panchayat. It is pleasure to observe that 92.00 percent women were participating actively in modern Panchayat meeting.

Table 8.19: Female Raised their Voice at Modern Panchyat Meeting

Response	*Number*	*%*
Yes	92	92.00
No	8	8.00
Total	**100**	**100.00**

8.1.4.3 Youth and Girls Participated at Gram Panchayat Samiti Work

Table 8.20 shows that youth and girls, they both participated in gram Panchayat Samiti work and there is no restriction for participation.

Table 8.20: Youth and Girls Participated at Gram Panchayat Samiti Work

Response	*Number*	*%*
Yes	91	91.00
No	9	9.00
Total	**100**	**100.00**

8.1.4.4 Panch Elected

Tribal women take vulnerable in their voting rights and about 2 percent of women in the study area exercised their right. Most of them follow the advice of their husbands or some of them are under pressure to accept the wishes of their husbands. Tribal speak little of statuses and roles when talking about their social life. What they do talk of are the skills for managing the environment for making a living. They also talk of marriage, married life, children and their socialisation within a community of relationships.

Table 8.21: Panch Elected

Sex	*Number*	*%*
Male	0	0.00
Female	2	2.00
Both	95	95.00
Don't Know	3	3.00
Total	**100**	**100.00**

8.1.4.5 Right to Decision for Panch Elected

This shows that women have a secondary importance in public affairs and community decision making. Women are generally bypassed and marginalized either they lack the requisite skills, or because women's heavy and unending domestic responsibilities makes attending meetings and participating in decision making difficult. It always happens that men take over the more profitable activities.

Table 8.22: Right to Decision for Panch Elected

Sex	*Number*	*%*
Male	5	5.00
Female	1	1.00
Both	94	94.00
Total	**100**	**100.00**

8.1.4.6 Conversation between Male and Female during Panchayat Meeting

Table 8.23 depicted that majority of the percentage (58.00 percent) relies, both male and female communicate to each other during Panchayat meeting while 35 percent respondents answered that female do not communicate to male. Panchayats play an important role in tribal villages. Disputes related to fields, pastoral land, and division of property among brothers or neglections of father by sons etc. were settled by the Panchayat. Traditionally, a council of elders did this and attempt was made to give unanimous judgments or compel the parties to have mutual agreement. Now this task has been taken by statutory village panchayats. Women have been traditionally discussing the disputes in the village and framed the rules in dormitories and thus used to assist the council of elders, which mainly consisted of male members.

Table 8.23: Conversation between Male and Female During Panchayat Meeting

Response	*Number*	*%*
Yes	58	58.00
No	35	35.00
Don't Know	7	7.00
Total	**100**	**100.00**

8.1.5 Position of Women in Society

There are three types of views about the status of tribal women expressed by different scholars. The *first view* holds that the status of tribal women is higher than their counterparts in caste ridden society. It emphasizes that they lead a very hard life and enjoy more freedom than their counterparts among Hindus. They can roam about freely, visit markets or friends, cut jokes with men without any reservations and are usually free to select their life partners. They are at liberty to divorce their husbands and remarry again. Divorce or widowhood is not taken as stigma in tribal society. The bride price itself is considered to be a mark of respect the value for a tribal woman. They have firm hand in most of the family matters and their social participation is not much curtailed as in the case of caste women. Thus, the popular and overall image and perception of the tribal women is that of being better off than their non-tribal counterparts. There is no child marriage and no stigma on widowhood. She enjoys the absolute right to decide about her marriage. Instead of dowry there is bride price indicating a high social status of the tribal women earn and are, therefore, to a great extent economically independent. Their contribution to the family and the community is more valuable and important in comparison to their counterparts in Hindu society.

According to *second view*, there are many facts, which indicate a low status for the tribal woman. For example, she does not have property rights except in a matrilineal society, which is a small proportion of the tribal population. She is paid fewer wages than her male counterpart for the same work. Several taboos discriminating against a tribal woman exist in certain tribal groups implying impurity and low status. She cannot hold the office of a priest. There are taboos related to menstruation as in non-tribal communities.

The *thrid view* has been expressed by Majumdar (1973), who has reported a higher status of tribal women on some indicators while lower on others, while Deshpandey, Shashi (1978) has concluded that the status of tribal women varies from tribe to tribe. The developmental projects have adversely affected the tribal women. With deforestation they have to travel longer distances to gather forest products. Incidentally, this has been one of the reasons for the participation of tribal women in the Chipko movement to save the trees. There are evidences of sexual exploitation of tribal women by forest and mining contractors. The incidence of sexual assaults on tribal women has increased.

Among tribals in the study area the concept of women's space is where only women may sit, work or enter freely at any time is relatively informal and flexible and depends on the separation of activities that result from the sexual division of labour. It is a characteristics feature of traditional societies to set apart, or see a distinction in physical space, which is used by men women (de Schlippe, 1956; Edelberg and Jones, 1979; Ladurie, 1979; Illich, 1982). In the study area, there are no such private or intimate spaces for women, though men have public space to hold meetings, settle disputes, and discuss political and farming issues. There is at least one such space in each of the settlements, either under a tree or in the open space. Women do not have a similar, formal sitting space. In the study area, the interaction between individual men and women varies according to kinship relation and relative age, which ranges from relaxed informality to extreme avoidance, marked by women covering their head and men averting their glances. Men who are not kin, especially elders do not come closer to an area where a group of women is sitting. By these standards the tribals also maintain the integrity of the gender divide. The courtyards are mainly women's space (except during threshing when men and women work together in the courtyard). All food processing is done here. Washing of clothes, spinning of wool, embroidery, providing bath to children etc is all carried out here. The kitchen is a woman' domain. The grazing grounds in and around the village, near water source are areas where old women, young girls and small boys sit with babies, to mind cattle and sheep and goat. That is to say, the pastures are spatially removed and are at different altitudes. Being seasonally used, they bring the concept of time. They provide gender differences in the utilization of resources and tool such as animals as opposed to field crops, male instead of female labour. The tribal women in the study area have been denied roles associated with masculinity as a result of ideology of the family and kinship, which identifies paternal roles with authoritative roles. Few women who have succeeded in acquiring some positions in communal life have found that their competence or their executive methods are frequently challenged or ridiculed.

Table 8.24 depicted that the position of women in the society where majority of respondents consider, women are lower in position (42.00 percent) than men. Women do sacrifices (28.00 percent) for family and for own need. Some respondent see the separated and older women as curse and bad eyes (18.00 percent) of evils. Thus the overviews are depending upon person to persons and their education level.

Table 8.24: Position of Women by Society

Type	*Number*	*%*
Scrifice	28	28.00
Low thinking	42	42.00
Bad eyes	18	18.00
Low mentality	12	12.00
Total	**100**	**100.00**

8.1.5.1 Equal Right defined by Society

Table 8.25 shows, 63 percent respondents opined that both female and male have equal rights given by their society. Tribal women in the study area recognizes the fact that they have been discriminated (34.00 percent) against in education, income, consumption, status and access to power; they have a worse health record than men; they suffer from social, cultural and legal discrimination and often from violence. They are discriminated on grounds of equity (which refers to equality of opportunities and choices) and efficiency. There is need for quantitative measurement, for a complete set of cultural and rights indicators to assess women's rights. A peculiar custom among the dhurwa was that generally a daughter inherited her mother's property like ornaments and clothes and not her daughter-in-law. Similarly, sons were entitled for their father's property and if the son wanted to give a share to their unmarried sisters, it was not objected to by the community. However, a daughter became eligible for her mother's property only after latter's death. In case a daughter decided, to remain unmarried, the same rule applied for inheriting mother's ornaments and clothes.

Table 8.25: Equal Right defined by Society

Response	*Number*	*%*
Yes	63	63.00
No	34	34.00
Don't Know	3	3.00
Total	**100**	**100.00**

8.1.5.2 Level of Women by Society

The women in the tribal community, as in other communities, constitute about half of the tribal population. The well being of the tribal community, as that of any other community, depends importantly on the status of their women. For a thorough understanding of the status of women, we have to dig in time and space, as the status of women has been like a moving equilibrium at various times in different societies, including the tribal ones. Theoretically, the low status of women is accepted (52.00 percent) even in a majority of tribal societies, exception being the matriarchal, matrilineal and polyandrous societies. Like Hindu women, the tribal women are also rated lower to men, in immediate response. But in actual practice, the tribal women enjoy comparatively more freedom and are devoid of many constraints that are still imposed on caste women. The traditional tribal norms are somewhat liberal to womanhood and most of them continue to live in their customary style including position and behaviour. In dhurwa very few respondents agreed that women are high in slandered (18.00 percent) in society.

Table 8.26: Level of Women by Society

Rank	*Number*	*%*
Low	52	52.00
Middle	30	30.00
High	18	18.00
Total	**100**	**100.00**

8.1.5.3 Both Male and Female Dancing and Singing Rights by Society

Women do take part in dancing but their movements are different from men. They are present only during festivals and certain ceremonies as spectators or at the time of earning merit for oneself. Women participate in dancing and singing (65.00 percent). There are no female counterparts but the religious

sphere is most dominating among tribals it constitutes a major field for male domination.

Table 8.27: Both Male and Female Dancing and Singing Rights by Society

Response	*Number*	*%*
Yes	65	65.00
No	35	35.00
Total	**100**	**100.00**

8.1.5.4 Female are treated as Daini by Society

Recent research indicates that violence against tribal women is increasing (Panda & Snehalata, 2008). The practice of eliminating widows through "witch hunting" has been condemned throughout the country. Table 8.28 depicted, majority of the respondents (63.00 percent) answered that separated and deserted women are treated as witch/daini by society.

Table 9.28: Female are treated as Daini by Society

Response	*Number*	*%*
Yes	63	63.00
No	37	37.00
Total	**100**	**100.00**

8.1.5.5 Male Outsider and Female insider Household Work

Awais, et al. (2009) point out that tribal women face problems and challenges in getting a sustainable livelihood and a decent life due to the environmental degradation and the interference of the outsiders. According to Fernandes, et al. (2001) in Andhra Pradesh, Orissa and West Bengal, tribal women deprived of natural resources that are their sustenance, complained of not having any work. In Dhurwa women are reduced to being housewives (61.00 percent) along with no opportunity to work outside the house and make a contribution to the family economy. It has long been recognised that men and women not only behave differently, but also have different attitudes to life.

Table 8.29: Responses of Female about Work

Response	*Number*	*%*
Yes	61	61.00
No	39	39.00
Total	**100**	**100.00**

There are various programmes running by state government and private institutions for the development of tribals people but inspite of all programmes illiteracy level is high. Because of the backwardness of these people permeates every department of their life. Poverty, ignorance, ill health and rudimentary culture of the tribals are parts of an integrated system. Attack, on any one of them will not be ultimately fruitful if the other sides are allowed to operate in full freedom.

Now the tribal people have begun to realise the benefit of gender equality and guardians send their boys as well as girls to the school and collages for education and away from home for employment/ job/work even at a loss to themselves own their children partly earn their own livelihood even at childhood and adolescence age nearby their homes.

8.2 Poor Health Status of Women as Compare to Men

In tribal region of Bastar during 2008 Maternal Mortality Ratio was 269.08, in 2009 was 277.33, 2010 was 226.33 and in 2011, M.M.R. is 239.03 per 100000 Live births (Data obtained from C.M.O Office, Jagdalpur (Bastar), Chattisgarh, India). In spite of all efforts taken by the central and state Government to ameliorate educational, socioeconomic status and occupational status, maternal mortality still remains a major cause of women mortality in tribal population of Bastar (Chhattisgarh).

8.3 A Comparison between Tribals and Urban General Communities

Table 8.30 depicted that women status is better than that of urban women in general communities. Much of the discrimination against women arises from India's dowry tradition, where the bride's family gives the groom's family money and/or gifts. Dowries were made illegal in India in 1961, however the law is almost impossible to enforce, and the practice persists for most marriages. Unfortunately, the iniquitous dowry system has even spread to communities who traditionally have not practiced it, because dowry is sometimes used as a means to climb the social ladder, to achieve economic security, and to accumulate material wealth. The model used to calculate the dowry takes the bridegroom's education and future earning potential into account while the bride's education and earning potential are only relevant to her societal role of being a better wife and mother. The bridegroom's demand for a dowry can easily exceed the annual salary of a typical Indian family, and consequently be economically disastrous especially in families with more than one or two daughters.

Table 8.30: Comparison according to Socio-cultural Status between Tribals and General Urban Communities

Type of Socio-cultural Status	*Tribals (n=100)*	*Generals (n=100)*
Dowry Tradition	2	100
Social Discrimination	35	85
Work Discrimination	7	97
Discrimination before Birth/As Infant	1	87
Nutritional and Health Discrimination as Child	49	67
Education	37	49
Child Marriage	79	17
Discrimination after Marriage	29	97
Discrimination against Women as Widow	33	100
Discrimination for Inheritance	69	57

The Indian constitution grants women equal rights to men, but strong patriarchal traditions persist in many different societal parts, with women's lives shaped by customs that are centuries old. Hence, in these strata daughters are often regarded as a liability, and conditioned to believe that they are inferior and subordinate to men, whereas sons might be idolized and celebrated. There are a couple of reasons, why men might be regarded an asset for a family:

- Considered capable of earning money
- Carry on the family line
- Able to provide for their aging parents
- Bring a wife (and with this a capable domestic helper) into the family

- Play an important role in death rituals in Hindu religion, which ensure, that the soul is released from the body and can go to heaven.

On the other hand, there are a couple of reasons why women might be regarded more of a liability for a family:

- Not considered capable of earning money
- Seen as economically and emotionally dependent on men
- While they help with domestic duties during childhood and adolescence, they go to live with their husband's family after marriage, which means less help in the household of their originating family and most importantly loss of money due to the dowry tradition.

This might explain why the birth of a daughter may not always be perceived as equally blissful as the birth of a son, and why "*May you be blessed with a hundred sons*" is a common Hindu wedding blessing.

8.3.1 Discrimination against Women

It should be noted that in a vast country like India - spanning 3.29 million sq. km, where cultural backgrounds, religions and traditions vary widely. The extend of discrimination against women also varies from one societal stratum to another and from state to state. Some areas in India being historically more inclined to gender bias than others. There are even communities in India, such as the Nairs of Kerala, certain Maratha clans, and Bengali families, which exhibit matriarchal tendencies, with the head of the family being the oldest woman rather than the oldest man. However, many Indian women face discrimination throughout all stages of their life, beginning at (or even before) birth, continuing as an infant, child, adolescent and adult. The stages can be divided in following sections:

- Before Birth / As an Infant
- As a Child
- After Marriage
- As a Widow

8.3.2 Discrimination against Women Before Birth / As an Infant

India is one of the few countries where males outnumber females; the sex ratio at birth (SRB) which shows the number of boys born to every 100 girls - is usually consistent in human populations, where about 105 males are born to every 100 females. There are significant imbalances in the male/

female population in India where the SRB is 113; there are also huge local differences from Northern / Western regions such as Punjab or Delhi, where the sex ratio is as high as 125, to Southern / Eastern India e.g. Kerala and Andhra Pradesh, where sex ratios are around 105. Though "prenatal sex discrimination" was legally banned in 1996, the law is nearly impossible to enforce and is not even familiar to all Indian families. Hence, the preference for a male child persists, quite often out of mere practical, financial concerns, because the parents might not be able to afford the marriage dowry for (another) daughter. This leads to some of the most gruesome and desperate acts when it comes to gender discrimination:

- Selective abortions
- Murdering of female babies
- Abandonment of female babies

Prenatal tests to determine the sex of the fetus were criminalized by Indian law in 1994, but the above mentioned imbalances in the sex ratio at birth, clearly point to gender selective abortions. While abortion is officially illegal in India there are some exceptions to this rule such as the failure of contraceptive device used by a couple; if the woman was raped; or if the child would suffer from severe disabilities. In total 11 million abortions take place annually and around 20,000 women die every year due to abortion related complications.

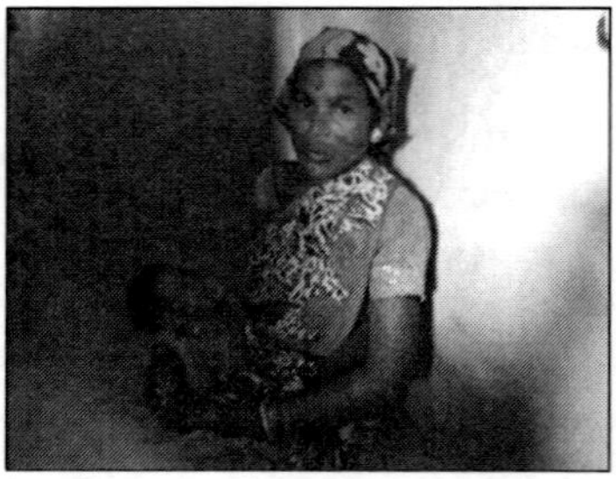

8.3.3 Discrimination against Women as Child Nutrition and Health

As a child, girls are often treated differently from male children in terms of nutrition and health care; where limited food or financial resources are available, the insufficient means are prone to be allocated unevenly in favour of the male offspring. This imbalance results in insufficient care afforded to girls and women, and is the first major reason for the high levels of child malnutrition. This nutritional deprivation has two harmful consequences for women: they never reach their full growth potential and Anaemia both consequences are risk factors in pregnancy, complicating childbearing and resulting in maternal and infant deaths, as well as low birth weight infants.

8.4 Education

India's constitution guarantees free primary school education for both girls and boys up to age 14. This has been repeatedly reconfirmed, but primary education in India is not universal, and often times not seen as really necessary for girls. Their parents might consider it more important, that they learn domestic chores, as they will need to perform them for their future husbands and in-laws. Another disincentive for sending daughters to school is a concern for the protection of their virginity. When schools are located at a distance, when teachers are male, and when girls are expected to study along with boys, parents are often unwilling to expose their daughters to the potential assault on their virginity, that would ultimately result in an insult to the girl's family's honor.

This results in one of the lowest female literacy rates in the world.

- Literacy Rate for Women: 54 percent
- Literacy Rate for Men: 76 percent

As a comparison, female literacy per 2009: Pakistan: 60 percent, Peru: 89 percent, Indonesia: 93 percent.Mothers illiteracy and lack of schooling directly disadvantage their young children. Low schooling translates into poor quality of care for children, consequently in higher infant and child mortality and malnutrition, because mothers with little education are less likely to adopt appropriate health promoting behaviors, such as having young children immunized.

Social sector programmes e.g. "Sarva Shiksha Abhiyan" (Education for Everyone) are promoting girls' education to equalize educational opportunities and eliminate gender disparities, but these initiatives will take time to unfold their whole effect.

8.5 Child Marriages

The Prohibition of Child Marriage Act 2006 bans marriage below age 18 for girls and age 21 for boys, but some 80 percent of Indians live in villages where family, caste and community pressures are more effective than any legislature. According to UNICEF's "State of the World's Children 2009" report, 47 percent of India's women aged 20–24 were married before the legal age of 18, with 56 percent in rural areas. The report also showed that 40 percent of the world's child marriages occur in India.

8.5.1 Reasons of Child Marriage

Child marriage is a traditional practice that in many places happens simply because it has happened for generations and straying from tradition could mean exclusion from the community. In many communities where child marriage is practised, girls are not valued as much as boys, they are seen as a burden. The challenge will be to change parents' attitudes and emphasise that girls who avoid early marriage and stay in school will likely be able to make a greater contribution to their family and their community in the long term. Where poverty is acute, giving a daughter in marriage allows parents to reduce family expenses by ensuring they have one less person to feed, clothe and educate. In communities where a dowry or 'bride price' is paid, it is often welcome income for poor families; in those where the bride's family pay the groom a dowry, they often have to pay less money if the bride is young and uneducated. Many parents marry off their daughters young because they feel it is in her best interest, often to ensure her safety in areas where girls are at high risk of physical or sexual assault

8.5.1.1 Financial Benefit

- As outlined above, due to the dowry tradition women are prone to be a (financial) burden for their families, thus seen as a liability.
- If the match is made at an early age, the dowry is usually much lower, as the dowry is calculated on the future husband's societal status and education, which obviously would be much lower at an early age.
- Common Hindu phrase: "The younger the groom, the cheaper the Dowry"

In addition marrying off girls at an early age, ensures, that they marry as virgins, thus protecting the girl's and their family's honour.

8.5.1.2 Historical Origins

- Child marriages started during the invasions of Northern India around 1,000 years ago, when unmarried girls were raped by invaders.
- To protect their women from abuse, family members began marrying their daughters at young ages.

8.5.1.3 Religious Origin

It has been observed that copying the myth that the goddess *Parvati* had decided to marry God *Shiva* when she was only eight, girls were married off as young as eight or nine years old. Girls between 15 and 19 are twice as likely to die of pregnancy-related reasons as girls between 20 and 24.

Girls married off as children sometimes stay in their parents' house until puberty, but it is just as common, that they move in with their husband and in-laws right after marriage. In that case, many child wives are inclined to experience domestic violence, marital rape, deprivation of food, and lack of access to information, healthcare, and education. Thus, the vicious cycle of illiteracy and abuse is likely to be continued and passed on to their own daughters.

8.5.1.4 Discrimination against Women

There is mainly a bias towards men and their superiority in marital relationships: while women ought to be respected, protected and kept happy by their husbands – their happiness being vital for the prosperity, peace and happiness of the whole family – they should also be kept under constant vigilance, since they cannot be completely trusted or left to themselves. Whereas as a child a girl is supposed to remain in the custody and care of her parents, after marriage she becomes the property and responsibility of her husband, who is supposed to take care of her and keep her in his custody. Under the existing cultural and social ethos of India a married girl / woman is no longer considered to be part of the family of her birth, instead she has become part of the family of the groom. Hence, after marriage the woman leaves her parental home and lives with her husband's family, where she is required to assume all household labour and domestic responsibilities. In certain parts of Indian society, women are conditioned from birth to be subservient not only to their future husbands, but also to the females in their husband's family especially, their mother-in-law. Accordingly, the surrounding society mandates a woman's obedience to her husband and her in-laws. Any disobedience would bring disgrace to both, the wife herself and her originating family, and might lead to the woman being ostracized and neglected by her very own family and in her own home.

8.5.1.5 Discrimination against Women after Marriage

There is no cultural or religious tradition behind one of the most ghastly incidents of female oppression, but the prevalence of the dowry tradition has supposedly lead to "Bride *Burning*" (or other form of murdering) of the newly wed wife by the husband and his family, who would claim, that she died in a domestic accident, so that the widowed husband would be free to marry again and collect another dowry. Indian law demands a formal criminal investigation when a newly married woman dies within the home within 7 years of marriage. According to Indian National Crime Record Bureau, there were 8,239 dowry death cases, 1,285 cases of attempted dowry deaths, and another 4,890 cases with pending investigations in 2009. The punishment for dowry deaths is a term of 7 years, which may extend to life imprisonment. Indian law clearly distinguishes the offence of dowry deaths from the offence of murder, for which a death sentence might be declared.

8.5.1.6 Discrimination against Women as a Widow

Indian government has enacted numerous laws to protect widow's rights, including prohibitions against traditional practices for which India has been discredited, such as the burning of widows (Sati). Whereas in India's contemporary culture, especially in the modern urban middle-class, these societal norms have given way to a more righteous conduct, the enforcement of the law continues to be challenging, where there are regional, religious or caste variants of family law, which tend to escape government jurisdiction. Hence, a widow is still seen as a liability in some part of the Indian society, which might result in her being abandoned by her inlaws. As her originating family is often unable or unwilling to take her back as well, she might be left on her own, without any education, skills, or financial assistance. Instead, she is subjected to many restrictions, and might be required to shave her head permanently, or to wear white clothes for the rest of her life; thus, stigmatized, she is not allowed to enter in any celebration e.g. weddings, because her presence is considered to be inauspicious. Moreover, a widow might face trouble securing her property rights after her husband's death, nor be allowed to remarry, disregarding at what age she became a widow. As the described discrimination against widows is likely to occur in the same societal surroundings as the above mentioned child marriages, this might lead to child or teenage widows, who are bound to be isolated and ostracized for the rest of their lives.

8.5.1.7 Discrimination against Women for Inheritance

While in the educated, urban middle class women's rights continue to improve, there remains a strong bias against gender equality in those societal parts of India, where patriarchal traditions prevail. Consequently, in these strata any inheritance of a deceased husband or father would be passed down to the oldest son, while his wife or daughters would not receive any financial benefit. There are laws in place to ensure legal protection for women's right to inheritance, but the enforcement of the law is challenging, when the woman is refused her right by the family, and when she is not confident or educated enough to claim her right.

8.5 Psychological Threatening Towards Women

This is a very cruel and barbaric form of violence against women seen in Chhattisgarh. The concept of *Tonhi* (Witch) is part of the state of Chhattisgarh. A woman is declared *tonhi* and is accused of spreading disease and bringing disaster to the village by performing *Jadu-Tona* (Witch craft). These women are insulted and humiliated publicly. Often it is accompanied by physical torture and they are ostracised from the community. In many cases the torture is so severe that they suffer from the wounds for months. If any child is suffering from illness, or the cattle is affected due to any reason, or any other adverse situation comes, the blame for all this is put on the witch or the *tonhi* of the village. To identify a *tonhi* a man who is known as a *baiga* is called and he randomly identifies the witch. Thereafter the whole village turns against her, subjecting her to the most cruel and inhuman forms of physical and mental assault. Generally, the women who are identified as tonhi are often single and to children involved in cases of property disputes. Too often, the accusations of witchcraft are prompted by the relatives wanting to get hold of the property and other assets of the *Tonhi.* We have never heard that any man is hunted as ghost or evil spirit from others but there is lot of examples about women who have faced physical violence and psychological torture from relatives and their own societies as well as others. In witch hunting cases often the village representatives and the government officials do not come forward in opposition on the pretext that this is an indigenous belief that is best left undisturbed. So the news does not reach the world beyond the village and the rule of the *Baigas* (Witch Doctors) gets established. These *Baigas* declare all disasters in the village to be due to *Jadu-Tona*. They charge any amount for catching a *tonhi,* branding her and bringing the whole village under his protection (*Gaon Bandhava*). These *Baigas* demand impossible tests from these women to prove that they are not *Tonhi*. When the whole village is against the *Tonhi,* it is impossible for her to prove herself innocent.

8.6 Other Analysis about Women of Chhattisgarh

The sex ratio is indicative of a favorable count of females per thousand males, with Chhattisgarh ranking next only to Kerala which has got the highest sex ratio in the country. But a closer examination of the situation of the women in the state reveals that this is only one side of the coin. Although women do have a big role to play in the process of production and are free of practices like *purdah* in this state, yet there are some socio cultural practices related to marriage, divorce and custodial rights that are discriminatory against women. For example men and women in Chhattisgarh have the liberty to break out of their present marriage and can establish a new relation, (with the exception of few upper castes). But on the separation of husband and wife, the custody of the child is given to the father. The phenomenon of child marriage and the marriage of the girls before they attain their puberty is quite common in this region. Married at a very young age, women also face early pregnancy when they are not even physically matured. The traditional practices observed during pregnancy and delivery also affect the health of the mother adversely. For example, the mother is kept without food for three days after delivery in the belief that the baby will not be able to digest the milk if the mother eats. Amongst some communities, notably section of the Gond community in Bastar, the woman about to give birth is left alone in the forest outside the village for the actual delivery. After the process of purification, she is brought to home.

Apart from above, women are the major agricultural workers in Chhattisgarh. This is so in the production of rice our main food crop, as well as in pulses, millets and the many oilseeds. They work in each and every aspect of crop production, preservation and storage. In certain parts of the state like Abujhmar and Sihawa, women are also known to use the plough, a function that is taboo and prohibited for them in almost all other parts of the country, indeed the world. Apart from crop weeding, manuring, harvesting, women are the leading players in all post harvest and storage operations. Women also play a major role in the collection and processing of the many kinds of uncultivated foods and medicinal plants found in Chhattisgarh. Many of these foods are collections from the forest, and women use them for maintaining household food security and nutrition needs outside the market system. Women are the primary gatherers of all uncultivated foods, and inheritors of an ancient knowledge system about food bio diversity. Women are also the keepers of the seeds. As stated above, women are responsible for all post harvest operations. In traditional Chhattisgarh, the crop to be harvested as seed is identified in the field of standing crop, and women take special care while reaping these. The extremely complex knowledge of seed storage and preservation including its technical aspects is in the hands of the women. The important economic position of women can be seen also among migrant workers from Chhattisgarh who are major contributors to the construction industry nationwide. Many of the metropolitan highways, buildings and national industries have been built by the migrant workers from Chhattisgarh, and the women of Chhattisgarh have been more than equal contributors in these efforts. In urban Chhattisgarh too, women have played an important part in the economy. In all aspects of city based wage labour, be it cart pulling, load bearing or as unskilled workers in industry, women presence is significant. However, the situation is not so good when we come to modern industry. Women work in many of our large scale industries including the Bhilai Steel Plant, although, their presence is as unskilled workers in the slag dump and in the mines. Women are seen as mine workers in open cast dolomite, iron ore and bauxite mines in the Bilaspur, Durg and Surguja districts of the state. It is important to note that women are almost nonexistent as skilled workers, are in management positions in the same industries that they woman so steadily. Today, with the state poised for major industrial development, this becomes an area of concern. Like women worldwide, the women of Chhattisgarh are also the major nurturers, care providers, and builders of our future generations. However, the situation is far more complex when it comes to the social and political spaces that women traditionally enjoy. Women's position in this regard presents a contrasting and complex picture of unrestricted and restricted spaces.

Chapter - IX

Recommendation and Conclusion

Gender inequality is the byproduct of individual mind and cultural element of the various societies. Along with this opinion one thing is very clear that women is ever a vulnerable group who ever face any kind of disparity in all over the world either educated or uneducated family. Inequality is directaly related to culture and capability.With anthropological point of view, we are nutral to recommend any suggestion towards cultural norms of inequality about gender but policy level planning, laws and implementation would work for improvement. Sociologically education and awareness can be the catalyst to sensitise the gender inequality at all level of the society. Thus we are suggesting some important recommendation at multidimention direction which can work for the improvement of women and establishment of the equality between men and women.

9.1 Policy Recommendation

Gender inequality remains key barrier to development of every society. There is a strong need for establishment of gender institute as a central body which will collect all gender disaggregated data, create databases and create new researches needed for clarification of gender issues – gender data should be opened for public and institute should distribute key findings to all key stakeholders dealing with public policies. Engendering the field of transitional justice will entail a fundamental rethinking of the goals, structures and foundational assumptions upon which the field is built as well as the future incorporation of a gendered perspective in all levels of planning and implementation. Whilst this may destabilize accepted practices in the short term, continuing to sideline this perspective only contributes to an unjust and partial reconciliation premised upon pre-conflict inequitable power relations; laying the foundations for future violence and conflict and subverting the very goals transitional justice mechanisms are intended to secure.

9.1.1 Periods of Conflict and Post Conflict Reconstruction

Whatever the context, causes or nature of a conflict, all have in common that they are impacted by, and in turn impact upon, gendered power relations. Periods of conflict and post-conflict reconstruction destabilize gender identities and assumptions during conflict women often assume positions that would have been unacceptable preconflict, either by joining one of the fighting parties, assuming the position of head of a household, or occupying positions in the public sphere or other spaces that were previously the exclusive domain of men.

9.1.1.1 Reconstruction of Social Infrastructure

These shifts in roles and identities can provide a double edged sword, where by conflict has an enormous and devastating impact on women's lives, but can also open new spaces, and challenges, for transformation. As conflict is brought to an end and peace agreements negotiated, societies are faced with the task of reconstructing not only their physical infrastructure, but social infrastructure including relationships to each other, and between citizens and the state.

Much has been made in feminist literature of the importance of this postwar moment for transforming unequal power relations and furthering gender justice. However it has also been noted that this moment is fleeting; and few, if any, examples can be pointed to where the gains that were made during this period were successfully consolidated and manifested in sustained gender equality and a transformed society.

9.1.1.2 Potentially Transformative Moment

In part this inability to harness the potentially transformative moment is a result of the demand during post-conflict situations that 'women' and 'gender' be placed on the back burner for later as priority is once more placed on other issues. Equally detrimental is that peace negotiations often downplay issues of justice in an effort to consolidate a peace which is defined narrowly as a silencing of the guns. Where justice issues are addressed, 'justice' is similarly narrowly defined and does not encompass transformative justice or challenge fundamentally unjust power relations within society; power relations that are often at the heart of the conflict itself.

It is during this moment of flux that transitional justice mechanisms are negotiated and established, with the express mandate to deal with past violations and contribute towards a blueprint for a new society based on principles of justice and equitable relations; and in doing so, ensure that the atrocities of the past will 'never again' occur.

These objectives of transitional justice mechanisms as well as the space they occupy during the transition pose challenges as well as opportunities for the further in gender justice. The following paper begins to explore how transitional justice mechanisms can capitalize on the opportunities presented in order to move beyond the reconstruction of pre-war gender relations and instead encourage fundamental transformation of relations and institutions in order to contribute towards comprehensive social justice.

9.1.2 Need Gender Justice

Gender justice can be defined as 'the protection and promotion of civil, political, economic and social rights on the basis of gender equality. It necessitates taking a gender perspective on the rights themselves, as well as the assessment of access and obstacles to the enjoyment of these rights for both women, men, girls and boys and adopting gender-sensitive strategies for protecting and promoting them.'

9.1.2.1 Incorporation of Gender Justice into Accountability Mechanisms

Incorporation of gender justice into accountability mechanisms has thus far emphasized two key objectives: acknowledging and seeking justice for women's experiences of sexual violence during conflict; and securing increased representation of women in arenas of policy making and decision making on post-conflict issues as well as in the transitional justice mechanisms themselves. The following sections assess the gains made in both these fields as well as select recommendations going forward. The paper then turns to the need to move beyond increased participation of women and the redress of specific violations to an engendering of the field of transitional justice as a whole in order to progress towards sustainable peace and transformative justice.

9.1.3 Addressing Sexual Violation as a War Crime

Without accountability for crimes against women, the legal foundations of new governments will be weakened, the credibility of governing institutions will be undermined and women will continue to suffer discrimination.

9.1.3.1 Acknowledging and Addressing Womens Experiences of Sexual Violence

In the realm of international law there has been considerable progress in recent years towards acknowledging and addressing womens experiences of sexual violence during conflict. Where crimes of this nature were once covered in a complicit silence by both sides in a conflict, both law and the interpretation of law has shifted in recent years.

The Rome Statute which established the International Criminal Court recognizes sexual crimes as well as persecution on the grounds of gender. In cases before the International Criminal Tribunal for the Former Yugoslavia (ICTY) and the International Criminal Tribunal for Rwanda (ICTR) rape has been confirmed as both crimes against humanity as well as an act of genocide. Other notable initiatives at an international level include Security Council Resolution 1325 which deals specifically with justice for womens experiences of violence during conflict and the 2004 Report of the Secretary General on 'The rule of law and transitional justice in conflict and postconflict societies' which confirms the need for women to be included in all initiatives which seek redress for past violations as well as assurances that these interventions will not re victimize marginalized and at risk groups, in particular women who have been victims of sexual violence.

9.1.3.2 Mechanisms for Redress in the Domestic Sphere

Similarly, mechanisms for redress in the domestic sphere have increasingly become gender-sensitive and inclusive. This is particularly visible in the way in which national truth commission processes have built upon the best practices of preceding commissions. The first truth commissions in Latin America were 'gender blind' and either did not address sexual violence or omitted from their analysis the context of gender inequality. Subsequent commissions have incorporated women's hearings, dedicated gender units and international technical support as well as a broader and more gendered definition of their mandate and harms covered.

9.1.4 Policy Implications

Governments, like individuals, increasingly turn to science as a basis for the decisions or policies they make. Although the policy making process is arguably far from rational, and faces competing influences, including financial and legal constraints, ideology and values, rigorous evidence forms an important part of the policy making process, at least if the rhetoric of 'evidence-based' policy is to be believed. There is, for example, a long history of the use of empirical research to aid the development of health policy. In criminal justice, by contrast, the relationship between evidence and policy has been more tenuous and cyclical, and there have been many examples of policies being influenced more by public opinion, ideology or pressure groups than by evidence (Wilcox, 2005; Wilcox and Hirschfield, 2007).

9.1.4.1 Precedent Setting Cases

Whilst there have been important gains in the international legal arena with regards to redressing sexual violence during conflict, these have been tempered by the actual number of convictions secured which have been few and far between. Moreover, despite these early victories, subsequent cases of sexual violence have not received the same levels of attention. Precedent setting cases make an important contribution to curbing impunity and sending a message that these violations will be treated with the condemnation due such atrocities, but these gains have little on the ground impact if they are not consistently applied or given sustained attention.

9.1.4.2 International Law; Driving Force for the Reform of National Law

Beyond the individual cases, international law is in a unique position to serve as a driving force for the reform of national law and the encouragement of domestic prosecutions of sexual violence. This is important as access to justice for the vast majority of women occurs at this level. With regards to legal reform and implementation, the Rome Statute has again been a positive step in this regard. By recognizing gender persecution and requiring state parties to bring their own laws into conformity with the provisions of the Statute, the ICC can influence the adoption of domestic remedies and thus broaden access to justice for women in post-conflict states. Again, real impact will require follow through: As states rarely have the political will to prosecute cases of this nature, progress will entail the prioritization of these crimes at an international level with the backing of a credible threat of referral to the ICC.

9.1.4.3 International Institutions; Support the Reconstruction of Local Police and Courts

Ensuring access to justice for women post-conflict also entails the rebuilding of national justice systems, legal reform and the implementation of effective policing bodies. International institutions and particularly peace keeping operations are in a unique position to support the reconstruction of local police and courts and address the vacuum often left by the absence of these institutions in a post-conflict period by taking over the functions whilst working to establish new ones. Violence against women in particular flourishes in a context of general insecurity, impunity and an absence of judicial mechanisms. United Nations Mission in Liberia (UNMIL) has played a positive role in addressing widespread and endemic levels of violence against women in that country as well as working with local police to rebuild and reform to meet these challenge son their own.

9.1.5 Gender Balance

Women's participation in all spheres of decision-making and policy formulation is both a form of justice and redress and a necessary element of real democratization. No policy process or institution can be credible which fails to incorporate the participation of a majority of the population; and this holds equally true for forums which determine and implement transitional justice policies. Moreover, marginalization and exclusion are often at the heart of the conflict being addressed, and transitional justice mechanisms are intended to both address these causes as well as contribute to the creation of a new society. Creating mechanisms which incorporate the voices of women and women's experiences begins to address old patterns of exclusion and actively lays down new patterns of engagement for the state. By doing so, it contributes to democratization in valuing equal participation in the public sphere, as well as vertical reconciliation as trust is built between previously marginalized populations and state institutions. Beyond being an important end goal in itself, gender balance in all areas of policy and implementation is a factor in sound policy formulation and implementation as it brings to the table an increased range of skills and perspectives.

Despite recognition of the need for gender balance in all policy processes concerned with dealing with the legacy of past crimes, actual progress towards this objective has been inconsistent. A United Nations Development Fund for Women (UNIFEM) study on Security Council Resolution (Women, Peace and Security) notes that rarely have women been 'consulted about the form, scope and modalities for seeking accountability. Women's stake in these processes has been minimized or denied and, in most cases, crimes against them go unrecorded.'

9.1.6 Women's Stake; Minimized Processes

- Democratization and social justice necessitate that women be involved at every step of postconflict reconstruction. Pressure should be brought to bear by international institutions and donor agencies for a minimum number of seats to be reserved for women during peace negotiations and in all forums where decisions are being made regarding justice for past crimes.

- A space at the table does not however guarantee that these voices will be heard. To increase effectiveness and impact, international agencies should work with local civil society, and particularly women's organizations, to build the capacity and,
- Expertise necessary to strategically represent the needs of previously marginalized constituencies during these deliberations.
- International agencies must reflect the practice they preach. Many such organizations continue to be dominated by men, particularly in those missions operating in a post-conflict context and particularly at higher levels of responsibility. To date, only 2 of the 27 UN peace keeping missions in postconflict countries have been headed by women.
- The full and equal participation of women is a goal in and of itself; it does not however necessarily lead to gendered policy. Equally important is the participation and involvement of gender experts both men and women, at all stages of peace negotiations, and particularly during the foundational discussion son transitional justice policies. This incorporation of gendered expertise should extend to all planning, implementation and evaluation of programs conducted by external agencies in a post conflict context.

9.1.7 Beyond Inclusion

While recent debate in the field of transitional justice has revealed a growing recognition of gender justice as an indivisible component of the overall postconflict justice and peace agenda, there are huge challenges which remain to be addressed. As the previous sections demonstrate, gains thus far have been predominantly concerned with increasing women's representation in existing mechanisms and addressing experiences of sexual violence. Both of these objectives are of fundamental importance, but neither can achieve in isolation the transformative justice required for sustainable peace and reconciliation.

New laws, seen in isolation, reduce women's experiences of conflict to only that of sexual crimes. They do little to challenge the fundamental assumptions of transitional justice mechanisms; the ways in which these assumptions are gendered or the extent to which such mechanisms take cognizance of or strive to further gender equality and justice as part of a 'justice' agenda. Whilst it is essential to make visible the use of rape as a weapon of war, this alone will not address the system of unequal power relations and the use of violence against women as a means to enforce these unequal relations. Gender justice can only be furthered if there is a focus not just on the crime but its context, motivation, and location within continuum violence.

There are two elements necessary to incorporating a gender justice agenda into the transitional justice field. The first requires acknowledging the specific needs of women in a system that has been designed to acknowledge and seek justice for crimes experienced and defined by men, as well as inclusion of women in all processes designed to deliver redress for the past. The second element moves beyond inclusion of women into existing mechanisms and instead seeks to examine the core assumptions of transitional justice from a gendered perspective, opening the field to a reassessment of these assumptions as well as the policies they inform. This second step moves beyond a limited reform agenda to addressing the root causes and consequences of conflict.

Incorporating a 'gender lenses, challenging core assumptions at its core, transitional justice is concerned with redress for victims of past violations and guarantees of non repetition. South Africa, a country often cited as a 'model' in the field of transitional justice for its innovative Truth and Reconciliation Commission premised on public victims hearings and conditional amnesty, is also a vivid example of the failings of such a mechanism to contribute substantially to gender justice. Today, it is a country with higher levels of violence against women than many countries currently mired in 'political' conflict. And it is by no means unique in this experience. Research across postconflict societies reveals that violence does not simply cease with the signing of a peace accord, but forvarious reasons including pervasive trauma, easy access to guns, militarized identities, normalization of conflict and the devastation of judicial systems, violence carries through and can even intensify during a transition period; playing out in ways which have continuity and a rooting in the causes and consequences of the conflict but which can also take on new forms. Ongoing insecurity and violence once again intersect with gendered hierarchies and disproportionately impact on certain sectors of society, those historically in positions of less power such as women, foreigners, children, and the elderly.

High levels of violence, specifically experienced by certain sectors, challenge some of the normative foundations of transitional justice. For example, 'non repetition' has been defined narrowly to cover only violent 'political' conflict which takes the same form as that experienced in the past. It has not been defined in a forward looking manner which repudiates all violence, prejudice and discrimination. The treatment of rape in war as exceptional, as has been the focus of international law to date, renders invisible the relationship between sexual violence in conflict and its ongoing and pervasive existence during and after the transition. These mechanisms may lend themselves to the denunciation of violence against women in a conflict setting, however their 'exceptional' focus does little to denounce violence in all forms, and in particular violence against women during peace.

The removal of war time rape from the continuum of violence against women in which it is inherently a part, the setting it aside as exceptional or not rooted in larger power relations, also reinforces a false dichotomy of conflict and post-conflict and detracts from the more fundamental goal of human security.

Similar to the false dichotomy of conflict and postconflict is the assumption of a dividing line between political and criminal (or 'private') acts. This focus on the political in transitional justice is not informed by the experiences of victims, but rather superimposes a false structure which fails to account for the common impact of violations and insecurity; missing as it does the way in which violence transforms through the transition, the merging of the criminal and the political and the ways in which Violence against women in particular becomes the response to transition, destabilization and the reinforcement of traditional norms.

9.1.8 Feminists

As the causes of violence against women, particularly during the post-conflict period, emanate directly from the political sphere and gendered power relations are very much a political construct the arena of what TJ mechanisms seek to address needs to be expanded beyond the current privileging of a patriarchal notion of what is 'political'. Just as feminists have strived over the years to breakdown the false dichotomy of public/private which entrenches and renders invisible larger structures of oppression, similarly, the false distinctions of conflict/post conflict and criminal/political implicitly entrenched in transitional justice policies must be equally addressed.

9.1.9 International Law

Other key assumptions that require revisiting include the very violations that transitional justice seeks to redress. International law reflects a male experience of conflict, failing to take into account the specific impact conflict has on women slaves, the consequences of a lack of access to basic services; ongoing insecurity; being forced to take on the roles of missing male family members but in a context of ongoing and systematic discrimination such as laws which prohibit women from inheriting land and property, force them to be married to a husband's relative, prevent them from accessing services from the state without a male intermediary etc. For women the post conflict period of rebuilding and restructuring their lives is very much focused on everyday survival needs. In this context, terms such as 'justice' and 'peace' take on a very different meaning. Women's experiences of injustice during conflict are also a result of existing inequalities and as such are not necessarily the crimes that are codified in international human rights law. For example, given existing patterns of feminization of poverty, the aggravation of poverty when a state chooses to shift its spending from social services to military disproportionately affects women and women headed households. Moreover, the gendered impact of forced displacement, of deliberate bombing and destruction of social infrastructure which places an increased burden on those assigned a care giving role by society, are all ways in which conflict has a gendered impact; one which is not captured or redressed through the rights which are codified in international law, and as such, the rights which are the concern and focus of transitional justice. A gendered analysis would require rethinking even what it is that we are seeking redress for. As noted above, the shift in thinking is beginning to occur as experiences of women are incorporated into the work of existing mechanisms, but this incorporation has been limited and has yet to secure justice for the full range of gendered harms.

A focus on gender can also begin to address some of the central questions regarding perpetrators providing needed information for the prevention of future violence. More attention also needs to be paid to the use of rape and sexual violence against male combatants and boys this too is a result of gender constructions and militarized masculinities.

Reassessing key notions of truth, justice and reconciliation from a gendered perspective will undoubtedly complicate the field of transitional justice by destabilizing core assumptions. But it will also lead to different questions being asked, different information being collected and therefore a fuller picture created which can inform policy that furthers a transformation agenda, rather than policy which reinforces unequal power relations.

Given the limited space available it is not possible to examine each of the core areas of transitional justice and assess how incorporating gender would further the end goals of justice and reconciliation. As such, the following section engages with just one key mechanism that of truth commissions and outlines briefly the potential contribution they can make to gender justice, key challenges to date and select policy recommendations before making some further general recommendations for the field.

9.1.10 Truth Commissions

Truth commissions have over the past two decades expanded from their limited institutional origins just a step beyond commissions of inquiry, to bodies that today are expected to deliver a range of social goods not just for victims, but for post conflict societies as a whole: documenting history, encouraging reconciliation, providing public acknowledgment for victims, social sanction for perpetrators and more. Most recently, truth commission reports have gained import as foundational documents of the new society; recording not just past history but providing a blueprint for legislation, policy and practice which address the root causes of the conflict and give impetus to the transition towards democracy and good Governance.

Early concerns with gender and truth commissions were very much focused on increasing the number of women commissioners, encouraging the employment of women statement takers and providing a safe space for women to tell their stories of sexual violence. As noted previously, given the history of silence which shrouds women's experiences of sexual violence and the lack of accountability or justice with which these crimes have been treated, creating spaces to hear, record and acknowledge these crimes is no small contribution. This concern with 'adding women' however has not adequately examined the core assumptions of truth commissions and how these assumptions may or may not fit the needs of women, gender justice and individual context.

With regards to the focus on recording sexual violence itself, assumptions regarding truth, public acknowledgement and healing need to be questioned regarding their applicability to the specific nature of sexual violations. The focus almost exclusively on sexual violence reinforces the view of women as victims and prescribes meaning to the event externally. The focus on the one event severs it from a context of violations and oppression that women endure as well as casts into the shadows the other roles that women have occupied. The truth commission is a forum where this emphasis has played out in a visible manner to silence women's complex identities. Some feminists have noted that because of what is valued by these institutions women are implicitly encouraged to assume a victim identity in order to be 'acknowledged'. The focus on 'the' incident strips it of meaning in a wider context, as well as subverts or fails to acknowledge resilience and the complexity of identities which are not frozen in a single identity of victim-hood. It has been noted that in this regard there is actually a tension established between justices and healing.

Some have argued that truth commissions can in fact undermine gains made by women during conflict, recording and naturalizing a gender biased history through its focus on specific types of violations, individual acts of violence perpetrated against largely 'politically active' figures or combatants, both of which categories have been historically defined to exclude women's roles and marginalizing the spaces occupied and the contribution of women. As one activist notes: 'Societies focus in the aftermath on finding the truth about atrocities and on the reconciliation process; this diverts women from looking at the advances they made during war and distracts them from creating new blueprints. Because public reward goes to those who died, women's advances the survival strategies that kept families alive and communities together are erased from the historical record.'

9.1.11 The Focus; The Power to Highlight the Structural Factors

The focus on the single violation also removes it from its context within a broader frame work of oppression and strips it of the power to highlight the structural factors. In South Africa for example, African women's unlawful detention and the fear and intimidation they felt at the hands of white security officers was informed by lifetime of oppression, humiliation, and abuse at the hands of a white minority state and its officials. To unravel a single element of the overall picture and convey the story as a single event, devoid of context, does little to promote healing and acknowledgement; and may in fact do harm. The primary focus that was placed on getting women to speak of their sexual violations denied the range of other abuses women endured and shaped the stories that were heard; until 'a diversity of harms, a story of sexual violation'. Whilst legal processes necessarily need to focus on the actual crime, transitional justice mechanisms do not have the same limitations, and in pursuit of redress, these bodies need to acknowledge context and address consequence and pain in a more nuanced way which takes into account where women are, what their experiences are, and how their live shave been impacted by the violation. Thus the applicable policies should be given below:

- International institutions and donor agencies should financially and technically support a research agenda during the transition.

Local civil society should be given the resources necessary to carry out research, document victim's perspectives and needs and learn from the experiences of other countries though horizontal networks. Within this research agenda, specific attention should be given to documenting the cultural and political context, power relations and the specific needs of women prior to the establishment of a truth commission or decisions on their mandate or modes of operation.

- There should be no assumptions about what victims of gender based violence (GBV) need for healing and justice; this needs to be context specific. For many victims, the difficulties of discussing one's suffering in the public sphere, particularly in a context where speaking of sexual violence will lead to are victimization and other consequences for the victim, the assumptions of atruth commission regarding revealing and healing may not 'restore dignity 'but may in fact compound harm. This has been well recognized by commissions to date and much effort has been expended on securing in camera hearings and ensuring adequate numbers of women statement takers. However the assumption does not hold true for all women in all contexts and the assumption should not be made that women don't want to speak out. Moreover, there has not been the same concerted focus on encouraging boys and men who have also been victims of GBV and suffer the same consequences of shame and silence to come forward. Gender based violence is not just about women and its use against male victims is equally about gendered power and may need to be addressed in unique ways.
- There must be adequate support given to those who do want to talk, and mechanisms of acknowledgement and redress constituted for those who cannot come forward. The linking of reparations specifically to the disclosure of the violation needs to be reassessed. Even for those that benefit from disclosure, once off unburdening of stories during a hearing is inadequate for full healing, and truth commissions should partner with and feed into a larger network of psycho-social support where available. Different spaces for therapeutic support should also be considered i.e., group hearings or the use of local or cultural traditions may not assist a truth commission to put numbers to the crimes, but they could be a more valuable space for victim-centered healing. Given that this

is the first priority for commissions, and that in many countries devastation and poverty limits access to any psycho social support beyond the commission itself, these options should be considered where appropriate. Where survivors do choose to testify in public, power over the story and exchange needs to be given to the survivor. The act of taking control over one's own story in a historical context of uneven power relations can be a form of redress itself and contribute to a sense of justice; it also allows the commission to model equal gender relations in its own dealings where the survivor is female.

- Public hearings should be harnessed for their potential value for public education. Special hearings on women that are held publicly should capture the full range of women's experiences not reflect them as passive victims or solely as victims of sexual violence. Truth commissions serve an important function in writing/ recording a new and ideally more inclusive history. The narrowing of women's stories in this forum merely perpetuates their ongoing invisibility from history and the marginalization of their roles and contributions; and further entrenches gendered notions of who is remembered and valorized and what the new society values and includes.
- Final reports can play an important role in guiding the transformation of society; however the best and most inclusive report serves little purpose if its recommendations are not implemented. It is here that multilateral and donor agencies can make an impact in holding governments to account in the implementation of recommendations, in particular those that concern gender justice where political will is often at its weakest. Tying loans, allocating dedicated program funding or incentivizing for the implementation of these recommendations can have substantial impact. This is particularly important with those recommendations that could be easily implemented given sufficient political will, and which would have a meaningful impact.

9.1.12 Further General Policy Recommendations

- Reparations as a tool for gender empowerment: Just as an exclusive focus one specific violation or incident undermines the ability of truth commission's to contribute to a broader agenda of social justice, so too with reparations does the linking of redress to a single incident similarly weaken the potential contribution to social justice. Reparations programs have enormous potential to empower women, address social and economic inequality linked to gender and contribute to a broad social justice agenda. Using reparations policies can serves a proactive vehicle to redress past harms which are not limited to 'the' violation, but rather serve to redress an overall context of oppression and violations of basic rights and a contribution towards furthering gender equality, empowerment and gender sensitive development.

- Lesson learning from other fields: Lessons learned from 'engendering' policy and practice in other fields should be assessed for their application and use in the field of transitional justice. For example, reparations policies in the past have failed to take into consideration the gendered hierarchies of individual families and the implications for how resources are provided, who benefits and what impact these programs have. In South Africa, reparations took the form of a once off payment of approximately $4000 USD. Despite the fact that the majority of beneficiaries were African women, the policy failed to take into consideration both power differentials within families as well as the historic lack of access to bank accounts amongst this population. Local victims groups reported that the money was often deposited into male family member's accounts and women were given limited or no control over the resources. In some cases, tensions over how money should be spent in households lent itself to family violence. Valuable lessons could be learned for reparations programs from the field of Gender Budgetary analysis that is the study of budgets and policy decisions for their gendered impact in order to inform how state spending can be used to target the causes of feminization of poverty; thereby breaking the cycle of poverty and furthering gender sensitive development strategies that foster real equality. By only seeing half the picture, policies can in fact do more harm than good as they are unable to answer questions regarding how resources should be distributed or services delivered and what impact it will have on gender relations or the ability of women to access these resources.
- Integration and coordination: An integrated approach is needed between various sectors and international and national bodies/ donor agencies engaged in all aspects of transitional justice and reconstruction.

- Use of existing resources: In planning transitional justice mechanisms, policymakers should draw upon and make use of relevant existing information which would allow them to understand the overall context with regards to gender relations.
- Funding of research: It is vital to have victim informed policies and research that is gender disaggregated and challenges cultural assumptions.
- Selective audit of mechanisms to date: A multi-country audit should be commissioned to review the range of Transitional Justice (TJ) policies and mechanisms to date and examine not just how women's participation can be increased but the relationship between transitional justice and gender justice; what these mechanisms have contributed to gender justice; how they should be restructured; and what additional policies or procedures would strengthen their impact to this end. There is scant research on these questions thus far.
- Dedicated funding: There is a need for dedicated funding to ensure that these issues are given adequate attention. For example, the dedicated funding provided by the UN's Office of the High Commissioner for Human Rights (OHCHR) in the case of the Peruvian truth commission and by UNIFEM in the form of technical support and expertise in the case of the Sierra Leone truth commission, ensured that these issues could not be relegated to the margins or constrained by an absence of resources.
- Increased representation of women in all levels of international institutions operating in a post-conflict setting. Initial evidence from Liberia in the months after the deployment of the UN's first all women peace keeping unit showed that not only were they making services more accessible to women who had experienced sexual violence but they were also becoming role models and challenging domestic thinking on the roles and abilities of women.
- Support for local women's organizations. Intervention, funding and technical support should be provided to women operating at a grass roots level to bridge the divide post-conflict and forge reconciliation based on shared needs and concrete projects. This is not to essentialism women as being inherently peaceful, but rather to acknowledge that given the traditional roles and place in society occupied by many women, there is evidence across conflict zones of marginalized women seizing these roles in order

to mobilize for change based on concrete projects. Examples such as the Women in Black in Yugoslavia, numerous initiatives by Hutu and Tutsi women to jointly care for children orphaned by the genocide in Rwanda, examples in Burundi, Israel/Palestine and elsewhere all demonstrate a mobilization across the divide based on concrete needs. Support for these initiatives encourages community level reconciliation whilst also supporting projects which address basic survival needs post conflict.

- The role of local mechanisms. Local or traditional rituals can play a strong and positive role in community reintegration of victims and combatants as well as for healing and reconciliation as they are likely to resonate with the local population and have buy in. However some of these practices may perpetuate inequality or undermine the rights of women and girls such as the practice of exchanging a girl of marriageable age as 'compensation' for a life taken or a crime committed. National governments and international institutions should aim to audit local practices in a country during the transition phase to look at what practices could contribute to reconciliation and reintegration, draw out the positive principles to be encouraged and address those that undermine justice and equality. Traditions are not static but evolve according to context. Building on the positive elements of these practices can contribute to establishing locally informed mechanisms for justice and healing and can also have a positive impact on society more generally by initiating the reform of practices that are antithetical to gender justice and leave a legacy of evolved traditions that are more conducive to the rights of all.
- Sustained and long term funding for a range of initiatives. Psychosocial support for example requires long term investment and is not a one off event. Dealing with trauma is integral to halting the cycle of violence and implementing sustainable reconciliation, but victims of gender based violence in particular may not be ready to access psycho social assistance until there has been some space and time from the actual conflict, and until immediate issues of security are addressed.

Security is a precondition to reconciliation and given the pervasive levels of insecurity experienced almost uniformly by women in post conflict situations, an integrated response is required which includes: rebuilding the justice and policing sector; implementing DDR programs which aim to demilitarize society and minds, not just collect weapons; removal of small arms from circulation; access to opportunities for both former combatants and marginalized populations; addressing of root causes; and rebuilding of social development networks amongst other issues. Donors and international agencies should create forums for coordination and regular feedback which involves and is driven by a national agenda. Also, there will be little impact if TJ mechanisms focus on gender equality within a context characterized by ongoing oppression and discrimination. There needs to be an integrated response with other key role players who are concerned with legal reform including the signing of all relevant human rights instruments, particularly CEDAW; establishment of quotas for all levels and spheres of government; public education to address cultural practices which disadvantage women, etc.

9.1.13 General

- An independent, empowered, and representative State womens Commission should be constituted at the earliest possible opportunity.
- All statutory committees aimed at women's empowerment like the committee aimed at dowry prevention should meet regularly, their powers should be well defined and information about their activities and mechanisms should be widely disseminated.
- The divorce and the maintenance provisions of women belonging to the minority community should be examined and a wide process of consultation should be ensured to ascertain womens views.
- Consultative processes should be undertaken to understand and document the many customary laws affecting women in Chhattisgarh, so that adequate steps can be undertaken for codification/ modification.
- NGO representation should be ensured in all state and lower level committees that are concerned with womens issues.
- The Chief Minister should reserve the daily Jandarshan programme at least once a week for women to place their problems before him directly.

9.1.13.1 Livelihoods, Labour and Employment

- To ensure equality of wages of men and women especially in agricultural and unorganized sector.

- Crèches for the children of working women and elementary education facilities at all workplaces of women at the responsibility of the employer.
- Separate toilets for women at all workplaces/offices should be ensured
- Special provision for the rehabilitation and education of girl child labourers should be put in place.
- Womens participation in management of water, forest and common property resources in land be ensured through adequate legal safeguards.
- Labour cases of women workers that are pending in court for long periods be shifted to fast track courts and speedy justice be ensured.
- Since seasonal out migration of rural worker families is a serious issue in the state, and since sexual and economic harassment of migrant women is a major problem, the government should immediately constitute an empowered regulatory body to put in place structures of Redressal and relief for cases pertain to migrant women.
- Womens SHGs should be encouraged to go into productive ventures and suitable marketing support should be given to them through Khadi and Village Industries Commission and other agencies.
- Cottage and small scale industries should be given a boost to provide maximum employment opportunities to women.
- Adequate provisions and separate resting facilities for women at all workplaces where women are employed at night.
- Reservation for women in all public sector employment to the extent of 50 percent, and reservation for promotion and career advancement.

9.1.13.2 Education

- Increase and extend facilities for girls education at all levels, especially in far-flung areas of the state.
- Family life education should be given to girls studying in 9 to 12 standard.
- Network of high schools for accessible in every Tehsil and district. Including special schools for girls.

- Ensure enabling provisions for higher education for girls, including financial assistance and grants for books.
- Girl's hostels should be set up at tehsil and district level with proper security and other facilities.
- Restarting of Adult Education Program and rehabilitation of girls who have dropped out from mainstream education through condensed courses/ innovative schemes.
- Separate toilets should be constructed for the exclusive use of girls at all schools and institutions of higher education.
- Special facilities be created for the education including vocational education of women in jails and their minor children.

9.1.13.3 Health

- Compulsory recruitment of at least one female medical officer in each primary health center. At present there is only one female doctor at the district level.
- Surveys of pregnant adolescent girls should be undertaken to identify nutrition status (BMI) and anemia. Adequate package of diet and supplementary nutrition should be conceptualized and put in place.
- Adequate facilities and treatment arrangements for women suffering from mental illness should be made. There should be a psychiatrist posted/attached to each district hospital, and a comprehensive residential care and rehabilitation facility should be put in place at every district.
- Compulsory recruitment of a female doctor in jail to attend to the female prisoners.

9.1.13.4 Legal and Criminal Justice

- Legal recognition to the proceedings and decisions of Family Counseling Centre and Parivarik Lok Adalats.
- Institutionalize a system of family counseling centers and setting up of family courts for a quick redressal of family disputes and to resolve family problems being faced by women.
- Put an absolute stop to the practice of husbands of elected PRI representatives negotiating with govt. officials on behalf of their spouses. Penalize officials found doing so,
- Strict penalties are enforced on those found guilty of crime of sexual violence and harassment, especially with minor girls.

- A law is enacted to make it mandatory for all decisions of PRI/ Gram Sabhas to be valid only if it has been passed by a 33 percent women's vote in the relevant constituency.
- Machinery should be put in place to ensure full and proper implementation of the provisions of the Prevention of PNSDT laws and female foeticide.
- Setting up of special women courts presided by a women Judge to ensure quick and easy disbursement on justice.
- The present situation in which the minimum penalty and easily available nature of offences of drinking and gambling should be proactively changed so that the penalties act as deterrents to those indulging in such abuse. Much of family violence on women is traceable to these vices.
- Financial compensation to women victims' sexual violence, currently available to SC, ST women only, should be generalized.
- Since many women currently in jails exist totally without family support, the government should constitute a cell to extend legal, counseling and other forms of support to such women.
- Since many women under trials are unable to attend hearings in their cases due to absence of women constables to escort them to court, recruitment and placement of relevant personnel be put into place forthwith.

9.1.13.5 Social Problems

- Unfair practice of branding vulnerable women as Tonhi followed by extreme torture, exploitation and social ostracism. Deal with this issue by increasing awareness, enforcing strict penalties to those found guilty of perpetrating this form of violence, and campaigning actively against superstitions and irrational belief. Police should be specially sensitized and trained to deal with this issue.
- Concentration of liquor shops around the industries, which results in men spending their wages on liquor. Such outlets should not be located near industrial areas or residential areas.
- Illegal sale of liquor in villages should be controlled.
- Adequate safeguards should be institutionalized to protect women against exploitation and harassment at their work place.
- To set up complain boxes at prominent public places for women to register their complaints against sexual harassment or violence.

- Committee on harassment and exploitation of women should be formed with increased representation of rural women.
- Adequate representation of women should be ensured in traditional caste panchayats as these bodies often legislate on family matters regarding women and at present are totally patriarchal.
- Adequate steps should be under taken to address the issue of child marriages in the state. A campaign strategy for awareness and action should be formalized in this regard.

9.1.13.6 Social Security

- Funds distributed to the deserted and the widowed women by the Panchayats should be monitored by the State Government.
- Special Police Thanas should be set up at every district and ordinary Thanas should be strengthened with Mahila Darogas or Women Constables. One of the functions of the Darogas should be the facilitation of FIR registration of cases against women.
- Easy and uncomplicated laws for Divorce for women to follow in genuine cases.
- Retrieval of alimony becomes particularly difficult in case of laborers or businessmen. In such cases, the Police should retrieve the money from the Husband and deposit the amount with the Court.
- If the Mother is in a position to be the caretaker of the child, in case of a divorce, the custody of the child should be given to the mother till the child attains adulthood.
- Old age homes for destitute women at the tehsil level set up by the State Government, although, if required, the private management can run them.
- Transparent and simplified system for identification of recipients of old age and social security pensions as well as disbursement of pensions by the government.
- The report of sexual exploitation of women should be kept confidential and a special team of five members, consisting of an advocate, a doctor, a lawyer, a journalist and a social worker should investigate the same.
- At present there are only three Nari Niketan in the State. There should be at least one Nari Niketan and one girl's juvenile home

in every district and the management on the institution should be in the hands on the representative panel, including government and non governmental persons.

- Institutional and community based rehabilitation for physically challenged women.
- Lack of information on various rules and schemes reduces the efficacy of functioning of voluntary organizations. Such information should be circulated through charts and other ways to increase awareness amongst women at the village level.
- Separate window set up for women to ensure ease of transaction.
- Ensure appropriate identification and procedures of families below poverty line taking into account cultural practices or behavior.

9.1.13.7 Media

- The problem of commercial representation of womens bodies and indecent exposure of womens bodies has become an increasingly serious issue. To tackle this, it was suggested that a panel be set up at State level to monitor the media in this respect and that on the recommendation of this committee, govt. advertisements to said media be stopped. Publicity and Awareness Rising.
- Extensive Camps in villages for spreading awareness about rational health practices, dowry, AIDS and other legal/essential issues. Both government as well as non-government organizations should organize such camps.
- Use of appropriate media channels to raise awareness of womens rights in remote areas.
- State government should publish a small booklet only stating womens laws and circulate it through the supervisory staff example the Aanganwadi Workers.

9.1.13.8 Rural/Urban Development

- Elected women representatives should be given on duty training about their rights and duties through workshops and other ways in rural areas.
- In urban areas, special cells should be constituted to take up cases of violence against women and to look into complaints of trafficking.

9.2 Conclusion

In India, a sex selection phenomenon has been in place since the 1980s, with men born during this period now at marriageable age then the urbanization since the 1990s where a lot of families and men have moved to cities to look for work. People are much wealthier but at the same time there's pressure to produce sons as an heir, so educated, wealthy families are now more likely to have sex selection. All these factors are coming to play and creating this toxic mixture, which has turned violence against women into a bigger issue today. India's social structure is a unique blend of diverse religions, cultures and racial groups with the great religion of the world, viz, the Hindus, the Muslims, the Christians, etc, are found here. The 18 major literary languages, apart from numerous other languages and dialects add to it. This leads to a striking diversity between various communities and groups in kinships and marriages rites, customs, inheritance and modes of living. Diversity is also seen in the pattern of rural as well as urban settlements, community life, cultural and social behaviour as also in the institutional framework.

In the ancient India women were held in high esteem and the position of a woman in the Vedas and the Upanishads was that of a mother (maata) or goddess (Devi). In the Manusmriti, woman was considered as a precious being and in the early Vedic age, girls were looked after with care. Then practice of polygamy deteriorated the status of woman and in the medieval period, the practices of purdha system, dowry and sati came into being. With the passage of time, the status of woman was lowered. After the development of science and technology, female foeticide is being practiced on a large scale. This has led to a drop in the female ratio. According to the census 2001, the sex ratio in India is 927 females to 1,000 males. And then dowry have become common and started Female infanticide practices in few areas. In many parts of India, women are viewed as an economic liability despite contribution in several ways to our society and economy. The crime graph against women is increasing at an alarming rate. The condition of an Indian widow is quite deplorable. At home, the woman's contribution towards home as a housewife is not recognized. Domestic Violence, Rape, Sexual Exploitation, molestation, eve-teasing, forced prostitution, sexual harassment at work places etc are a common affair today and in some cases its too tragic that it gets the global attention. The major reasons for this inequality are identified as the need of a male heir for the family, huge dowry, continued financial support to girl child, poverty, domestic violence, farming as major job for poor and the caste system.

At work, this disparity is visible through a different working environment for women, unequal wages, undignified treatment, sexual harassment, higher working hours, engagement in harmful industries, occupational hazards, working roughly twice as many hours as men and a nearly 27 percentage of women are accounted by unpaid activities. Violence against women is also prominent in India which leads to every 42 minutes a sexual harassment occurring, every 43 minutes a woman kidnapped and every 93 minutes a woman is burnt for dowry. And by the pre quarter of reported, rapes involve girls under the age of 16 years. Every 26 minutes a woman is molested and every 34 minutes a rape take place.

Poor health care is another attitude towards women which makes them neglected during illness, recognition of illness by herself, health services as a last resort and reluctance to be examined by male doctors. Lack of education in women has lead to poor literacy leading to gender gap in literacy rate and no higher education. Economic constraints are also imposed to women in India by keeping them as dependents, no equal property rights (as against law), loans of men is paid back by women, economic uncertainty and denial in inheritance of properties to orphaned/ deserted. Discriminative socialization process is another aspect of inequality towards women which leads to customary practices, more involvement in household activities only (boys not allowed), restricted to play, isolation, separation in schools and public places and restrictions to move freely. Detrimental cultural practices like after marriage husbands dominating the family, dominance from In-laws family, members, never or rarely considered for any decision making, limitations in continuing relationships with brothers, sisters, relatives, child or early marriage, patriarchal attitudes and not able to continue girl or boy friendship after marriage are also contributing factor to the inequality. In Governance this inequality is visible, after over sixty years of independence women are still exploited, the 73rd and 74th constitutional amendments have provided 33 percent reservation for women in the Panchayati Raj System ,Panchayat and Parliament totally 790 seats by filling 6.6 - 8.4 percentage, women Reservation bill delayed, cast disparity and the men domination in administration.

Strategies for advancement of women should be higher literacy, more formal education, and greater employment opportunity. In education it needs to be reducing primary and secondary dropout of female child. In post literacy, the basic literacy skills at speaking, reading, and writing and problem solving shall be imparted. Women learners should educate their children which further enhances social advancement. In job opportunities there shall be reservation or expenditure or provision of services or special provisions. In governance all rights and all legal measures should be available for women's protection and support. Human rights education, know how to take control of their circumstance, help to achieve their own goals, helping themselves, enhancing their quality of life and motivating for lobbying or advocacy are also enablers for their advancement. Collaborators such as NGO, INGOs, NPOs, SHGs, CBOs, policy makers, local leaders, information disseminators, health care providers, teachers and family members should help in the social advancement of women

Gender gaps favoring males in education, health, personal autonomy, and more are systematically larger in poor countries than in rich countries. Poor countries by no means have a monopoly on gender inequality. Men earn more than women in essentially all societies. However, disparities in health, education, and bargaining power within marriage tend to be larger in countries with low GDP per capita. It hampers the overall well being, because blocking women from participation in social, political and economic activities can adversely affect the whole society. Many developing countries including India, have displayed gender inequality in education, employment and health.

It is common to find girls and women suffering from high mortality rates. There are vast differences in education level of the two sexes. India has witnessed gender inequality from its early history due to its socio-economic and religious practices that resulted in a wide gap between the position of men and women in the society.

Statistics reveal that in India males significantly outnumber females and this imbalance has increased over time. The sex ratio according to 2001 census report stands at 933 per 1000 males. Out of the total population, 120 million are women who live in abject poverty. The maternal mortality rate in rural areas is among the world's highest.

From a global perspective, India accounts for 19 percent of all live births and 27 percent of all maternal deaths. The deaths of young girls in India exceed those of young boys by over 300,000 each year, and every 6th infant death is specifically due to gender discrimination. Women face discrimination right from the childhood. Gender disparities in nutrition are evident from infancy to adulthood.

In fact, gender has been the most statistically significant determinant of malnutrition among young children and malnutrition is a frequent, direct or underlying, cause of death among girls below age 5. Girls are breast fed less frequently and for a shorter duration in infancy. In childhood and adulthood, males are fed first and better. Adult women consume approximately 1,000 fewer calories per day than men according to one estimate.

Imagine a country where the most powerful political figure, two billionaires, three of the most dominant regional politicians, several prominent CEOs, and half of local government representatives are women. Now imagine that, in that same country, one third of adult women are illiterate, spousal rape is not illegal, and sex selective abortion and female infanticide are still widely practiced.

It may be hard to reconcile these two realities, but modern India somehow manages to be, at the same time, the land of Indira Gandhi and Mother Theresa and of child brides and dowry deaths. The standing of women in Indian society received unprecedented national and international attention last year following the brutal gang rape and subsequent death of a young woman in Delhi. The incident sparked widespread public protests in the Indian capital and gained further attention after one of the accused perpetrators was found hanged in jail on Monday. While the tragedy has led to some long overdue reforms, it is far too early to declare it a turning point for the fate of the majority of India's women.

"No nation, no society, no community can hold its head high and claim to be part of the civilized world if it condones the practice of discriminating between men and women." The only concern here is gender inequality. The widespread practice of aborting female foetuses happens every day: the reality of gender inequality in India, origin of gender inequality and how to deactivate it.

The reality of gender inequality in India is very complex and diversified, because it is present in many ways, many fields and many classes. Fields like education, employment opportunities, where men are always preferred over women. Consider the case a girl taking admission in mechanical engineering. Doesn't it sound a bit awkward because it's always considered a man's field.

There again comes this menace gender inequality. The gender inequality faced by women was so much that many women claimed May God give sons to all. This is a fact and India has witnessed gender inequality from its early history due to its socio-economic and religious practices that resulted in a wide gap between the position of men and women in the society. Clearly, then gender gaps that are widespread in access to basic rights, access to and control of resources, in economic opportunities and also in power and political voice are an impediment to development.

The origin of this gender inequality has always been the male ego. At least in India, a woman still needs the anchor of a husband and a family. Their dominating nature has led women to walk with their head down. It was all practiced from the beginning and is followed till date. Consider the woman's reservation case in parliament. The opposing party believes that women are born to do household work and manage kids, and not to corrupt the country by taking hold over politics. Here, just as women's domestic work is undervalued, so are their skills in the world of employment. Most are concentrated in the poorly paid, low skilled 'women' sectors of the economy.

What we need today are trends where girls are able not only to break out of the culturally determined patterns of employment but also to offer advice about career possibilities that look beyond the traditional pail of jobs. It is surprising that in spite of so many laws, women still continue to live under stress and strain. To ensure equality of status for our women we still have miles to go. Things do not always work out in our favor (women are still subjected to the glass ceiling and unequal pay) but we still have the freedom to speak, resist, challenge and change. Thus, it is rightly said that Man and Woman are like two wheels of a carriage. The life of one without the other is incomplete.

Bibliography

Abrevaya , J. (2009) Are There Missing Girls in the United States? Evidence from Birth Data, *American Economic Journal: Applied Economics,* 1:34.

Accra Agenda for Action (2008) www.oecd.org/dac/effectiveness.

Action Aid (2007) "Gender Mainstreaming since Beijing: A Review of Success and Limitations in International Institutions". *Gender and Development* Vol. 13, No. 2, *Mainstreaming a Critical Review*. Taylor & Francis on behalf of Oxfam GB. pp. 11–22.

Adukia, A. (2014) Sanitation and Education, "Working paper, University of Chicago. Albanesi, S. and C. Olivetti (2009): Gender Roles and Medical Progress," Working Paper 14873, National Bureau of Economic Research.

Ahmed, S. (2004) *Gender Issues in Agriculture and Rural Livelihoods Volume* 1. Chennai: M. S. Swaminathan Research Foundation and Thrissur: Kerala Agricultural University.

Alesina, A. et al. (2013) On the Origins of Gender Roles: Women and the Plough, Quarterly *Journal of Economics,* 128, 469, 530.

Almond, D. and Edlund, L. (2008) Son-Biased Sex Ratios in the 2000 United States Census," Proceedings of the National Academy of Sciences, 105, 5681, 5682.

Anand, P., Hunter, G., Carter, I., Dowding, K., Guala, F. and Hee, Van. M. (2010) "The Development of Capability Indicators", *Journal of Human Development and Capabilities* 10(1): 125–152.

Anderson, S. (2003) Why Dowries Payments Declined with Modernization in Europe but Are Rising in India, *Journal of Political Economy,* 111, 269-310.

Anderson, S. (2007) The Economics of Dowry and Bride price, *Journal of Economic Perspectives*, 21, 151,174.

Anderson, S. and Bidner, C. (2014) Property Rights over Marital Transfers," Mimeo, Simon Fraser University.

Anderson, S. and Genicot, G. (2014) Suicide and Property Rights in India," Working Paper 19978, National Bureau of Economic Research.

Anker, R. (1997) "Theories of occupational segregation by sex", in *International Labour Review*, Vol.136, No.3 pp. 315-339, Geneva.

Anker, Richard (1987) Preface, in L. Goldschmidt-Clermont, *Economic evaluations of unpaid household work: Africa, Asia, Latin America and Oceania*, ILO, Geneva, Switzerland.

Appadurai, A. (1981) 'Gastro-Politics in Hindu South Asia', *American Ethnologist*, 8(3), pp. 494–511. Available at: http://www.jstor.org.gate2.library.lse.ac.uk/stable/644298

Arkles, Gabriel. and Gehi, Pooja S. (2007) "Unraveling injustice: Race and class impact of medicaid exclusions of transition-related health care for transgender people". Sexuality Research & Social Policy 4 (4): 7–35. doi:10.1525/srsp.2007.4.4.7.

Arnold, F., et al., (1998) Son Preference, the Family-Building Process and Child Mortality in India," Population Studies, 52, 301-315.

Asifa Quraishi (1997) "*Her Honor: An Islamic Critique of the Rape Laws of Pakistan from a Woman-Sensitive Perspective", Michigan Journal of International Law,* Vol. 18, No. 2.

Awais, et al. (2009) Socio-economic empowerment of tribal women: An Indian perspective, *Int Jrnl of Rural Studies (IJRS),*vol-16, no-1 Article 5.

Azmat, et al. (2007) Gender Gaps in Unemployment Rates in OECD Countries, *Journal of Labor Economics*, 24(1): 1-37.

Bairathi, S. (1991) "Tribal Culture, economy and health" Rawat Publishers, Jaipur.

Bardasi et al (2011) 'How do Female Enterpreneurs Perform? Evidence from Three Developing Region", *Small Business Economics,* 37 (4), pp. 417-441.

Barro, R. and Lee, J.W. (2010) "A New Data Set of Educational Attainment in the World, 1950–2010." NBER Working Paper No. 15902. *www.barrolee.com/data/dataexp.htm.*

Basu, Alka M. (1993) "Women's Roles and the Gender Gap in Health and Survival", mimeograph, Institute of Economic Growth, Delhi University.

Besley, T. and A. Case (2003) "Political Institutions and Policy Choices: Empirical Evidence from the United States", *Journal of Economic Literature* 41: 7-73.

Bettio, F. and Verashchagina, A. (2009) Gender segregation in the labour market: Root causes, implications and policy responses in the EU, Luxembourg: Publications Office of the European Union.

Bhasin, K (1999) *Tribals of Ladakh: Ecology, Human Settlements and Health*. Delhi: Kamla-Raj Enterprises.

Bhasin, K. (1998) Understanding Gender', Kali For Women, New Delhi.

Bhasin, V. (2007) *Status of tribal woman in Indi*a. Retrieved from http://www.krepublishers.com/02-Journals/S-HCS/HCS-01-0-000-000-2007-Web/HCS-01-1-001-07-Abst-Text/HCS-01-1-001-07-001-Bhasin-V/HCS-01-1-001-07-01-Bhasin-V-Tt.pdf Accessed on 23 September, 2011

Bhat, P. N. Mari and A. J. Francis Zavier (2003) Fertility Decline and Gender Bias in Northern India, *Demography, 40(4),* Population Association of America Northern India,637-657.

Blackden, M., S. Canagarajah, S. Klasen, and D. Lawson (2006) "Gender and Growth in Sub-Saharan Africa: Issues and Evidence." UNU-WIDER Research Paper No. 2006/37.

Blaydes, Lisa. and Drew, A. Linzer (2006) The Political Economyof Women's Support for Fundamentalist Islam. Working paper, Department of Political Science, University of California, Los Angeles.

Bloch, F. and Rao, V. (2002) Terror as a Bargaining Instrument: A Case Study of Dowry Violence in Rural India," American Economic Review, 92, 1029-1043.

Bockrath, T. (2003) "Bhartia Hijro Ka Dharma: The Code of India's Hijra", Legal Studies Forum 83.

Borooah, V. and Iyer, S. (2005). Religion, Literacy, and the Female-to-Male Ratio, "*Economic and Political Weekly,* 40, pp. 419-427.

Boserup, E. (1970) Woman's Role in Economic Development, London: George Allen and Unwin Ltd.

Brandon, R.R. & Dixit, B.N. (1983) Sericulture for Tribal Women In Singh, J.P., Vyas, N.N. and Mann, R.S. (Eds.). *Tribal Women and Development.* MLC Tribal Research and Training Institute, Tribal Area Development Dept., Udaipur, Rajasthan.

Bruce, J.S and Clark (2004) *The implications of early marriage for HIV/AIDS policy*. Brief prepared for Population Council and UNFPA.

Burde, D. and Linden, L.L. (2013) Bringing Education to Afghan Girls: A Random- ized Controlled Trial of Village-Based Schools," American Economic Journal: Applied Economics, 5, 27-40.

Buss, D.M. (1989) Sex Deference in Human Mate Preferences: Evolutionary Hypothe- ses Tested in 37 Cultures, "Behavioral and Brain Sciences, 12, 1; 14.

Butler, Judith. (1990) Gender Trouble: Feminism and the Subversion of Identity, New York & London: Routledge, Chapter 1: Subjects of Sex/Gender/Desire, p346.

Caijing.Com.Cn (2010) China's labor share of GDP declined for 22 consecutive years, http://english.caijing.cn/2010-05-12/110437827.html.

CEDAW (1993) www2.ohchr.org/english/bodies/cedaw/docs/.../CEDAW-C-BHS-1_4.doc

Census of India (2011) Office of the Registrar General & Census Commissioner, India.

Census of India (2001) *Primary Census Abstract General Population, Scheduled Casters and Scheduled Tribes,* Ministry of Home Affairs, Government of India, New Delhi.

Chakraborty, T. and Kim, S. (2010) "Kinship Institutions and Sex Ratios in India." *Demography* 47(4):989–1012.

Chakravarty, Indira (1972) *Saga of Indian Food: a Historical and Cultural Survey*. New Delhi: Sterling.

Chatterjee, P. (1993) *The Nation and its Fragments: Colonial and Postcolonial Histories,* Princeton, Princeton University Press.

Chen, Lincoln C., Huq, Emdadul and D'Souza, Stan (1981) "Sex Bias in the Family Allocation of Food and Health Care in Rural Bangladesh." *Population and Development Review* 7(1):55–70.

Chen, M. (1995) A Matter of Survival: Women's Right to Employment in India and Bangladeshh, in Women, Culture and Development, ed. by M. Nussbaum and J. Glover, Oxford, UK: Clarendon Press.

CIA (2010) The World Factbook: Online. Available at: www.cia.gov/library/publication the world-factbook/index.html(accessed April 2010).

Cohen, L. (1995) The Pleasures of Castration: the postoperative status of hijras, jankhas and academics, in Paul R. Abramson, Steven D. Pinkerton (eds), Sexual Nature, Sexual Culture, (University of Chicago Press, 1995.

Corden, W.M. and Neary, J.P. (1982) Booming Sector and De-Industrialization in a Small Open Economy, *The Economic Journal*, vol. 92(368): pp. 825-848.

Correa, Sonia and R. Petchesky (1994) "Reproductive and Sexual Rights: A Feminist Perspective." In *Population Policies Reconsidered: Health, Empowerment, and Rights*, eds. G. Sen, A. Germain, and L.C. Chen. Boston, MA: Harvard University Press, 107-123.

Costa Rica (2000) UNICEF (2000). Estado de los Derechos de la Niñez y la Adolescencia en Costa Rica (1999). San José, Costa Rica: UNICEF.

Crystallising Queer Politics-The Naz Foundation Case and Its Implications For India's Transgender Communities (PDF) (2009) http://www.liiofindia.org/in/journals/NUJSLawRw/2009/26.html.

DAC (1999) Guidelines on Gender Equality and Women's Empowerment in Development Co-operation.

Dalton, E.L. (1872) Descriptive Ethnology of Bengal. Calcutta: Office of the Superintendent of Government Printing Press, West Bengal.

Das Gupta, M. (1987) "Selective discrimination against female children in rural Punjab, India." Population and Development Review13: 377-400.

Das Gupta, M. et al 2003) Why Is Son Preference So Persistent in East and South Asia? A Cross- Country Study of China, India and the Republic of Korea, *"Journal of Development Studies,* 40, 153-187.

de Schlippe (1956) *Shifting Cultivation in Africa: The Zande System of Agriculture*. Routledge and Kegan-Paul, London.

Deininger, K. et al (2013) Women's Inheritance Rights and Intergenerational Transmission of Resources in India," Journal of Human Resources, 48, 114-141.

Deolankar, V. (2003) "A Profile of Entrepreneurship Development Yojana, May.

Derne, S. (2000) *Movies, Masculinity, and Modernity: An Ethnography of Men's Filmgoing in India*. Greenwood Press.

Desai, et. al (2010) "Gender Scripts and Age at Marriage in India." *Demography* 47(3):667–87.

Deshpande , A. (2007) "Overlapping identities under liberalization: gender and caste in India", Economic Development and Cultural Change, 55(4): 735-760.

Deshpandey, Shashi (1978) *A Matter of Time*. New Delhi: Penguin Books India, 1996. Print.

Dodoo, F. Nii-Amoo, and Ashley E. Frost (2008) "Gender in African Population Research: The Fertility/Reproductive Health Example." *Annual Review of Sociology* 34(1):431–52.

Dorothy, E.R. et al (2006) "Race and Gender in the Law Review," 100 Northwestern University Law Review 27-70 (with Cynthia Bowman & Leonard Rubinowitz).

Drucker, P. (1986) *Toward the next economics and other essays.* New York: Harper and Row.

Dyson, T. and Moore, M. (1983) On Kinship Structure, Female Autonomy, and De- mographic Behavior in India, "Population and Development Review, 9, 35-60.

Ebenstein, A. (2014) Why do parents abort girls? Patrilocality and its historical origins, "Mimeo, Princeton University.

Ebenstein, A. and Leung, S. (2010) Son Preference and Access to Social Insurance: Evidence From China's Rural Pension Program, "Population and Development Review, 36, 47-70.

EC (*European Commission)* (2007) European Commission's database on women and men in decision-making: http://ec.europa.eu/justice/gender-equality/gender-decision-making/database/index_en.htm

Eckel, Catherine C., and Philip J. Grossman. (2008) "Differences in the Economic Decisions of Men and Women: Experimental Evidence." In C. Plott and V. Smith (eds.) *Handbook of Experimental Economic Results*: 509-519. New York: Elsevier.

Economic Census (2005) unstats.un.org/.../economic.../Economic_Census/ Economic%20Census%20TR.pdf

Edelberg, L. and Jones, C. (1979) *Nutristan, Academische: Druck-Urid-Verlagsab State* Australia: Graz.

Emerick, Y. (2002) 'The Fight for the Soul of Islam in America', in Wolfe, M. (ed.) Taking Back Islam: American Muslims Reclaim Their Faith, pp. 196–202. United States: Rodale.

Ferm, N. (2008) 'Non-traditional agricultural export industries: conditions for women workers in Colombia and Peru', Gender & Development 16(1): 13-26.

Fernandes, et al (2001) Women's Rights and Development," Journal of Economic Growth, 19, 37-80.

Fernandez, et al (2004) Mothers and Sons: Preference Formation and Female Labor Force Dynamics, *"Quarterly Journal of Economics,* 119, 1249-1299.

Fernandez, R. and Fogli, A. (2009) Culture: An Empirical Investigation of Beliefs, Work, and Fertility, "*American Economic Journal: Macroeconomics,* 1, 146-177.

Field, E. and Ambrus, A. (2008) Early Marriage, Age of Menarche, and Female Schooling Attainment in Bangladesh, *"Journal of Political Economy,* 116, 881-930.

Field, E. et al (2010) Do Traditional Institutions Con- strain Female Entrepreneurship? A Field Experiment on Business Training in India, *"American Economic Review,* 100, 125-129.

Field, E. et al (2014) Friends at Work: Can Peer Support Stimulate Female Entrepreneurship?" Mimeo, Northwestern University.

Florentino, R.F., et. al (2003) Dietary and physical activity patterns of 8- to 10-year-old urban schoolchildren in Manila, Philippines. *Food and Nutrition Bulletin*, 2002, 23(3):267–273.

Franzmen, M. (2000) *Women and Religion*. Oxford University Press, Oxford.

Furer- Haimendor(1943) The Chenchus: Jungle folk of Deccan, London: Macmillan and Company.

Gadgil, D. R. and Dandekar, V. M. (1991) *Primary Education in Satara District: A Report*, Gokhale Institute of Politics and Economics, Pune.

Garcia, Michelle (2013) "Women's College Returns Transgender Student's Application". Advocate.com.

Geertz, Clifford. (1983) Local Knowledge: Further Essays in Interpretive Anthropology, New York: Basic Books, p81.

Gender Inequality Index (2010) eige.europa.eu/sites/default/.../Gender-Equality-Index-Country-Profiles.pdf

Genicot, G. (2014) *Aspirations and Inequality*, NBER Working Paper 19976, Cambridge MA: National Bureau of Economic Development.

Germaine Greer (2001) "*The Female Eunuch"*, Farrar, Straus, and Giroux.

Global Expat Network India (2014) *"Lesbian, Gay, Bisexual and Transgender Communities in India". Angloinfo; the Global Expat Network INDIA.*

GOI, Educationforallindia.com, Selected Educational Statistics (2007-08) www.educationforallinindia.com/ses.htm

GOI, NSSO, Report No. 516, Employment & Unemployment Situation among Social Groups in India, 61st Round, (July 2004 – June 2005), October 2006 and NSSO (2009-10)www.indiaenvironmentportal.org.in/.../NSS_Report_employment%20and%20unemployment.pdf

Goldin, C. (1990) Understanding *the gender gap: an economic history of American women*. New York: Oxford University Press. 1990. 287pp.

(NBER series on long-term factors in economic development). ISBN: 978-0-19-505077-6.

Goldin, C. and Katz (2009) The Race Between Education and Technology, Harvard University Press.

Goldschmidt Clermont, L. (1987) *Unpaid Work in the Household: A Review of EconomicEvaluation Methods*. International Labour Office, Women, Work and Development Series No. 1. 148 pp.

Grant, Jaime M., Harrison, Jack, Herman, Jody L., Keisling, Mara, Mottet, Lisa, A. and Tanis, Justin (2015) "Injustice at Every Turn: A Report of the National Transgender Discrimination Survey Executive Summary". National Transgender Discrimination Survey. National Center for Transgender Equality, National Gay and Lesbian Task Force. Retrieved 19 April 2015.

Grigson, W.V. (1938) The Maria Gonds of Bastar. Oxford: OxfordUniversity Press.

Gurnug, J. (1998) 'Gender dimension of biodiversity management: Cases from Bhutan and Nepal.' *ICIMOD, Sustainable Mountain Development* (31): 6–7.

Hadhrat Mirza Tahir Ahmad (1992) "*Islam's Response to Contemporary Issues*", Islam International Publications, Ltd.

Halila, H. (1984) www.ukessays.com/.../understanding-of-gender-equality-and-islam-sociology-essay.php

Hausmann, R. et al. (2010) *The Global Gender Gap Report 2010*. World Economic Forum. Retrieved May 18, 2011. (http://www.weforum.org/pdf/gendergap/report2010.pdf).

Hawkley, Louise C. et al. (2005) "Stress, Aging, and Resilience: Can Accrued Wear and Tear Be Slowed?" *Canadian Psychology* 46(3): 115–25.

Hertzman, Clyde. and John Frank. (2005) "Biological Pathways Linking Social Environment, Development, and Health." in *Healthier Societies: From Analysis to Action*, edited by Jody Heymann, Clyde Hertzman, Morris L. Barer, and Robert G. Evans. New York: Oxford University Press.

Hirschman, C. (1985) "Premarital Socioeconomic Roles and the Timing of Family Formation: a Comparative Study of Five Asian Societies." *Demography* 22(1):35–59.

Hogan, M. et al. (1999) Maternal Mortality for 181 Countries, 1980–2008: A Systematic Analysis of Progress towards Millennium Development Goal 5. The Lancet, 375 (9726), 1609-1623.

Horrie, C. and Chippindale,P. (2001) *What is Islam? A Comprehensive Introduction*, pp. 96-100. Virgin Books, 1991. ISBN 0 7535 0827 3.

http://indianexpress.com/article/india/india-others/rajya-sabha-passes-private-bill-to-protect-the-rights-of-transgenders/99

http://owa.netxtra.net/indepth/project.jsp?project=206

http://www.cdc.gov/healthyyouth/physicalactivity/facts.htm

http://www.ghazali.org/ihya/english/index. html

http://www.hcmadras.tn.nic.in/jacademy/Article/PSJ-CJO-SPEECH-Royappetah.pdf

http://www.hrln.org/hrln/womens-justice-.html#ixzz3ia8VHyyu

http://www.newkerala.com/news/2015/fullnews-72086.html)

https:/en.wikipedia.org

https:/www.ncbi.nlm.nih.gov/pmc/articles/pmc2928103

Hunter, W.W. (1973) Orissa. London : Smith Elder.

Hutton, J.H. (1922) The Sema Naga. London: Macmillan.

IANS (2014) news.biharprabha.com.

ICRW (2000) 'Domestic Violence in India: Part 3, A Summary Report of a Multi-Site Household Survey', International Centre for Research on Women and The Centre for Development and Population Activities.

IFC (2009) 'Growth Orientated Women Enterprise', www.ifc.org/ifcext/africa.nsf/Content/GOWE_Home

IGHRC (2005) Institutional Memoir of the 2005 Institute for Trans and Intersex Activist Training, p8 http://www.iglhrc.org/files/iglhrc/LAC/ITIAT-Aug06-E.pdf)

IIPS and Macro International (2007) National Family Health Survey 2005-2006, India.Mumbai: International Institute for Population Sciences.

Illich (1982) *Gender*, Pantheon Publications, New York.

In *Oliphant v. Suquamish Indian Tribe*, 435 U.S. 191 (1978) https://supreme.justica.com > cases > federal

International Center for Research on Women (2007) Engaging Men and Boys; To Achieve Gender Equality: www.icrw.org/.../Engaging-Men-and-Boys-to-Achieve- ender-Equality-How-Can-We-Build-on-What-We-Have-Learned.pdf

International Gay and Lesbian Human Rights Commission (IGLHRC) (2005) Institutional Memoir of the 2005 Institute for Trans and Intersex Activist Training, p. 8. http://www.iglhrc.org/files/iglhrc/LAC/ITIAT-Aug06-E.pdf

International Labor Organization (1997) http://www.ilo.org/ilolex/english/convdisp1.htm *Promoting gender equality: a resource kit for trade unions* http://www.ilo.org/public/english/employment/gems/advance/trade.htm *ABC of women workers' rights and gender equality* http://www.ilo.org/dyn/gender/docs/RES/68/F1962744474/ABC%20of%20women%20workers

International Labor Organization (2009) http://www.ilo.org/ilolex/english/convdisp1.htm *Promoting gender equality: a resource kit for trade unions* http://www.ilo.org/public/english/employment/gems/advance/trade.htm *ABC of women workers' rights and gender equality* http://www.ilo.org/dyn/gender/docs/RES/68/F1962744474/ABC%20of%20women%20workers

Jacobsen, J.P. (2007) *The economics of gender, third edition*, Wiley-Blackwell, Malden, MA.

Jannatul Ferdaush, K. M. Mustafizur Rahman (2011) *Gender Inequality in Bangladesh, Unnayan Onneshan-The Innovators.*

Jayachandran, S. (2014) Fertility Decline and Missing Women, "Working Paper 20272, National Bureau of Economic Research.

John Stuart Mill (1997) "*The Subjection of Women*", Dower Publications, Inc.

Johnson, Hanks, et al. (2011) *Understanding Family Change and Variation: Toward a Theory of Conjunctural Action*. New York: Springer.

Johnson, Julia R. (2013) Johnson, Julia R. (1 March 2013). "Cisgender Privilege, Intersectionality, and the Criminalization of CeCe McDonald: Why Intercultural Communication Needs Transgender Studies". Journal of International and Intercultural Communication 6 (2): 135–144. doi:10.1080/17513057.2013.776094.

Jones, S.R. (1993) Creating gender equality: cross-national gender stratification and mathematical performance. *Sociol. Educ.* 66(2):91–103.

Kanbur,R. and Haddad, L. (1994) "Are Better off Households More Unequal or Less Unequal?" *Oxford Economic Papers*, 46: 445-458.

Kapsos,S. (2009) The Gender Wage Gap in Bangladesh, "ILO Asia-Pacific Working Paper Series, International Labour Organization.

Kar, P.V. (1993) Samajtatta. Calcutta: West Bengal State Book Board.

Kazianga, et al. (2013) The Effects of "Girl- Friendly" Schools: Evidence from the BRIGHT School Construction Program in Burkina Faso, *"American Economic Journal: Applied Economics,* 5, 41-62.

Kim, et al. (1999) Can Private School Subsidies Increase Enrollment for the Poor? The Quetta Urban Fellowship Program, *"The World Bank Economic Review*, 13, 443-465.

King, M. et al. (2009) *Indigenous health part 2: the underlying causes of thehealth gap*: *Lancet,* Elsevier; 374: 76–85.

Kishore, S. (1993) May god give sons to all: Gender and child mortality in India. *American Sociological Review,* 58(2), 247–265.

Klasen, S. and Lamanna, F. (2009) "The impact of gender inequality in education andemployment on economic growth: New evidence for a panel of countries," *Feminist Economics*, 15: 3, pp. 91-132.

Kusum (1993) The Use Of Pre-Natal Diagnostic Techniques for Sex Selection*: The Indian Scene," Bioethics,* 7, 149-165.

Ladurie Le Roy (1979) *The Territory of Historian*. Chicago: translated by Ben and Sian Reynolds.

Landefeld, J. et al. (2009) Accounting for household production: a prototype satellite account using the American Time Use Survey, *Review of Income and Wealth*, 55(2), 205-225.

Liddle, J. and Joshi, R. (1986) *Daughters of independence: Gender, caste and class in India.* (United Kingdom. London: Zed Books Ltd, Rutgers University Press).

Luke, N. and Munshi, K. (2011) Women as Agents of Change: Female Income and Mobility in India*, Journal of Development Economics,* 94, 1-17.

Majumdar, D.N. (1973) A Glimpse of Garo politics in North Eastern Affairs. London: Longman.

Mandelbaum, David G. (1970) Society in India, Volumes 1 and 2, Berkeley, CA: University of California Press.

March of dimes (2010) www.who.int/pmnch/media/news/2012/201204_borntoosoon-report.pdf

Mason, Karen Oppenheim. (1986) "The Status of Women: Conceptual and Methodological Issues in Demographic Studies." *Sociological Forum* 1(2):284–300.

Mawar, N. et al (1999) Children and young people in context of HIV/AIDS: Listen, learn and live! World AIDS Day campaign with children and young people. *ICMR Bull; 29:* 125-35.

McEwen, Bruce S. (2002) *The End of Stress as We Know It*. Washington, D.C: Joseph Henry Press.

McPherson, M.A. (1996) "Growth of micro and small enterprises in Southern Africa", *Journal of Development Economics*, 48: 253–277.

Mead, D.C. and Liedholm, C. (1998) "The dynamics of micro and small enterprises in developing countries", *World Development*, 26: 61–74.

Memoli, Michael A. (2013) "Senate passes workplace protections for gay, transgender Americans". LA Times.

Menon, Geetha (1992) Ecological Transitions and the Changing Context of Women's Work in Tribal India. In: *Purusartha*, 1991, p.291-314.

Miller, Barbara D. (1981) *The Endangered Sex: Neglect of Female Children in Rural North India*. Ithaca, NY: Cornell University Press.

Ministry of Health and Family Welfare (2000) mohfw.nic.in/WriteReadData/.../FAMILYWELFARE-38385935.pdf

Ministry of Palestinian Health (2006) www.jica.go.jp/english/our_work/.../gender/.../pdf/e07pal_02.pdf

Muhammad Zafrulla Khan (1980) "*Muhammad: Seal of the Prophets*", Routledge & Kegan Paul.

Muralidharan, K. and Prakash, N. (2013) Cycling to School: Increasing Secondary School Enrollment for Girls in India," Working Paper 19305, National Bureau of Economic Research.

Nanda, S. (2003) "Hijra and Sadhin". Constructing Sexualities. Ed. LaFont, S., New Jearsey: Pearson Education.

Nanda, S. and Herdt, G. (1996) "Hijras: An Alternative Sex and Gender Role in India; Third Sex, Third Gender: Beyond Sexual Dimorphism in Culture and History. Zone Books.)

Narrain, Siddharth (2003)". *Frontline* (The Hindu Group*) 20.*

National Population Policy (2000) countryoffice.unfpa.org/india/.../NationalPopulation-Policy2000.pdf

National Transgender Discrimination Survey (2015) "Injustice at Every Turn: A Look at Asian American, South Asian, Southeast Asian, and Pacific Islander Respondents in the National Transgender Discrimination Survey" (PDF).

Nelsen, Aaron (2013) "La Feria high school transgender student gets OK for photo". Houston Chronicle. Retrieved 17 November 2013.

news.biharprabha.com.

NFHS-1 (1991-92) hetv.org/india/nfhs/india1.html

NFHS-2 (1998-99) hetv.org/india/nfhs/india2.html

NFHS-3 (2005-06) hetv.org/india/nfhs/india3.html

Niederle, M. and Vesterlund, L. (2007) Do women shy away from competition? Do men compete too much? *Quarterly Journal of Economics* 122(3): 1067–1101.

Ortner, Sherry B. (1974) 'Is female to male as nature is to culture?' in Rosaldo, M Z and Lamphere, L (eds) *Women, Culture and Society*, Stanford: Stanford University Press.

Oster, E. (2009) Does Increased Access Increase Equality? Gender and Child Health Investments in India, *"Journal of Development Economics",* 89, 62-76.

Pakko, M. (2004) Labor's share, *National Economic Trends* (August), Federal Reserve Bank of St. Louis.

Panda, Snehalata. (2008) "Socio-Economic Status and Domestic Violence against Tribal Women", *Man & Development*, Vol. XXX, September 2008; No. 3, pp. 55-68.

Pandey, Rohini P. (2003) Selective Gender Differences in Childhood Nutrition and Immunization in Rural India: The Role of Siblings, *Demography, 40(3),* Population Association of America.

Pareek, U. and Nandkarni, M. S. (1978) "Development of Entrepreneurship: A Conceptual Model", In Developing Entrepreneurship, In T.V. Rao & Udai Pareek (Eds.), Learning System, New Delhi, 208 - 215.

Prased ,Narmadeswer (1991) Change strategy in a developing society. India, Meerut, Meenakshi Prakashan.

Ramakrishnan, et al. (2011) Gender Deferences in the Utilisation of Surgery for Congenital Heart Disease in India, Heart, 97, 1920-1925.

Rao, Rama. (1993) The Rising Price of Husbands: A Hedonic Analysis of Dowry Increases in Rural India," Journal of Political Economy, 666-677.

Rao, S. (1999) 'Fractioned states and negotiated boundaries, gender and law in India', in H. Afshar and S. Barrientos, *Women, Globalization and Fragmentation in the Developing World*, New York: St. Martin's Press.

Raworth, K. (2004) 'Trading Away Our Rights: Women working in global supply chains', p.76. Oxford: Oxfam.

Read, J.G. and Gorman, Bridget K. (2010) "Gender and Health Inequality." *Annual Review of Sociology* 36(1):371–86.

Reddy, S. and Balachandra, P. (2003) Integrated Energy-Environment-Policy Analysis", Utilities Policy, Vol. 11(2).

Rivers, H.R. (1973) The Todas. London: Macmillan.

Rose, E. (1999) Consumption Smoothing and Excess Female Mortality in Rural India, Review of Economics and Statistics, 81, 41-49.

Rosenzweig, M. R. & Schultz, T. P. (1982) 'Market Opportunities, Genetic Endowments, and Intrafamily Resource Distribution: Child Survival in Rural India.' *American Economic Review*, 72 (September), Pp.803-15.

Ross, M. (2008) "Oil, Islam and Women" *American Political Science Review* 102(1):107-123.

Roy Burman, B.K. (1988) Challenges of development and tribal women oflndia, in J.P. Singh, N.N. Vyas & R.S. Mann (Eds.). Tribal women and development. Udaipur: MLV Tribal Research and Training Institute, Tribal Area Development Department, Rajasthan.

Roy, S. (2013) Empowering Women: Inheritance Rights and Female Education in India,"Mimeo, Warwick University.

Salamacis, B. (2006) Gender Politics: Citizenship, Activism and Sexual Diversity, London: Pluto Press, p47.

Satyanarayana and Behera (1986) Socio-economic responsibility of tribal women: A micro-study of the Kissan of Western Orissa. Tribal women and development. Agenda Papers, Theme I, P.15.

Scott, John W. (1988) *Gender and the Politics of the History.* Columbia University Press, New York.

Seguino, S. (2010). "Gender, Distribution, and Balance of Payments Constrained Growth in Developing Countries", *Review of Political Economy* 22(3): 373–404.

Sen, Amartya (2001) Many Faces of Gender Inequality (Volume 18 - Issue 22, Oct. 27 - Nov. 09.

Sen, G. and Batliwala, S. (2000) 'Empowering Women for Reproductive Rights' in in Harriet B. Presser and Gita Sen, *Women's Empowerment and Demographic Processes*, Oxford University Press, New Delhi, pp. 15-36.

Sered (1994) *Priestess, Mother, and Sacred Sister*. Oxford University Press, Oxford.

Sewell, William H. (1992) "A Theory of Structure: Duality, Agency, and Transformation." *American Journal of Sociology* 98(1):1–29.

Sewell, William H. (2005) *Logics of History: Social Theory and Social Transformation*. Chicago: University of Chicago Press.

Shackle, Samira. (2013) "Politicians of the third gender: the "shemale" candidates of Pakistan". New Statesman. Retrieved 11/05/2013.

Sharma, Preeti. (2012a) "Historical Background and Legal Status of Third Gender in Indian Society" (PDF).

Sharma, Preeti. (2012b) "Awareness about sexually transmitted infections among Hijra sex workers of Rawalpindi/Islamabad" (PDF). Pakistan Journal of Public Health.

Shelah S. Bloom, David Wypij, Monica Das Gupta. (2001) Dimensions of Women's Autonomy and the Influence on Maternal Health Care Utilization in a North Indian City, *Demography, 38(1),* Population Association of America.

Simonton, D. (1998) *A history of European women's work: 1700 to the present*, Routledge, London and New York.

Singh, B. (1993) An outline of work to be taken up on tribal women. Working Papers: NCW.

Singh, S.K. (1988) "Role ofHousehold Economy in child Nutrition at low Incomes," Occasional Paper No. 95 (Ithaca: Dept. of Agricultural Economics, Cornell University.

Spencer, S. (2009) The 2009 Spencer Stuart Board Index, http://content.spencerstuart.com/sswebsite/pdf/ lib/SSBI2009.pdf

SRS (2009) Office of the Registrar General and Census Commissioner, India; Report No.1, Ministry of Home Affairs, Government of India, New Delhi.

Sugumar, M., and Rajaram, V. (1996) "The Relation between General-Aggression; Assertiveness and Job Satisfaction among the P.T.C. Bus Conductors", *Journal of Psychological Researcher,* Vol.37, Number 1&2, 1993, PP. 23-26.

Swamy, et al (2001) "Gender and Corruption." *Journal of Development Economics* 64 (1): 25–55.

The World Bank's Gender Statistics database for 2012.

Timmons, J.A. (1986) "Characteristics and Role Demands of Entrepreneurship".*American Journal of Small Business,* 3, (1), 5-17.

Tinkler, J. E., Li, Y. E., & Mollborn, S. (2007) Can legal interventions change beliefs? The effect of exposure to sexual harassment policy on men's gender beliefs. *Social Psychology Quarterly*, 70, 480-494.

Towle, R. B. and Morgan, L.M. (2006) "Romancing the Transgender Native: Rethinking the Use of the 'Third Gender' Concept", in S. Stryker and S. Whittle (eds), Transgender Studies Reader, p. 116.

Transequality.org.

Transgenderdor.org

Tzannatos, Z. (2010) Decreasing the gender gap in employment and pay in the Arab world: Measuring the gains for women, youth, and society. Paper presented at the International conference , Number on women and youth in Arab development, &Cairo, 22-24 March.

U.S. Bureau of the Census (1976) Economics and Statistics Administration ,Bureau of The Census: https://www.census.gov/prod/1/pop/p25-1130.pdf

UN (2009) 'World Survey on the Role of Women in Development: Women's Control over Economic Resources and Access to Financial Resources, including Microfinance'. New York: United Nations.

UN (1975) *Conference on Women in Mexico City.* New York: United Nations.

UNICEF (1998) The impact of HIV/AIDS on education systems in the eastern and southern Africa region and the response of education systems to HIV/AIDS: life skills programmes" By D. Gachuhi: www.unicef.org

United Nation Development Programs Human development report (2013) United Nations Human Development Report, p. 356

United Nations (1995a) *Lokking Back Moving Forward: Second Review and Appraisal of the Implimentation of the Nairobi, Forward-Looking Strategies for the Advancement of Women,* E.95.IV.New York.

United Nations (1995b) *Internally Displaced Persons,* Report of the Representative of the Secretary General Mr. Francis M. Deng (E/CN.4? 1995? 50) New York.

Usmani, Basim (2009) "Politicians of the third gender: the "shemale" candidates of Pakistan". *New Statesman.and Pakistan.*

Venkat, Vidya (2008) "From the shadows". *Frontline (*The Hindu Group*) 25 (4, 16–29 February).*

Wagman, Barnet and Nancy Folbre (1996) Household services and economic growth in the United States, 1870-1930. *Feminist Economics,* 2, 43–66.

Weischelbaumer, D. and Rudolf, Winter Ebmer (2007) The effects of competition and equal treatment laws on gender wage discrimination, *Economic Policy,* 2007, 22(50), 235-287.

Wilchins (2006) Gender Politics: Citizenship, Activism and Sexual Diversity, London: Pluto Press, p. 30.

Wilcox, A. (2005) *The Validity of Reconviction Studies* (Unpublished PhD Thesis) Oxford: University of Oxford.

Wilcox, A. and Hirschfield, A. (2007) *Pathways into Policy: A Study of the Relationship between Research, Policy and Government* Huddersfield: Applied Criminology Centre.

Wong, Curtis (2012) "Transgender Employees Now Protected By Anti-Discrimination Law After 'Landmark' EEOC Ruling". Huffington Post.

World Bank (2010) 'Swimming Against the Tide: How developing countries are coping with the global crisis', background paper prepared by World Bank staff, 13–14 March 2009, www.un.org/ga/president/63/PDFs/WorldBankreport.pdf

World Bank (2012) 'Women, Business & The Law: Measuring Legal Gender Parity for Entrepreneurs and Workers in 128 Economies'. Washington DC: The World Bank.

World Health Organization (2001) Transforming health systems: gender and rights in reproductive health, http://www.who.int/reproductive-health/gender/glossary.html)

World Health Organization (2010) *Mental health: Stop exclusion. Dare to care*. Geneva.

World Health Organization (2002) Gender and Reproductive Rights: Working Definitions, http://www.who.int/reproductive- health/gender/sexual_health.html#1)

World Health Organization (1989) *Preventing Maternal Deaths*. Geneva: WorldHealth Organisation.

World Health Organization (2001) Transforming health systems: gender and rights in reproductive health, http://www.who.int/reproductive-health/gender/glossary.html

www.lambdalegal.org

www.un-instraw.org/en/index.php?option=content&task=view&id=37&Itemid=76

Index

C

D

M

N